Autobiographical Memory and the Construction of a Narrative Self

Developmental and Cultural Perspectives

Autobiographical Memory and the Construction of a Narrative Self

Developmental and Cultural Perspectives

Edited by

R O B Y N F I V U S H
Emory University

C A T H E R I N E A. H A D E N
Loyola University Chicago

LAWRENCE ERLBAUM ASSOCIATES, PUBLISHERS
2003   Mahwah, New Jersey   London

Chapter 10: Self-Making Narratives by Jerome Bruner. Reprinted from "The Narrative Creation of Self" from MAKING STORIES: LAW, LITERATURE, LIFE by Jerome Bruner. Copyright © 2002 by Jerome Bruner. Reprinted by permission of Farrar, Straus and Giroux, LLC.

Lawrence Erlbaum Associates, Inc., Publishers
10 Industrial Avenue
Mahwah, NJ 07430

Cover design by Kathryn Houghtaling Lacey

LIBRARY OF CONGRESS CATALOGING-IN-PUBLICATION DATA

Autobiographical memory and the construction of a narrative self : developmental and cultural perspectives / edited by Robyn Fivush, Catherine A. Haden.
    p.   cm.
    Includes bibliographical references and indexes.
    ISBN 0–8058–3756–6 (alk. paper)
    1. Autobiographical memory—Social aspects. 2. Self-presentation.
    I. Fivush, Robyn. II. Haden, Catherine A.
BF378.A87 A883 2002
153.1'3—dc21   2002072668

Books published by Lawrence Erlbaum Associates are printed on acid-free paper, and their bindings are chosen for strength and durability.

Printed in the United States of America
10 9 8 7 6 5 4 3 2 1

Contents

Introduction:
Autobiographical Memory,
Narrative and Self

Robyn Fivush
Emory University

Catherine A. Haden
Loyola University Chicago

It is a truism in psychology that self and autobiographical memory are linked, yet we still know surprisingly little about the nature of this relation. Recent theorizing on the role of narrative in human cognition suggests that it is through the construction of a life story that self and memory are intertwined (Bruner, 1987; Fivush, 2001; MacAdams, 1996; Neisser, 1988; Nelson, 1993). In this volume, we approach this relation from a social and developmental constructivist position. Although individual authors offer their own unique perspectives in illuminating the nature of the link between self and memory, the contributors share a perspective that both memory and self are constructed through specific forms of social interactions and/or cultural frameworks that lead to the formation of an autobiographical narrative. Taken together, the chapters weave a coherent story about how each of us creates a life narrative embedded in sociocultural frameworks that define what is appropriate to remember, how to remember it, and what it means to be a self with an autobiographical past.

The work that motivates this volume crosses ideas both within psychology and across the social sciences. Scholars from multiple disciplines, including cognitive psychology (Conway, 1990; Neisser & Fivush, 1994; Pillemer, 1998;

Rubin, 1986), developmental psychology (Fivush, 2001; Nelson, 1993; Nelson & Fivush, 2000; Stein, Wade, & Liwag, 1996; Welch-Ross, 2001), anthropology (Scheifflin & Ochs, 1986), and philosophy (Barnes, 1997) have begun theorizing and writing about the ways in which autobiographical memory is organized, the role that narratives play in the development of autobiographical memory, and the relations between autobiographical memory, narrative, and self concept. If narratives are a critical link between memory and self, then it becomes apparent that the roles of language and social interaction are paramount. By their very nature, narratives are culturally prescribed forms for organizing events through canonicalized linguistic frameworks. Although events in the world may be organized in space and time, it is through narrative that events take on human shape and human meaning (e.g., Carr, 1986; Ricouer, 1991). Narrative forms allow for more complex organization and understanding of experienced events through the provision of subjective evaluations of what occurred and the formation of thematic relations among events separated in time and space but linked through personal meaning making, such as relationships, careers, and so on (Fivush & Haden, 1997; Labov, 1982; Linde, 1993).

To focus on the role of narrative in linking autobiographical memory and self also highlights individual differences. The ways in which any given individual constructs a life narrative are influenced both by the larger cultural frameworks available for understanding what a self is (e.g., Oyserman & Markus, 1993) and what it means to remember one's past. Even within culture, individual pathways in the emergence of autobiographical memory are clearly evident (Harley & Reese, 1999). Developmentally, children are learning the forms and functions of autobiography through participating in conversations about the past with adults (Fivush, Haden, & Reese, 1996), and as adults, the way in which we share our memories with others modulates the way we think about our experiences and, ultimately, ourselves (Pasupathi, 2001). If we take seriously the assumption that autobiographical memory is formed in social interaction, then it becomes necessary to examine the ways in which cultural constructs of the self and autobiography come to shape the kinds of interactions children and adults engage in, and thus the kinds of autobiographical selves that are formed.

The chapters that animate this volume portray a fresh, new set of theoretical and empirical perspectives on these issues. More specifically, individual chapters revolve around the following three sets of issues: (a) the development of autobiographical memory and self-understanding; (b) cross-cultural variation in narrative environments and self-construal; and (c) the construction of gender and identity concepts in developmental and situational contexts.

PART I: THE DEVELOPMENT
OF AUTOBIOGRAPHICAL MEMORY
AND SELF-UNDERSTANDING

Chapters 1 through 3 focus on the impact the linguistic and social "milieu" that surrounds the developing child—as captured in mother–child conversations about personally experienced events—may have on autobiographical memory and self-understanding. In chapter 1, Katherine Nelson proposes a model of the development of self in which she characterizes children's movement over the first 6 years of life to increasingly sophisticated levels of understanding of the extent to which the self's experiences in the world are like, but distinct from, others'. Narrative discourse that occurs between parents and their young children about the present, the past, and the projected future is argued to underlie this progression. Thus, for Nelson, as for the other contributors to this volume, the self emerges from a collaborative constructive process. Language is thought to play a critical role in gradually moving children to new levels of understanding of the contrasts between the self and other selves. As Nelson puts it, "The use of language to exchange messages about 'my' experience, 'your' experience, and 'our' experience . . . constitutes a major 'taking off' point for further development of self understanding." In fact, the author "tentatively" posits that although practice in talking about events hastens children's achievement of a representational self (Level 4), the transition to the final level (Level 5), a "cultural self," *requires* experience in the use of language to tell stories about one's past.

Consistent with Nelson's view of the importance of language for autobiographical memory and self development, the following two chapters by Elaine Reese and Kate Farrant, and by Catherine Haden discuss evidence from a growing body of work focusing on mother–child conversational interactions about ongoing and previously experienced events as they link to children's remembering. In chapter 2, Reese and Farrant are particularly concerned with contextual and child characteristics that might shape parents' style of reminiscing about the past. Evidence reviewed from a large-scale longitudinal study of children from 1½ to 3½ years of age documents the importance of both the child's own early participation in memory conversations and maternal reminiscing style in predicting children's subsequent skills for remembering. Reese and Farrant also consider the early attachment relationship between the mother and child as a potential contributor to both maternal reminiscing style and children's autobiographical memory. Their findings place the development of autobiographical memory and the self in a larger context of interpersonal relationships.

The impact of language-based interactions that occur while novel events unfold has not been explored as thoroughly as adult–child talk about the past. But as Haden argues in chapter 3, parent–child interchanges during events can serve to focus attention on salient aspects of an activity and provide information about it, in turn, affecting children's sense making and remembering of personal experiences. Haden discusses a longitudinal investigation in which young children were tracked between the ages of 2½ and 3½, with the major emphasis being placed on linkages between mother–child communication during specified events and children's subsequent memory performance. In this work, even the youngest children showed mnemonic benefits from conversations about events as they were unfolding, reinforcing the view that mother–child discourse during events is linked in important ways to what is encoded and subsequently remembered. Haden's analysis emphasizes that cultural differences in remembering may reflect not only differences in reminiscing but also differences in the ways parents and children jointly encode experienced events.

PART II: CROSS-CULTURAL VARIATION
IN NARRATIVE ENVIRONMENTS
AND SELF-CONSTRUAL

The second section of the book turns to more specific consideration of cultural differences in autobiographical memory development. Here the contributors focus on questions of cultural differences in the age and content of adults' earliest recollections, and whether these differences might be rooted in early differences in parent–child conversations about the past in families from different cultural backgrounds.

In chapter 4, Michelle Leichtman, Qi Wang, and David Pillemer report on cross-cultural differences in the content and style of autobiographical remembering in Chinese, Korean, Indian, and North American adults and children. Across several studies, differences in autobiographical memory reports of adults in these groups were associated with the extent to which the cultural values favored independence or interdependence. As such, adults who had grown up in independent cultures told earlier, lengthier, and more elaborated childhood memories than adults who had grown up in interdependent cultures. In considering possible mechanisms by which cultural values impact autobiographical memory, the authors go on to review an impressive body of literature related to four potentially key factors: variations in narrative environments, self-construal, emotion understanding, and beliefs about the personal past. The authors conclude that the interaction of several of these factors are likely responsible for cultural differences in autobiographical memory.

Harlene Hayne and Shelley MacDonald then present data on how cultural belief systems and values impact remembering in the White, European Pakeha New Zealanders as compared with the indigenous Maori, who have a strong oral tradition stressing past ancestry and lineage. Hayne and MacDonald found that, on average, Maori adults remembered childhood experiences several months earlier than the Pakeha sample. When looking at mother–child reminiscing in these two cultures, Hayne and MacDonald found that the Maori parents adopted a more repetitive reminiscing style. Whereas in White, Western cultures, an elaborative, descriptive style of talking about the past has been shown to facilitate memory (e.g., Reese, Haden, & Fivush, 1993), Hayne and MacDonald propose that the cultural values, beliefs, and experiences of the Maori culture might result in an emphasis on recitation or repetition in the telling of personal narratives.

The final chapter in this section by Robert Schrauf and David Rubin focuses on exciting new clinical and experimental data examining differences in autobiographical recall in bilingual adults depending on the language used at encoding and retrieval. The authors asked a relatively simple question — "Will memories cued in one language trigger retrievals in that same language?" — and found a complicated answer. Bilinguals showed no differences in their abilities to report their memories in same versus different language from experience. In other words, memories can be translated quite readily to another language that the bilingual speaks when called for by the situation. However, when asked in which language the memories "came to them," bilinguals across several studies reported that the memories were retrieved in the language of experience, and then translated. These findings prompt the authors to question prior notions of the linkages between language and memory, and to suggest that bilinguals do not have two interchangeable codes for the world, but rather have two linguistic networks for understanding their experiences and themselves. In a very real sense, these authors argue, bilingual immigrants possess "language-specific selves."

PART III: THE CONSTRUCTION OF GENDER AND IDENTITY CONCEPTS IN DEVELOPMENTAL AND SITUATIONAL CONTEXTS

The chapters in the final section concern connections between autobiographical narratives and the development and expression of self-understanding over the life course. In particular, Robyn Fivush and Janine Buckner construct a case for the idea that the way aspects of male and female identity are presented in one's life story is, to a considerable extent, influenced by the narrative context. To support this position, Fivush and Buckner review evidence to suggest that there are striking gender differences in the ways that boys and girls describe their experiences in early and middle childhood—a time when gender concepts are being formed and elaborated. But although both mothers and fathers tell more emotional and social-relational stories about past events with their daughters than with their sons, research suggests that adult women and men do not differ from each other in the ways they reminisce with their children. Moreover, the narratives about academic achievement of college-aged males and females are more similar than different. The authors suggest that in situations such as these—when parents are focusing on their relationships with their children, and college students are focusing on issues of professional identity—gender is "backgrounded," and presentations of the self would not be expected to differ along gendered lines. When gender is in the "foreground"—as in the developmental periods of early and middle childhood, and in discussions of emotionally significant events—gender differences would mostly likely be apparent. Thus, the images of gendered identity that are reflected in autobiographical narratives have much to do with when, where, why, and to whom the story is being told.

Like Fivush and Buckner, Avril Thorne and Kate McLean focus on gender and emotional expression in event narratives, in this case, stories about personally traumatic experiences. The way that these event narratives are told, the authors suggest, is affected by cultural conventions concerning the reporting of events, particularly, what is appropriate to tell depending on one's audience. Analyses of narratives collected from European-American college students are presented to illustrate the different stances, or "master narratives" that males and females favor in telling about their responses to trauma. A consideration of audience reaction to tough, empathetic, vulnerable, and existential awe narratives further indicated that how these tellings are received by others can vary according to cultural beliefs and values concerning gender and emotion.

In chapter 9, Dan McAdams reviews his life-story theory of identity formation. Although the beginnings of life-story making can be traced to young children's early conversational interactions with their parents, from this perspective, it is not until late adolescence that "selves begin to take identity shape" and individuals begin to "effectively put their lives together into a story" McAdams traces the development of the life story, illustrating how by adolescence, individuals start to construct stories together that have temporal, biographical, causal, and thematic coherence (Habermas & Bluck, in press). The author provides quantitative evidence from his work and others' to illustrate how individual differences in life stories are linked to social motives, personality characteristics, and to mental well-being. A prominent theme in this chapter is that life stories are based on autobiographical episodes, but to a considerable extent reflect efforts to portray oneself in a way that makes sense within one's social and cultural context.

In the final chapter, Jerome Bruner provides us with a theoretical and philosophical treatise on how and why narrative and self are so inextricably intertwined. Using historical examples of self making through narrative, Bruner shows how selves are constructed over time through cultural lenses. Most important, autobiographical selves are continuously in the making and re-making. Bruner poses critical questions: Are selves constructed through narrative or do narratives convey an existing deep sense of self? Do selves exist as independent entities or only in relation to and as a reflection of others? These are questions that are both enduring and unanswerable, as reality must lie in the tension between these alternatives. Ultimately, as Bruner reminds us, we are both expressions of our cultural and developmental history and we come to express that history through the creation of our narrative selves.

REFERENCES

Barnes, H. E. (1997). *The story I tell myself: A venture in existential autobiography.* Chicago: University of Chicago press.

Bruner, J. (1987). Life as narrative. *Social Research, 54,* 11–32.

Carr, D. (1986). Narrative and the real world: An argument for continuity. *History and Theory, 25,* 117–131.

Conway, M. (1990). *Autobiographical memory: An introduction.* Buckingham: Open University Press.

Fivush, R. (2001). Owning experience: The development of subjective perspective in autobiographical memory. In C. Moore & K. Lemmon (Eds.). *The self in time: Developmental perspectives* (p. 35–52). Hillsdale, NJ: Lawrence Erlbaum Associates.

Fivush, R., & Haden, C. (1997). Narrating and representing experience: Preschoolers' developing autobiographical recounts. In P. van den Broek, P. A. Bauer, & T. Bourg (Eds.), *Developmental spans in event comprehension and representation: Bridging fictional and actual events.* Hillsdale, NJ: Lawrence Erlbaum Associates.

Fivush, R., Haden, C., & Reese, E. (1996). Remembering, recounting and reminiscing: The development of autobiographical memory in social context. In D. Rubin (Ed.), *Reconstructing our past: An overview of autobiographical memory* (pp. 341–359). New York: Cambridge University Press.

Habermas, T., & Bluck, S. (in press). Getting a life: The emergence of the life story in adolescence. *Psychological Bulletin.*

Harley, K., & Reese, E. (1999). Origins of autobiographical memory. *Developmental Psychology, 35*, 1338–1348.

Labov, W. (1982). Speech actions and reaction in personal narrative. In D. Tannen (Ed.), *Analyzing discourse: Text and talk.* Washington, DC: Georgetown University Press.

Linde, C. (1993). *Life stories: The creation of coherence.* New York: Oxford University Press.

MacAdams, D. P. (1996). Narrating the self in adulthood. In J. E. Birren, G. M. Kenyon, J. Ruth, J. J. F. Schroots, & T. Svensson (Eds.), *Aging and biography: Explorations in adult development* (pp. 131–148). New York: Springer.

Neisser, U. (1988). Five kinds of self-knowledge. *Philosophical Psychology, 1*, 35–59.

Neisser, U., & Fivush, R. (Eds.). (1994). *The remembering self: Construction and accuracy in the life narrative.* New York: Cambridge University Press.

Nelson, K. (1993). Explaining the emergence of an autobiographical memory in early childhood. In A. Collins, M. Conway, S. Gathercole, & P. Morris (Eds.), *Theories of memory.* Hillsdale, NJ: Lawrence Erlbaum Associates.

Nelson, K., & Fivush, R. (2000). The socialization of memory. In E. Tulving & F. Craik (Eds.), *The Oxford handbook of memory.* London: Oxford University Press.

Oyserman, D., & Markus, H. (1993). The sociocultural self. In J. Suls (Ed.), *Psychological perspectives on the self: The self in social perspective* (Vol. 4, pp. 187–220). Hillsdale, NJ: Lawrence Erlbaum Associates.

Pasupathi, M. (2001). The social construction of the personal past and its implications for adult development. *Psychological Bulletin, 127*, 651–672.

Pillemer, D. (1998). *Momentous events: Vivid memories.* New York: Cambridge University Press.

Reese, E., Haden, C. A., & Fivush, R. (1993). Mother–child conversations about the past: Relationships of style and memory over time. *Cognitive Development, 8*, 403–430.

Ricoeur, P. (1991). Life in quest of narrative. In D. Wood (Ed.), *On Paul Ricoeur: Narrative and interpretation* (pp. 20–33). London: Routledge.

Rubin, D. (Ed.). (1986). *Autobiographical memory.* New York: Cambridge University Press.

Schieffelin, B. B., & Ochs, E. (1986). *Language socialization across cultures.* New York: Cambridge University Press.

Stein, N. L., Wade, E., & Liwag, M. D. (1996). A theoretical approach to understanding and remembering emotional events. In N. Stein, P. A. Ornstein, C. A. Brainerd, & B. Tversky (Eds.), *Memory for everyday and emotional events.* Hillsdale: NJ: Lawrence Erlbaum Associates.

Welch-Ross, M. (2001). Personalizing the temporally extended self: Evaluative self-awareness and the development of autobiographical memory. In C. Moore & K. Lemmon (Eds.), *The self in time: Developmental perspectives* (pp. 97–120). Mahwah, NJ: Lawrence Erlbaum Associates.

List of Contributors

Jerome Bruner
NYU School of Law
New York University
New York, NY

Janine Buckner
Department of Psychology
Seton Hall University
South Orange, NJ

Kate Farrant
Department of Psychology
Otago University
Dunedin, New Zealand

Robyn Fivush
Department of Psychology
Emory University
Atlanta, GA

Catherine A. Haden
Department of Psychology
Loyola University Chicago
Chicago, IL

Harlene Hayne
Department of Psychology
University of Otago
Dunedin, New Zealand

Michelle Leichtman
Department of Psychology
University of New Hampshire
Durham, NH

Shelley MacDonald
Woolf Fisher Research Institute
University of Auckland
Auckland, New Zealand

Dan McAdams
School of Education and Social
    Policy
Northwestern University
Evanston, IL

Kate C. McLean
Department of Psychology
University of California, Santa Cruz
Santa Cruz, CA

Katherine Nelson
Developmental Psychology
Graduate School of the
    City University of New York
New York, NY

David Pillemer
Department of Psychology
Wellesley College
Wellesley, MA

Elaine Reese
School of Psychology
Clark University
Worcester, MA

David C. Rubin
Department of Psychology
and Brain Sciences
Duke University
Durham, North Carolina

Robert W. Schrauf
Buehler Center on Aging
Northwestern University
Chicago, IL

Avril Thorne
Department of Psychology
University of California, Santa Cruz
Santa Cruz, CA

Qi Wang
Department of Human
Development
Cornell University
Ithaca, NY

I

The Development
of Autobiographical Memory
and Self-Understanding

Chapter 1

Narrative and Self, Myth and Memory: Emergence of the Cultural Self

Katherine Nelson
City University of New York Graduate Center

The major developmental transition in the preschool years can be viewed as a move toward a social–cultural–linguistic self in society This transition to a new level of social-cognitive consciousness is apparent in major shifts between the 2- and 5-year-old levels of functioning in myriads of situations, experimental and everyday, that are now well documented in the developmental literature. How the emerging capacity for autobiographical memory narratives contributes to the newly emerging concept of self during this period is the theme of this chapter. The theoretical framework builds on previous work (Nelson, 1996, 2000b, in press), while the discussion here relates the theory to current work on autobiography and the development of self understanding. I use the term *self understanding* in preference to *self concept* here to emphasize changes in how self is constructed and understood as development proceeds.

This account of the preschool transition includes the following assumptions. The changes observed are not caused by some single factor, but are dependent on the achievements of many related skills unique to human development. Nor are they the product of a sudden shift in cognitive level, but of a continuous, overlapping process of developing functions. Among the achievements of this period of development, the most powerful and profound is that of an advanced level of social and cultural language functions. The transition to a "cultural self" depends on the experiences of language in social use, thus

3

on social practices, but its effects are also profoundly personal, involving the child's social and cognitive awareness and capacity for new levels of mental representation and reflective thought. This process is slow and massively interactive, eventuating in a culturally saturated concept of self, an autobiographical memory self with a specific self-history and imagined self-future that reflects the values, expectations, and forms of the embedding culture.

To substantiate these claims, I first propose developmental distinctions among levels of self understanding that become evident during the first 6 years of life. I then consider the onset of autobiographical memory as both a reflection of the achievement of a new level of self understanding in this sequence, and as a contributor to further self development. I next set these proposals into the context of theories of the origins of autobiographical memory and of the function of this kind of memory in human evolution and culture.

LEVELS OF SELF UNDERSTANDING

Developmental psychologists have made varying proposals about the development of self awareness and the self concept. (For reviews of this literature see Snodgrass & Thompson, 1997; Rochat, 1995, on self awareness in infancy; and Harter, 1998, on later development of the self concept in childhood.) Recent work on autobiographical memory and childhood amnesia has drawn on this literature in different ways. The scheme outlined here draws in part on the standard literature, but makes some cuts that others would not necessarily agree on. I hope to identify some gaps in our knowledge of how this crucial understanding may develop.

In the scheme that follows, I suggest that the elaboration of self understanding rests on the successive ability to make increasingly distinct *contrasts* between the self and other aspects of the world of experience. These are made explicit in the phases outlined in Table 1.1. In laying out a developmental scheme in terms of levels, I want to emphasize again that the idea is not that there is a discrete advance from one level to the next. Rather, as the infant/ child interacts with the world from one developmental perspective, contrasts become evident in these experiences that contribute to attainment of the next level of understanding. Also, a given level never disappears from view; rather, as development proceeds the perspectives become more complex, composing a mosaic of self understanding that eventually may encompass all of the dimensions that James (1890/1950) discussed in his discourse on this baffling concept, and that include the five aspects of self that Neisser (1988) invoked.

TABLE 1.1
Levels of Self Understanding

Level of Self Understanding	Onset Age	Mental Content	Self–Other Contrast	Self–World Contrast
Physical	Postnatal	Emotional attachment	Physical boundary	Physical boundary
Social	6–12 mo.	Social sharing	Attention, Intention, Communication	Routines, Object kinds, words
Cognitive	18–24 mo.	I–you perspective	Object–other perspective	Self/Object-in-world
Representational	2–4 years	Continuing me	My mind/ your mind	Mental–physical
Narrative	3–6 years	Story of me	Stories of me/ stories of others	Past-future, worlds outside this one
Cultural	5–7 years	Story of us/ in world	Cultural roles	Cultural knowledge, institutions

The scheme here departs, however, from Neisser's conception in its details (for a developmental account of this theory see Neisser, 1997).

Level 1. The Physical Self

From early infancy, the individual is aware of the *difference* between the physical self and the world outside that boundary (Butterworth, 1990). In addition, according to Meltzoff (Meltzoff & Moore, 1999), the infant makes a distinction between self and other, with the nascent idea that the self is *like* conspecifics, as indicated by the primitive kind of imitation in neonates that Meltzoff and Moore documented. At this level, there is not an understanding of self per se but awareness of aspects of the world that are outside the self and that provide opportunities for interaction, initially with caretakers and other social beings, then with inanimate objects as well. Gradually, understanding of the physical self is expanded as the infant gains mobility in the context of increasingly wide exploration of space.

Level 2. Social Understanding of Self

At this level, which emerges sometime in the second half of the first year, according to most observers, the infant makes relational contrasts, understanding the roles that the other and self play in routines such as feeding, dressing, and play, and understanding the relational differences between people—for example, mother and stranger. This stage is characterized initially by shared attention with the other (Tomasello, 1995) and leads into the early stages of language acquisition and intentional communication.

Level 3. Cognitive Understanding of Self

This is the terminology used by Howe and Courage (1997) to refer to the "mirror recognition" stage, somewhere between 1½ and 2 years of age, where the child recognizes his or her image in the mirror. The child at 18 to 27 months also begins to refer to the self with linguistic terms, *I, Me, My,* or the child's own name. The contrastive distinction that the child of this age is making is a contrast in the *perspective* of self and other. This is indicated by the beginnings of a capacity to take another's perspective into account, such as when looking at pictures. The perspective contrast is also evident in a new kind of self awareness—awareness of the self as an object that can be viewed by others, such that shyness, embarrassment, and inhibition come into play in the 2-year-old (Lewis, 1997).

Level 4. The Representational Self

The evidence of self–other perspectives at the third level does not establish the self as a representational object, however. The 2-year-old may view the self as an object in the ongoing activity, but does not represent the self outside the context of present experience. The representational self has a continuing mental reality that can be decontexted from the present; it is not just the experiencing self, or the self in action, but a contemplated conceptual object.

DeLoache (1990) documented important deficiencies in the 2-year-old's understanding of representational objects such as models and pictures. Recent evidence from her laboratory (DeLoache, 2000) indicates that, contrary to common assumption, children younger than about 4 years have difficulty viewing a doll or a picture of themselves (even a life-size picture) as a representation of themselves. For example, they fail to see the analogy when asked to touch the same place (e.g., a knee) on a doll as on their own body. They are able to perform this task when the two "objects" are both dolls or are both other people. This finding supports the claim that the 2- and 3-year-old does not view the self as a *representable object.* Povinelli's work showing that 3-year-old children fail to recognize their former selves on videotape suggests the same conclusion (Povinelli, Landau, & Perilloux, 1996).

The move to the 3½- to 4-year-old understanding then involves a new *contrast* between self as present object and as represented "permanent" self, representing the self as a "permanent object" to be tracked over time. The younger child's failures of objectivity may be connected to failures on other tasks at the same ages, such as theory of mind, and source monitoring (Perner & Ruffman, 1995; Wellman, 1990). It is during the 2- to 3-year-old period that children begin to engage in episodic memory recounting with parents, suggesting a new appreciation of reporting in language experiences of the self in the past. Despite the extensive attention to this level of understanding (the transitional stage from 3 to 5 years), there is much still to be learned about it in terms of the self perspective.

Level 5. Narrative Self Understanding

Autobiographical memory emerges during the latter part of the preschool years and suggests a new level of self understanding. This level of self understanding integrates action and consciousness into a whole self, and establishes a self-history as unique to the self, differentiated from others' experiential histories. It follows on the simpler representational self of the prior level, and adds to that level a new awareness of self in past and future experiences and the contrast of that self to others' narratives of their past and future experiences, including the representation of these in stories and personal recounts. This is the beginning point of the establishment of a unique life story that has coherence across different life phases, initially starting with the phases from babyhood to childhood, and looking forward to the future as an adult.

Level 6. Cultural Self Understanding

The child's self history comes to be set into a cultural framework that differentiates it in terms of cultural settings and time frames, babyhood, adulthood, school, home, playground, each with its own rules and participant roles. Henceforth, typically at the school level, an autobiographical memory can come into existence, culturally framed, full of incidents and meanings for the self. The self then may make contrasts between the ideal self portrayed by the culture and the actual self as understood, and then may strive to achieve a more ideal self (Higgins, 1991).

Again, these levels are overlapping, not discrete. While operating at one level of understanding, the child is becoming aware of the next, and is being led by adults into the next level of understanding through the kind of conversational exchanges that have been studied extensively in the pursuit of understanding the development of autobiographical memory. The view that autobiographical memory serves as self history requires examining the evidence for the emergence of a specific form of memory, *autobiographical memory,* in relation to these developmental changes.

DEVELOPMENTAL DIFFERENCES
IN PERSONAL MEMORY

Autobiographical memory is constituted by those personal memories of one's life events that begin to accumulate sometime during early to mid-childhood. The period prior to this beginning point from the perspective of adults is termed *childhood amnesia.* We now know, after decades of extensive research on memory in infancy and the toddler years, that the term childhood amnesia does not apply to children but to adults; infants and children do have memory of events of varying kinds. But this fact makes the emergence of autobiographical memory more puzzling: Why does a new kind of memory emerge in early to mid-childhood? The answer here involves the self and its development, but before this can be explored in full, it is necessary to explicate the kind of memory that autobiographical memory represents and how it differs from the memory kinds observable in earlier periods.

Autobiographical memory has a clear beginning point for most people, on average at about 3½ years, although there are wide individual differences and some people have few or no memories earlier than 8 or 10 years of age. Although many if not most adults' episodic memories may be fleeting, autobiographical memories may persist for years and even decades. Thus, whereas autobiographical memory may be considered a subtype of episodic memory, as defined by Tulving (1983; see discussion in next section), not all episodic memories are autobiographical memory. Autobiographical memory has personal significance that goes beyond that of much of episodic memory (such as memory for word lists or yesterday's breakfast), which may account for its long-term retention, as most theorists would agree; but exactly what determines personal significance is uncertain.

Studies of memory in the infant and toddler years show a quite consistent increase in the duration of event memories with development during this period (Bauer, Hertsgaard, & Dow, 1994; Rovee-Collier & Shyi, 1992; Sheffield & Hudson, 1994). By the age of 2 years, some salient memories are retained for at least 2 more years, and by 4 years it appears that they may last well into middle childhood, if not longer (Fivush, 2000). Thus a simple restriction on retention time does not seem to explain the difference between memory before and after the period of childhood amnesia.

There are two discernible short periods in the move beyond childhood amnesia, the earlier constituting what we might call the emergence of auto-biographical memory, and the second its consolidation. According to Pillemer and White (1989), the first period (typically involving memories from about 2 to 3 years) tends to be characterized by memories of brief but vivid scenes (akin to flashbulb memories in later life), often scenes that are evocative but for which the adult cannot assign an unambiguous meaning. Studies of children's early memory also suggest that what is remembered in the first 3 years is typically fragmentary and context-bound, consisting largely of visual scenes, situations, events, actions, and associations. It may be that the fragments that appear in later memory from this period with elusive meaning and uncertain temporal dating are thus remnants of the kind of specific memory typical of this early period.

Pillemer and White (1989) indicated that for the second period of the emergence of autobiographical memory (4 to 6 years), access to memories begins to increase, but they are still relatively few in number (Wetzler & Sweeney, 1986). Like later autobiographical memory, personal memory for an episode during this period tends to be in the form of a complete narrative (even if missing pieces), which is usually visual and verbal and has personal meaning for the individual. Memories can usually be located temporally within a life scheme and are often felt to contribute to self-knowledge.

THEORIES OF THE DEVELOPMENT OF AUTOBIOGRAPHICAL MEMORY

Over the past decade, a number of theories have been advanced to explain the demise of childhood amnesia and the origins of autobiographical memory. Three main approaches are considered briefly here with respect to their relation to the development of the representational, narrative, and cultural aspects of self.

Memory and the Cognitive Self

Howe and Courage (1993, 1997) focused on the self component of the puzzle of childhood amnesia and autobiographical memory. They argued that self-awareness as evaluated by the mirror recognition test is the key to the emergence of episodic memory, and that distinctive episodic memories are those that will be retained into the autobiographical memory system. They proposed that a "cognitive self" is established by 2 years of age, reflected in two achievements: recognition of the self in the mirror and use of personal pronouns to refer to oneself. They state further that childhood amnesia declines at the same age.

As already noted, toddlers at 18 to 27 months show a different awareness of self than they did in the infancy period, indicated by the mirror recognition test and also by the kind of inhibition and embarrassment noted in the 2-year-old. This level of self-awareness is indicative of the cognitive differentiation of self and other, justifying the term *cognitive self,* Level 3 in the scheme presented earlier. It marks an advance in social and self understanding that may be partly achieved through the acquisition of the language used for self and other. In turn, this use and practice in talking with others makes possible further differentiations.

Nonetheless, the level reached by the 2-year-old is still very limited—in language, in self-conceptualization, and in memory. The assertion by Howe and Courage that autobiographical memory begins at 2 years (and thus the demise of childhood amnesia) goes against the major consensus, based on a century of research with adults, which shows the mean age of earliest memories to be 3½ years for educated middle-class European-American adults (Pillemer & White, 1989).[1] For many such individuals and for people raised in other cultures, the age is much later in childhood.

The early signs of self-consciousness in toddlers may well relate to later memory developments, as they emanate from other developments of social awareness and social interaction, and as later memory development is part of an encompassing change that takes place in the preschool years. For example, Reese (2000) found a positive correlation of mirror self-recognition at 20 months with children's episodic memory productions at 3 years. It is certainly likely that early self understanding contributes to the later development of specific personal memory, mediated through language. Reese's work also showed that early experience with past talk with elaborative mothers is correlated with children's memory productions at age 3, and together these influences may establish a threshold from which further development of self and self history in the form of autobiographical memory may proceed.

---

[1] Howe and Courage rely on Usher and Neisser (1993), who queried college students about four specific salient events of their childhood, such as the birth of a sibling, using a set of standard probes, and found that some students could remember something about an event that had happened when they were younger than 3 years (i.e., 2 years old).

Autonoesis and Episodic Memory

Tulving (1972, 1983) made a distinction between episodic and semantic memory where *semantic memory* was seen as a general knowledge base, common in form and function to that of many sentient creatures. In contrast, Tulving and Lepage (2000) claimed that *episodic memory* is uniquely human and alone is concerned with awareness of the past. Most forms of memory, they stated, "have nothing to do with the past" (p. 209) with the single exception of episodic memory. This distinction is also one that I made with regard to developmental changes in children's memory, as well as in phylogeny, based in part on Tulving's (1983) discussion, and emphasizing that basic memory forms are oriented to the present and the future, not to recall of the past (Nelson, 1988, 1989b, 1993b, 1993c). The importance of this characteristic, however, has not been sufficiently recognized in developmental work on memory.

Related to the awareness of the past as a distinctive characteristic of episodic memory is its specificity in terms of location of an event in time and space, and the specific awareness of personal experience—the feeling that "I was there, I did that." Tulving and his colleagues (Wheeler, Stuss, & Tulving, 1997; Tulving & Lepage, 2000) called this aspect *autonoesis or experiential awareness* and they viewed it as definitive of episodic memory. Autobiographical memory is clearly episodic in these terms, being quintessentially autonoetic. Tulving contrasted autonoetic with *noetic* remembering; the latter consciously draws on the personal knowledge base, but does not "relive" the past or "travel backwards in time," as Tulving put it. This contrast distinguishes semantic memory from episodic memory—knowing versus remembering—but both are considered *declarative* memory.[2]

There is no convincing evidence that the infant or toddler who appears to remember an object or sequence of actions consciously remembers that a particular experience was experienced at a singular time and place in the past, and that the infant remembers the self experiencing the occasion, that is, remembers autonoetically. The alternative is that the infant or toddler is reminded of the sequence by the sight of the associated object or context but does not place the remembering as having been specifically experienced ("I was there"), only as a recallable sequence of actions (Nelson, 2000a). This phenomenological distinction is, of course, difficult if not impossible to make for a nonverbal organism, which the 1- to 2-year old is. Tulving and his colleagues (Tulving & Lepage, 2000) are currently carrying out research using modern brain

---

[2]Because of the disagreement in the literature as to whether early memory is or is not declarative, this joint characterization and distinction may help to clarify the issues.

imaging techniques (PET, fMRI) showing that the distinction is not just subjective, but can be identified in the different patterns of neural activity under different recall (knowing vs. remembering) conditions. They have found that there are distinctive neurological pathways in the right frontal lobes associated with autonoetic as opposed to noetic processing in adults. Future research should enable us to determine whether and when similar distinctions are evident in children's accessing of memories, but this will require rather different experimental paradigms from those used with adults. Moreover, as I have previously suggested, developing forms of memory might not map perfectly onto fully mature forms. For example, in considering the episodic implications for autobiographical memory in its development, the meaning of an early episode for the individual may account for its retention in a form that makes it autonoetically accessible at a later time.

An approach to the issue of the emergence of autobiographical memory, based in Tulving's theory of autonoesis, was put forth by Perner and Ruffman (1995). They viewed the development of connections of the prefrontal cortex—that involves the so-called *executive function*—to the pathways that establish memory in the limbic system as the critical development that enables memory of the self to be distinguished from simply memory in general. This is a developmental proposal that relates memory to developments in areas such as theory of mind, understanding of knowledge source, and metarepresentational levels. Thus it puts memory development into context with the other dramatic changes that are taking place during the preschool years.

In contrast to Perner, many developmental memory researchers have concluded that children as young as 1 year have episodic memory, that is, memory for specific episodes. As previously noted, it is difficult to establish the characteristics of episode recall by children before they are able to express themselves in language; thus it is difficult to set definitive lower limits on autonoesis. What Perner insisted on, and where I agree, is that when *episodic* is defined as autonoetic ("I was there; it happened to me one time"), there is little evidence that most children under about 3 years have episodic memory specifying time, place, and personal involvement (in some of Perner's work he puts the age at 5 years). There are, however, suggestions of brief segments of autonoetic awareness in younger children (Nelson, 1988, 1989a). These cases suggest a gradual development of a new function. Evidence for such representation of self in the past may be related to the representational self (Level 4) and it may appear in linguistic representation before becoming evident in the external objects or pictures that DeLoache (2000) has been exploring. These matters need further investigation.

Hereafter, following Perner, I make a distinction between *memory for episodes* (which may be quite brief and fragmentary) and *episodic memory*, which implies experiential (autonoetic) awareness. How the development from one to another comes about is not explained, however, simply by identifying possible different neural pathways operating for each. Rather, what we need to understand is how children make the passage from *episode* to *episodic* in the early childhood years, and what conditions make it possible for them to do so.

Social Interaction and Autobiographical Memory

The theory most enthusiastically embraced by the authors represented in this book is *social-interaction theory* (Fivush, 1991; Nelson, 1993a; Pillemer & White, 1989; Welch-Ross, 1997). This theory proposes that children *learn* to remember in a new way and for a new purpose during the preschool years; as a result, memory takes on a new form during this time that is apparent during the ensuing years as autobiographical memory develops. The context of this learning is conversation with adults about happenings in the present and past, as well as the future.

Parents often engage the child in talk about their previous experiences together beginning at 2 years or earlier, and provide probes and scaffolding to encourage the child to contribute to the conversation. Some parents do more of this than others, and some provide more exciting stories based on their own experiences or those shared with the child. There is ample evidence that these experiences of sharing memories have effects on the child's later memory, both specific and general (Haden, Didow, Ornstein, & Eckerman, 1997; Nelson & Fivush, 2000). Many social interaction studies have emphasized the significance of narrative in the construction of memory talk, making stories of personal experience (Engel, 1986; Miller, Potts, Fung, Hoogstra, & Mintz, 1990; Nelson, 1989b, 1993a; Tessler & Nelson, 1994). Moreover, there is evidence that parents who provide the framework and components of a narrative influence the child's own structure of the remembered event (Fivush, 1994; Nelson & Fivush, 2000). The narrative form takes a mundane event, gives it a setting of time and place, provides a central action or goal, a motivation, highlights a highpoint of surprise, success, or failure, an emotion, a conclusion, and an evaluation. The verbal form both organizes the experience and provides a rationale for remembering it as significant personally or socially. Thus experiences with the form of personal story telling can lead the child gradually into the level of the narrative self (Level 5).

The point is not that rehearsal of memories makes them stick, contrary to some interpretations of the social interaction model. The point is that engaging in these experiences serves the child as a framework for reconstructing his or her own specific memories, whether to share with others or to savor for the self. It is this process that leads to the emergence of autobiographical memory and thereby to the preservation of memory over time.

Functional Systems and Autobiographical Memory

A functional systems approach to development, wherein memory is seen not as a singular structure but as a set of functions that employ similar processes to achieve different ends, provokes additional questions and helps to integrate these theoretical strands (Nelson, 1989c). What are the ends served by memory in the infant and toddler period, and what new ends are served by memory later in development, specifically by autobiographical memory? As already emphasized, most forms of memory are present- and future-oriented (Nelson, 1993c; Tulving & Lepage, 2000). The future-oriented function of memory is basic to all organisms that have memory. To be able to predict the unfolding of events is to gain control, by anticipating what actions of one's own are called for in a situation. Evolution does not provide memory for the purpose of simply thinking about the past but to solve problems in the present, in particular to anticipate the next moves that are required by a situation. Recognizing a predator, for example, requires memory of the predator's appearance and threat for the purpose of undertaking action to avoid being its victim. Thus the past provides the experience that evokes reaction in the present and action in the future to avoid dangerous encounters or to achieve desired ends.

For the infant and young child, as for adults and other creatures, the basic function of memory is to establish knowledge of everyday situations that have been experienced and are likely to occur again in the future, are likely to present danger, or are critical to achieving goals. This kind of memory does not depend on recall out of context, but only the capacity for accessing the appropriate memory to support action in context. A standard form of such memory is *script knowledge* that helps the child anticipate what will happen next, for example in the bath or getting dressed or being fed. Anticipation enables relaxation of anxiety, enjoyment, cooperation, and excess attentional capacity to bring to other aspects of the situation. It thus fosters further social relationships and cognitive growth.

Memory in infancy is functional both within the infant's experience of activities in the world and for further psychological development. These functions are more or less automatic. They follow general "laws" of memory, as

Rovee-Collier and Shyi (1992) and Howe and Courage (1997) emphasized, but they are not deliberately employed. During the second year, memory may undergo a subtle change. It still serves basic present- and future-oriented functions, but with a component of directional control involved in such activities as delayed imitation and word learning. That is, memory is no longer simply automatic, but for some purposes comes under cognitive control and is called up out of context.[3] Memory comes to incorporate specific episodes and not just recurrent or traumatic events. As argued earlier, such early *episode* memory, however, is not *episodic;* it is not located in a specific time and does not display the sense of self that "owns" the memory; there is not yet in place a contrast between a memory of one's own as distinguished from a general knowledge storehouse.

The functions of memory that emerge from the practice of talking with others about one's own past are both social and personal. Exchanging memories with others solidifies the social and affectional bond and provides an important source of understanding the perspective of others that goes beyond awareness of visual orientation. These practices require deliberate organization, linguistic articulation, specific location in time and place, and the unique perspective of the self as narrator; in other words, they require the character of episodic memory. Thus these functions incorporate the characteristics of all memory, but they call on additional cognitive processes, which are developed collaboratively with others in the child's social world (Nelson, 1996). Most important for the establishment of long-lasting autobiographical memory is the personal function of retaining memories that are meaningful to the self. This, too, is collaboratively constructed as parents provide a perspective on the child's experience that may be adopted as the child's own, or may contrast with the child's perspective and is therefore resisted (Fivush, 1991; Nelson, 1996).

The period of sharing past talk overlaps in time the fourth and fifth levels of development of self understanding that are outlined in Table 1.1, the representational and narrative levels. I tentatively suggest that achievement of the representational level is accelerated by these practices, and that the narrative self level is highly dependent on such experiences. This suggestion depends on future research for support or amendment.

---

[3] Some would claim that this aspect of control is present in the first year. For the purposes of this argument, the precise timing of the emergence of controlled encoding and recall are not at issue. It seems certainly in place by 2 years.

LANGUAGE, SELF, AND AUTOBIOGRAPHICAL
MEMORY

Previously I argued (Nelson, 1996) that language plays a number of roles in the establishment of autobiographical memory between the ages of 3 and 6 years. It provides a second mode of encoding and accessing memories (Bauer & Wewerka, 1997). It also provides a narrative framework for organizing memory, turning an event into a story (Reese, Haden, & Fivush, 1993). Further, it may provide a unique modality for reinstating a memory that might otherwise be forgotten, through talking about it with others or ruminating on it alone, as in crib monologues (Nelson, 1989b). More generally, language contributes critically to the many dramatic changes in the social-cognitive functioning of the child during the early childhood period. Because children of 3 or 4 years are able to engage in brief colloquies with others, they can begin to receive verbal messages about aspects of the world that have not been personally experienced. Some of these come in the form of stories in books, some come in the form of conversations about the child's own personal past, some about others' experiences (Miller et al., 1990).

   Without access to these sources, uniquely available through language, personal memory is confined initially to the child's own experience. Likewise, initial representations must constitute a "single reality" view of the world, one in the present, with a common past undifferentiated with regard to source or ownership, and no specific sense of the mental as contrasted with external reality (Fonagy & Target, 1997). This state implies that, for the young child, memory for episodes is not distinctively his or her own but part of common knowledge. Miller and her colleagues (Miller et al., 1990) suggested that children do not distinguish between own memories and others' memories at the age of 2 or 3, taking others' accounts of experiences and repeating them as their own. At the same age, they often seem to merge their own lives with those of story characters (Miller, Hoogstra, Mintz, Fung, & Williams, 1993; Wolf & Heath, 1992).

   To the extent that experience, shared or not, is viewed by the child as common knowledge, experiential memory is not located in a particular time or with a particular point of view. This early period, then, is one in which there is *no contrast* for the child between his or her own world and that of anyone else's. It is not that there is a confusion between his or her view and others, or a fusion of self and other; it is simply that there is no recognition of differently owned mental states that represent experiences different from one's own, and thus no awareness of mental states such as memory that may differ from one person to another.

A telling example of the confusion that can follow from the lack of differentiation of self and other experience and memory is found in the following excerpt from a mother–child dialogue when the child participant (K) was 42 months (3½ years):

K: You know something?
M: What? (Pause)
K: Let me think. (Pause)
K: What's her name again?
M: What?
K: What's her name again?
M: Who?
K: That girl.
M: Who?
K: Don't you remember her?
K: You've seen her before.
M: No.
K: Yes.
M: Where is she?
K: I don't know.
M: Oh.
K: I don't know her name.
K: Somebody has a rocket.
K: That can turn into a big rocket.
M: Yeah?
K: (nods)
M: Who is this person?
K: I don't know her.
M: Where'd you meet her?
K: At our house!
M: At our house?
M: Somebody with a rocket came to our house?
K: Uh huh.
M: Was I home for this?
K: (shakes head)
M: No. So how would I know who this is?
(Original in Shaw, 1999)

It is obvious from this exchange (Nelson & Shaw, 2002) that the child does not understand that her mother, who was not present during the rocket episode, cannot identify the child who had the rocket and thus produce the child's name. In other words, the child has not yet differentiated her own memory and knowledge state from her mother's. The reason this excerpt sounds amusing to us rather than pathological is that we recognize it as a common state of a young child's confusion. (Further discussion between the two led to the mother's deducing from clues the name of the friend.) Experiences such as this presumably encourage children to reflect on their own and eventually to make the distinction between "mine" and "yours" in the mental domain.

Understanding that someone else may have a different (false) view of a real world situation than the self does—that is, the achievement, in the current parlance, of a "theory of mind"—is generally found to be achieved at about 4 to 4½ years of age. During the transition to this level of understanding, the child gradually comes to recognize that certain mental states exist independently of the physical world, for example, dreaming (surely in this case the child is given some help from parents, who explain that dreams are not real). The child at this time expresses emotional and conative states and attributes them to others (such as anger, love, happiness, wants, and likes). But epistemic states of knowing, thinking, and remembering remain unrecognized, even as the child is coming to use the language of the mind (Bartsch & Wellman, 1995; Shaw, 1999).

The relevance of theory of mind understanding to the present argument is that a child without a differentiated understanding of own and others' mental states[4] has not achieved a *conceptual* understanding of the self as a distinctive whole objective person, that is, at Level 4, the represented self. As James (1890/1950) noted, the continuity of self in time is critical to the self concept. If others' personal experience can be appropriated to the self, there can be no sense of self-continuity in time. The fluid boundary between self and other's experience in the early years blocks the establishment of this singularity—that is, "my past," not yours, not someone else's, not common to all.

The unique function of autobiographical memory is to establish a sense of personal history in a social world where others have their own unique personal histories that differ from the child's own, and thus to establish the "conservation of self" as existing independently through time (Nelson, 1997). Attaining this sense of self in time depends critically on the use of language to exchange messages about "my" experience, "your" experience, and "our"

---

[4]I prefer this way of stating the development to the term *theory of mind,* which implies that the child has an objective *concept* of mind constructed in terms of a theory (Nelson, Plesa, & Henseler, 1998).

experience. This constitutes a major taking-off point for further development of self understanding.

Thus the distinctiveness of the Level 5 narrative self involves two critical moves: distinguishing self experience from others' experience, and in consequence one's own past and future from others' past and future; and one's own knowledge states, thoughts, and memories from others'. There is no evidence that such a complex understanding of self and other emerges prior to the age of 4 years. There is evidence that there is a slow accretion of knowledge of this kind over the years from 2 to 5 and on into the early school years (Henseler, 2000; Nelson, 2000a; Nelson, Plesa, & Henseler, 1998). For example, Henseler found that 3- to 5-year-old children, asked to provide a narrative about playing a game with another child, focused at the youngest ages on their own action, then on both self and other, but even at 5 years did not incorporate any statements about mental states or attitudes in their narratives, although they could do so in retelling a story and in responding to theory of mind tasks.

NARRATIVE, MYTH AND MEMORY: TOWARD A CULTURAL SELF

The other side of the duality of self and other is the contribution made by the parent (and others) to the child's taking up of the values and constructions of the social and cultural world within which they are mutually interacting and narrating their lives together. This process constitutes the attainment of Level 6, the emergence of the cultural self. At this point, the proposal that autobiographical memory uniquely integrates the social and the cultural with the personal, and that the self that emerges from this process is formulated not only in terms of similarities and contrasts with other selves, but with explicit and implicit social and cultural norms, can be fully elaborated. A central question raised by this proposition is asked by Shore (1996): How does culture get into our minds? This question is clearly related to one that I posed in 1985: How does language get into our minds? Similar processes seem to be at work in both domains, not surprisingly, but the processes are subtle and require extensive time for consolidation. Neither language nor culture are acquired as objects in themselves; that is, they are by-products of activities that are focused on other goals. One of the main activities that provide the context for acquisition is the practice of engaging in story telling, whether the stories are about personal experience, fictional tales, or cultural myths.

The anthropologist Crapanzano (1990), who has written extensively on self, made the point that in the parent–child dialogues of the preschool years, where experiences are being recounted and reformulated, there is always a "third voice" present. The third voice is the voice of the culture, the social milieu, the society speaking through the parent (or other adult). This voice monitors and censors what the parent says and the way that the parent shapes the child's understanding of a situation. The various pieces that we have studied in the parent–child exchanges about the past, present, and future—the child's experience in and understanding of the world, self, and other, the social interchange that scaffolds and shapes that understanding into something more closely resembling the adult's, and that provides the model for auto-biographical memory—are integrated into a whole that in turn reflects the cultural models residing in the society's narratives. These can be found in explicit forms in stories and in school and are present implicitly through the parental voice from the earliest years, reflecting as well his or her perspective within those narratives. This is a point that Hendriks-Jansen (1996) made even more strongly, proposing that the child from birth is surrounded by the narratives of the culture, filtered through the parent's actions and arrangements of the infant's surroundings and care.

As these authors and others emphasized (Bruner, 1997; Donald, 1991), narrative plays a special role in human cognition and social relations. An autobiographical memory itself can be considered as one very long narrative, the story of one's life with many ministories incorporated into it. So far as we know, no other animals engage in story telling (although some seem to have complex communicative systems), yet people in all cultures studied do so. It seems reasonable to consider narrative as a thread that binds our memories, our selves, our social partners, and our culture together, and to explore the ways in which it does so.

Bartlett's (1932) original studies provided the first clues about the effect of narrative on memory, and also provided evidence that cultures differ in the preferred structures of narrative, especially of cultural myths. He showed that people of different cultures might reconstruct what is heard as a story in the course of remembering and recalling it at a later time in order to make it better fit their own cultural patterns. Embedded in Bartlett's work are several points of interest here: Narrative structure is acquired by individuals and used in the comprehension and remembering of verbal material; cultures differ in terms of the kinds of narratives they favor. How then do individuals acquire common cultural structures and content?

Autobiographical memory, as it has usually been studied in terms of episodes and narratives, develops not only through social language practices, but in the context of cultures that value the individual personal histories of their members. Autobiographical memory from this perspective is a product not only of the social world, but of the cultural world. For example, it is clear that learning to "tell your story" is highly valued in individualistic European-American cultures, and appears to be more highly valued there than in Asian cultures (Mullen, 1994). Children are not only inducted into this practice by their parents, but learn to produce their own stories beginning in preschools, kindergartens, and early school grades in terms of the practice of "sharing time" or "show and tell." These practices appear as one type of the cultural shaping of memory, much of which takes place in school. School memory is familiar to all of us in terms of memorization of facts and organization of material to be learned and remembered, but personal narratives are fostered there as well. The point here is that autobiographical memory is a favored cultural memory practice in Western society, learned not unlike other cultural memory practices that can be observed in both oral and literate societies (Rubin, 1995). It depends on specific cultural frameworks; to practice it well is to employ the narrative framework of setting, sequence, motivation, high-point, and evaluation.

Narrative as cultural practice, of course, is not confined to autobiography. Carrithers (1991) claimed that human societies depend on narrative to provide the meaning that ties the group together not only in the present but over generations and across social hierarchies. It is only within societal story telling and myths that social structures and the personages defined therein (such as royalty, professional identities) can be understood and maintained by individuals within them. Donald (1991) made an even stronger claim, that language itself was developed by early humans to express cultural understandings, myths that served to explain the world and its people to themselves. Thus according to Donald, narrative was from the beginning the "natural product" of language.

Constructing one's own self-history (or autobiography) typically involves the history and mythology of the culture within which one grows up, although these sources may not be recognized as such by the individual. In part, the autobiography serves to explain to the self why certain things happened the way they did, and their significance for the living present. Without the cultural frame of place, time, and social structure, the self-history lacks context. The sociocultural temporal frame of one's life—school, jobs, marriage —provides the narrative structure that situates specific episodes within the whole. Cultural memory practices such as national celebrations also provide frameworks for social and personal memory (Casey, 1987).

The implication from these various writers on memory, narrative, and myth is that the middle-class mothers who are generally studied in the paradigms of recalling events with their children are following acquired cultural patterns of how to tell a story, replicating the pattern with their children (although there are individual differences showing that not all parents use these patterns to the same extent). They may also situate their own stories within a specific historical period different from the present. The children in turn take up the cultural pattern from the model and from other social sources. The sources in societal models of varying kinds have become clearer with recent research, but the individual process of "taking up" remains obscure.

Within this larger perspective, autobiographical memory derives in all probability from social story telling and cultural myth making. All cultures convey myths to their members, some explicitly through language, both oral and written, others through ritual (Shore, 1996). The values of the cultural world are manifested in the cultural mythologies that are found in the representative stories and religious symbolisms of the society at large, which reach the young child primarily through the linguistic materials—songs, stories, games, and lessons—of their everyday experiences with parents and other adults. This is true not only of "primitive" or historical cultures, but of social and political structures of present-day modern societies.

Thus I believe that we can think of the cultural symbolisms available in literate and oral forms in our own society as mythological materials on which parents, teachers, and children draw to form their own ideas of the world in which they live. Through these materials, the child's own autobiographical memory takes on a cultural patina, and the child's sense of ideal self comes to resemble the cultural models that are included in the current mythologies. It may be noted that some myths are outworn and others are newly invented. Their relation to real societal history, sociology, and government as written by historians and other scholars may be very loose, in fact utterly detached. Nonetheless, they provide general understandings of how individuals do or should relate to their social and spiritual worlds. In this sense, they provide models for the ideal self that the Level 6 child begins to use as a comparison self.

Cultural myths incorporate models of the ideal life, on the basis of which individual lives may be led or reformulated in terms of a life story that conforms to the model. Of course, there are different models, such as those for boys and girls, and in many cultures there are many roles incorporated within the myths of the society that provide differentiated models (e.g., kings and knaves, queens and courtesans). The possible roles open on which to model a life are limited by the overarching mythology of the society's history and structure. American society is no different in this respect, although its rate of change over the past century may be greater than most, challenging old cultural myths and fostering the emergence of new cultural forms to take their place.

1. EMERGENCE OF THE CULTURAL SELF

Remnants of the old myths can be found strikingly in the stories of preschoolers as reported by Nicolopoulou and Weintraub (1998). In their studies, common story forms that vary by gender are identified. Preschool boys, when encouraged to tell a story, focused on superheroes and constructed loosely related episodes of overcoming one antagonist after another, stories with neither clear beginnings nor ends. Preschool girls, on the other hand, composed stories based on family and home life or on kings, queens, and princes. Their stories began in specific locations, went on to short adventures, and returned to home base at the end. One can see the formula suitable to each gender very visibly in these productions, as Nicoloupoulou pointed out (Nicolopoulou & Weintraub, 1998). Whether these reflect the actual individual "life models" of the children involved or only the dominant peer cultural expectations is not clear at this point.

The questions these reflections open up concern the importance of personal aspirations to achieve a cultural ideal in formulating autobiographical memory, anticipating one's future life course, and planning goals. The cultural values of personal power, self-actualization, and individualism appear today to be as strong as, if not stronger than, ever. Thus within this aspect of the cultural mythology, children are urged to develop their own expressions of self, distinct from parents and peers. Under this understanding of the cultural mythology, children and adults alike should value even more highly than ever the construction of a personal story, an expectation supported in contemporary works of both fiction and nonfiction, such as the current popularity of memoir writing.

NARRATIVE AND SELF, MEMORY AND MYTH TOGETHER

The idea of the parent, and thus the child, being enveloped in a society's metaphors and narratives (Crapanzano, 1990; Hendriks-Jansen, 1996) draws these observations and the context of mother–child talk about the past together. It is the fact that the culture is instantiated in the parental mind and is made visible through and in the language used to communicate that gives these exchanges their cultural power. Just as the child's talk about past and future is supported and scaffolded by the parent, so too the parent has been and continues to be supported, scaffolded, and shaped by experience in the surrounding culture. Autobiographical memory emerges from this mix; in the end, it is highly personal and idiosyncratic but never escapes its social and cultural boundaries. The best the individual can do is to challenge the boundaries and the myths that define them. It is this mix that implies that during the early school years, a narrative and cultural self emerges from the social, cognitive, and representational self established in the years from age 2 to 6. The cultural self is further shaped in school and in society. Other forms of memory and self understanding continue to operate for their different functions, but only with some recognition of self significance do they become part of the autobiographical memory self, the "Continuing Me."

Let me briefly summarize how the cultural perspective proposed in these last sections speaks to the earlier proposed explanations of the emergence of autobiographical memory to compose a more complete story. Early experience in constructing the personal past with parents provides the threshold for the emergence of a new function of memory, the autonoetic reference to personal experience in the past. Autonoesis emerges in concert with other developments of the preschool period, in particular with the attainment of psychological understanding of self and other (theory of mind), and reflects or is reflected in the establishment of frontal lobe processing through specific neural pathways that serve both autonoeseis and other executive functions, such as planning. These developments in turn open up the child's capacity to understand the self as a continuing person from a definite unique past into an indefinite but unique future, situated within a cultural complex. The child, of course, need not be aware that this is a specific cultural complex, any more than the fish is aware of water. However, as we now know, cultures vary in the values they hold for self-expression in its varying forms, and thus for the shape of autobiographical memory.

Let me add the following caveat. Because the child begins as an individual experiencer and rememberer, closed off from the different experiences of others for lack of effective representational language, she never becomes completely open to others' framing of her experiences, but can always reshape them to fit her own understanding, from her own developmental and personal perspective. Thus there may always be a tension between the parental and cultural shaping of her understanding of the past and the future, and her own account of it. This tension presumably accounts for individual aspirations and achievements, as well as for fiction, memoir, and the psychotherapists' practice.

REFERENCES

Bartlett, F. C. (1932). *Remembering: A study in experimental and social psychology.* Cambridge, UK: Cambridge University Press.

Bartsch, K., & Wellman, H. M. (1995). *Children talk about the mind.* New York: Oxford University Press.

Bauer, P. J., Hertsgaard, L. A., & Dow, G. A. (1994). After 8 months have passed: Long-term recall of events by 1- to 2-year-old children. *Memory, 2,* 353–382.

Bauer, P. J., & Wewerka, S. S. (1997). Saying is revealing: Verbal expression of event memory in the transition from infancy to early childhood. In P. W. van den Broek, P. J. Bauer, & T. Bourg (Eds.), *Developmental spans in event comprehension and representation* (pp. 139–168). Mahwah, NJ: Lawrence Erlbaum Associates.

Bruner, J. (1997). A narrative model of self construction. In J. G. Snodgrass & R. L. Thompson (Eds.), *The self across psychology* (pp. 145–162). New York: The New York Academy of Sciences.

Butterworth, G. (1990). Self-perception in infancy. In D. Cicchetti & M.. Beeghly (Eds.), *The self in transition* (pp. 99–119). Chicago: University of Chicago Press.

Carrithers, M. (1991). Narrativity: Mindreading and making societies. In A. Whiten (Eds.), *Natural theories of mind: Evolution, development and simulation of everyday mindreading* (pp. 305–318). Oxford: Basil Blackwell.

Casey, E. S. (1987). *Remembering: A phenomenological study.* Bloomington: Indiana University Press.

Crapanzano, V. (1990). On self characterization. In J. W. Stigler, R. A. Shweder, & G. Herdt (Eds.), *Cultural psychology: Essays on comparative human development* (pp. 401–423). New York: Cambridge University Press.

DeLoache, J. S. (1990). Young children's understanding of models. In R. Fivush & J. Hudson (Eds.), *Knowing and remembering in young children* (pp. 94–126). New York: Cambridge University Press.

DeLoache, J. (2000). *Becoming symbol minded.* Paper presented at Memory Theme Symposium, University of Otago, Dunedin, New Zealand.

Donald, M. (1991). *Origins of the modern mind.* Cambridge, MA: Harvard University Press.

Engel, S. (1986). *Learning to reminisce: A developmental study of how young children talk about the past.* Unpublished doctoral dissertation, City University of New York Graduate Center.

Fivush, R. (1991). The social construction of personal narratives. *Merrill-Palmer Quarterly, 37,* 59–82.

Fivush, R. (1994). Constructing narrative, emotion, and self in parent–child conversations about the past. In U. F Neisser & R. Fivush (Eds.), *The remembering self: Construction and accuracy in the self-narrative* (pp. 136–157). New York: Cambridge University Press.

Fivush, R. (2000). Children remembering childhood. *Memory Research Theme Symposium. Memory Development: Biological, Cognitive and Social Perspectives.* Dunedin, New Zealand.

Fonagy, P., & Target, M. (1997). Attachment and reflective function: Their role in self-organization. *Development and Psychopathology, 9,* 679–700.

Haden, C. A., Didow, S. M., Ornstein, P. A., & Eckerman, C. O. (1997, April). *Mother–child talk about the here-and-now: Linkages to subsequent remembering.* Biennial Meeting of the Society for Research in Child Development, Washington, DC.

Harter, S. (1998). Developmental changes in the self-system across the 5 to 7 shift. In A. Sameroff & M. Haith (Eds.), *Reason and responsibility: The passage through childhood* (pp. 207–236). Chicago: University of Chicago Press.

Hendriks-Jansen, H. (1996). *Catching ourselves in the act: Situated activity, interactive emergence, evolution, and human thought.* Cambridge, MA: MIT Press.

Henseler, S. (2000). *Young children's developing theory of mind: Person reference, psychological understanding and narrative skill.* Unpublished doctoral dissertation, City University of New York Graduate Center, New York.

Higgins, E. T. (1991). Development of self-regulatory and self-evaluative processes: Costs, benefits, and tradeoffs. In M. R. Gunnar & L. A. Sroufe (Eds.), *Self processes in development* (pp. 125–166). Hillsdale, NJ: Lawrence Erlbaum Associates.

Howe, M. L., & Courage, M. L. (1993). On resolving the enigma of infantile amnesia. *Psychological Bulletin, 113,* 305–326.

Howe, M. S., & Courage, M. L. (1997). The emergence and early development of autobiographical memory. *Psychological Review, 104,* 499–523.

James, W. (1950). *The principles of psychology.* New York: Dover Publications. (Original work published 1890)

Lewis, M. (1997). The self in self-conscious emotions. In J. G. Snodgrass & R. L. Thompson (Eds.), *The self across psychology* (pp. 119–142). New York: New York Academy of Sciences.

Meltzoff, A. N., & Moore, M. K. (1999). A new foundation for cognitive development in infancy: The birth of the representational infant. In E. K. Scholnick, K. Nelson, S. A. Gelman, & P. H. Miller (Eds.), *Conceptual development: Piaget's legacy* (pp. 53–78). Mahwah, NJ: Lawrence Erlbaum Associates.

Miller, P. J., Hoogstra, L., Mintz, J., Fung, H., & Williams, K. (1993). Troubles in the garden and how they get resolved: A young child's transformation of his favorite story. In C. A. Nelson (Ed.), *Memory and affect in development* (Vol. 26, pp. 87–114). Hillsdale, NJ: Lawrence Erlbaum Associates.

Miller, P. J., Potts, R., Fung, H., Hoogstra, L., & Mintz, J. (1990). Narrative practices and the social construction of self in childhood. *American Ethnologist, 17,* 292–311.

Mullen, M. K. (1994). Earliest recollections of childhood: A demographic analysis. *Cognition, 52,* 55–79.

Neisser, U. (1988). Five kinds of self-knowledge. *Philosophical Psychology, 1,* 35–39.

Neisser, U. (1997). The roots of self knowledge: Perceiving self, it, and thou. In J. G. Snodgrass & R. L. Thompson (Eds.), *The self across psychology* (pp. 19–34). New York: New York Academy of Science.

Nelson, K. (1988). The ontogeny of memory for real events. In U. Neisser & E. Winograd (Eds.), *Remembering reconsidered: Ecological and traditional approaches to the study of memory* (pp. 244–276). New York: Cambridge University Press.

Nelson, K. (1989a). Monologue as the linguistic construction of self in time. In K. Nelson (Ed.), *Narratives from the crib* (pp. 284–308). Cambridge, MA: Harvard University Press.

Nelson, K. (Ed.). (1989b). *Narratives from the crib.* Cambridge, MA: Harvard University Press.

Nelson, K. (1989c). Remembering: A functional developmental perspective. In P. R. Solomon, G. R. Goethals, C. M. Kelley, & B. R. Stephens (Eds.), *Memory: Interdisciplinary approaches* (pp. 127–150). New York: Springer-Verlag.

Nelson, K. (1993a). Events, narratives, memories: What develops? In C. Nelson (Ed.), *Memory and affect in development: Minnesota symposium on child psychology* (Vol. 26, pp. 1–24). Hillsdale, NJ: Lawrence Erlbaum Associates.

Nelson, K. (1993b). Explaining the emergence of autobiographical memory in early childhood. In A. Collins, M. Conway, S. Gathercole, & P. Morris (Eds.), *Theories of memory.* Hillsdale, NJ: Lawrence Erlbaum Associates.

Nelson, K. (1993c). The psychological and social origins of autobiographical memory. *Psychological Science, 4,* 1–8.

Nelson, K. (1996). *Language in cognitive development: The emergence of the mediated mind.* New York: Cambridge University Press.

Nelson, K. (1997). Finding oneself in time. In J. G. Snodgrass & R. Thompson (Eds.), *The self across psychology. Annals of the New York Academy of Sciences* (Vol. 818, pp. 19–33). New York: New York Academy of Sciences.

Nelson, K. (2000a). Memory and belief in development. In D. L. Schacter & E. Scarry (Eds.), *Memory, brain and belief* (pp. 259–289). Cambridge, MA: Harvard University Press.

Nelson, K. (2000b). Narrative, time and the emergence of the encultured self. *Culture and Psychology, 6,* 183–196.

Nelson, K. (in press). The role of narrative in the emergence of conscious awareness. In T. McVay, O. Flanagan, & G. Fireman (Eds.), *Narrative and consciousness: Literature, psychology, and the brain.* New York: Oxford University Press.

Nelson, K., & Fivush, R. (2000). Socialization of memory. In E. Tulving & F. Craik (Eds.), *Handbook of memory* (pp. 283–295). New York: Oxford University Press.

Nelson, K., Plesa, D., & Henseler, S. (1998). Children's theory of mind: An experiential interpretation. *Human Development, 41,* 7–29.

Nelson, K., & Shaw, L. K. (2002). Developing a socially shared symbolic system. In E. Amsel & J. Byrnes (Eds.), *Language, literacy and cognitive development* (pp. 27–58). Mahwah, NJ: Lawrence Erlbaum Associates.

Nicolopoulou, A., & Weintraub, J. (1998). Individual and collective representations in social context: A modest contribution to resuming the interrupted project of a sociocultural developmental psychology. *Human Development, 41,* 215–235.

Perner, J., & Ruffman, T. (1995). Episodic memory and autonoetic consciousness: Developmental evidence and a theory of childhood amnesia. *Journal of Experimental Child Psychology, 59,* 516–548.

Pillemer, D. B., & White, S. H. (1989). Childhood events recalled by children and adults. In H. W. Reese (Ed.), *Advances in child development and behavior* (Vol. 21, pp. 297–340). New York: Academic Press.

Povinelli, D. J., Landau, K. R., & Perilloux, H. K. (1996). Self-recognition in young children using delayed versus live feedback: Evidence of a developmental asynchrony. *Child Development, 67,* 1540–1554.

Reese, E. (2000). *A model of the origins of autobiographical memory.* Memory Research Theme Symposium: Memory Development: Biological, Cognitive and Social Perspectives. Dunedin, New Zealand.

Reese, E., Haden, C. A., & Fivush, R. (1993). Mother–child conversations about the past: Relationships of style and memory over time. *Cognitive Development, 8,* 403–430.

Rochat, P. (Ed.). (1995). *The self in early infancy: Theory and research.* Amsteram: North-Holland Elsevier.

Rovee-Collier, C., & Shyi, G. (1992). A functional and cognitive analysis of infant long-term retention. In M. L Howe, C. J. Brainerd, & V. F. Reyna (Eds.), *Development of long-term retention* (pp. 3–55). New York: Springer-Verlag.

Rubin, D. C. (1995). *Memory in oral traditions.* New York: Oxford University Press.

Shaw, L. K. (1999). *The development of the meanings of "think" and "know" through conversation.* Unpublished doctoral dissertation, City University of New York Graduate Center.

Sheffield, E. G., & Hudson, J. A. (1994). Reactivation of toddler's event memory. *Memory, 2,* 447–466.

Shore, B. (1996). *Culture in mind: Cognition, culture, and the problem of meaning.* New York: Oxford University Press.

Snodgrass, J. G., & Thompson, R. L. (Eds.). (1997). *The self across psychology: Self-recognition, self-awareness, and the self-concept. Annals of the New York Academy of Sciences* (Vol. 818). New York: The New York Academy of Sciences.

Tessler, M., & Nelson, K. (1994). Making memories: The influence of joint encoding on later recall. *Consciousness and Cognition, 3,* 307–326.

Tomasello, M. (1995). Understanding the self as social agent. In P. Rochat (Ed.), *The self in early infancy: Theory and research* (pp. 449–460). Amsterdam: North Holland-Elsevier.

Tulving, E. (1972). Episodic and semantic memory. In E. Tulving & W. Donalson (Eds.), *Organization of memory* (pp. 382–403). New York: Academic Press.

Tulving, E. (1983). *Elements of episodic memory.* New York: Oxford University Press.

Tulving, E., & Lepage, M. (2000). Where in the brain is the awareness of one's past? In D. L. Schacter & E. Scarry (Eds.), *Memory, brain, and belief* (pp. 208–228). Cambridge, MA: Harvard University Press.

Usher, J., & Neisser, U. (1993). Childhood amnesia and the beginnings of memory for four early life events. *Journal of Experimental Psychology: General, 122,* 155–165.

Welch-Ross, M. (1997). Mother–child participation in conversations about the past: Relations to preschoolers' theory of mind. *Developmental Psychology, 33,* 618–629.

Wellman, H. M. (1990). *The child's theory of mind.* Cambridge, MA: MIT Press.

Wetzler, S. E., & Sweeney, J. A. (1986). Childhood amnesia: An empirical demonstration. In D. C. Rubin (Ed.), *Autobiographical memory* (pp. 191–201). New York: Cambridge University Press.

Wheeler, M. A., Stuss, D. T., & Tulving, E. (1997). Toward a theory of episodic memory: The frontal lobes and autonoetic consciousness. *Psychological Bulletin, 121,* 331–354.

Wolf, S. A., & Heath, S. B. (1992). *The braid of literature: Children's worlds of reading.* Cambridge, MA: Harvard University Press.

Chapter 2

Social Origins of Reminiscing

Elaine Reese
Kate Farrant
University of Otago
Dunedin, New Zealand

Reminiscing, or talking about the past with others, is a critical part of our autobiographical memories. Autobiographical memories are private and uniquely our own, but they are simultaneously public property because they usually involve other people. A primary function of reminiscing is social (Hyman & Faries, 1992): We talk with others about our past to highlight events that were meaningful to those involved, as well as to illustrate our own personality characteristics. Thus, reminiscing is inherently social as well as a means of self-presentation.

Is reminiscing a universal phenomenon, or is it restricted to the population in which it has been studied most often, Western White middle-class adults and young children? Universality is difficult to prove because the possibility of a disconfirming culture always exists. At least with the present data, however, reminiscing does appear to occur in a number of disparate cultures, including middle-income Maori, Chinese, and Korean families, and lower income African-American families (e.g., Hayne & MacDonald, chapter 5, this volume; Miller, Potts, Fung, Hoogstra, & Mintz, 1990; Miller, Wiley, Fung, & Liang, 1997; Mullen & Yi, 1995). Of course, the form and function of reminiscing in these different cultures may differ dramatically (e.g., Hayne & MacDonald, chapter 5, this volume; Miller et al., 1997).

In this chapter, we are particularly interested in the way that reminiscing occurs between primary caregivers and children. If reminiscing is a culturally variable activity, then it is important to explore the way that young children are inculcated into the form and function of reminiscing in a culture (Nelson, 1993, 1996). Caregivers' styles of reminiscing could conceivably have an impact on children's autobiographical memory, and ultimately in their organization of knowledge about the self. We explore this issue primarily intraculturally, because individual differences in this activity exist within as well as between cultures. We integrate findings from a longitudinal study of caregiver–child reminiscing from 1½ to 3½ years of age to illustrate the point that caregivers socialize children into the form of reminiscing, but that children play an active role in the development of reminiscing from its inception. Moreover, we argue that reminiscing arises in part from the earlier attachment relationship between caregiver and child. Children's attachment to their caregivers appears to be a universal phenomenon (van Ijzendoorn & Sagi, 1999). Like reminiscing, however, the quality of attachment is variable within and between cultures (Harwood, Miller, & Irizarry, 1995). Finally, we discuss the implications of intracultural and intercultural variability in both attachment security and reminiscing for autobiographical memory and the development of self.

INDIVIDUAL DIFFERENCES IN CAREGIVERS' REMINISCING STYLES

A number of studies have now demonstrated the existence of individual differences in caregivers' styles of reminiscing with young children. To date, these within-culture studies have all focused on Western samples, usually White and middle-class (but cf. Hayne & MacDonald, chapter 5, this volume). The basic finding in these studies is that there are two distinct styles of caregiver reminiscing (Engel, 1995; Fivush & Fromhoff, 1988; Hudson, 1990; McCabe & Peterson, 1991; Reese & Fivush, 1993; Reese, Haden, & Fivush, 1993; Tessler & Nelson, 1994). The first style, which becomes more common as children grow older, is termed a highly elaborative, topic-extending, or narrative style. Caregivers who use this style follow in on their children's responses and then elaborate on them, ultimately providing a great deal of information about the event in the course of their statements and questions. The information they provide is often rich with descriptive and evaluative terms. These high elaborative caregivers collaborate with their children in producing a narrative about the past. In contrast, caregivers who adopt a low elaborative, topic-switching, or paradigmatic style repeat their own questions about the event, do not always follow in on children's responses when offered, and seem to be after a particular piece of memory information from the child. Their conversations about the past tend to result in less information being produced over-all, with less collaboration, and possessing less of a story-like quality. Research with non-Western cultures has not yet examined individual differences in caregivers' reminiscing style *within* those cultures. The overall degree of elab-oration does appear to vary across cultures, however, with caregivers in non-Western samples studied to date using fewer elaborations than caregivers in Western samples (Hayne & MacDonald, chapter 5, this volume) and initiating shared past-event conversations less often than Western caregivers (Mullen & Yi, 1995).

These caregiver styles of talking about the past tend to be stable across time with the same children (Reese et al., 1993), across types of past-event discus-sions (Reese & Brown, 2000), and across caregivers' conversations with differ-ent children in the same family (Haden, 1998). Thus, caregiver styles for talk-ing about the past are not completely dependent on children's characteristics. Neither, however, does reminiscing style appear to reflect a general conversa-tional style on the part of caregivers. Haden and Fivush (1996) demonstrated that mothers' reminiscing style was not related to their speech style in a free-play context with their preschoolers. Instead, reminiscing style appears to be specific to past-event discussions and may have to do more with the value placed on talking about the past rather than general personality characteris-tics of the caregiver.

OUTCOMES OF INDIVIDUAL DIFFERENCES IN CAREGIVERS' REMINISCING STYLE

Children whose caregivers adopt a high elaborative style report richer accounts of past events with caregivers, both concurrently (Fivush & Fromhoff, 1988; Reese & Fivush, 1993) and over time (Reese et al., 1993; McCabe & Peterson, 1991). These effects appear to generalize to children's independent memory reports with an experimenter (Hudson, 1993), and exist both in the quantity and quality of information reported. Children whose mothers used more orienting (who, where, when terms) and evaluative (how, why, and emotion terms) utterances early in the preschool years used more orienting and evalu-ative terms themselves later on when discussing past events with an experi-menter (Haden, Haine, & Fivush, 1997). Particularly convincing evidence of the causal nature of this relation is provided by a small-scale intervention study conducted by Peterson, Jesso, and McCabe (1999). Mothers trained to use an elaborative style of reminiscing with their 3½-year-old children effec-tively increased their children's general language ability at age 4½ and the quality of their personal narratives at age 5½, compared to children of a control group of mothers who were not specifically trained in a high elaborative style.

THE ROLE OF THE CHILD
IN CAREGIVER–CHILD REMINISCING

Children undeniably play a role in their own reminiscing. Vygotsky (1978) and Rogoff (1990) proposed that children are active shapers of their own cognitive development. Until fairly recently, the research on caregiver–child reminiscing tended to take a caregiver-driven approach. In particular, Reese et al. (1993) noted that children were essentially socialized into reminiscing by their mothers from the early preschool period, but that between 5 and 6 years of age, children started to take a more active role in reminiscing and could actually influence their mothers' reminiscing style. Recent research has attempted to explore the role of the child in these interactions in more depth. Reese and Brown (2000) noted that preschool children were initially more interested and capable at recounting or discussing events at which the mother was not initially present, than reminiscing or discussing events at which the mother was initially present. Harley and Reese (1999) found that at even younger ages, child characteristics such as self-recognition ability and language skill predicted children's later verbal memory skill, although Reese (2002) determined that the impact of children's self recognition on verbal memory was later mediated by maternal reminiscing style.

BIDIRECTIONALITY IN CAREGIVER–CHILD
REMINISCING

The bidirectionality between caregiver and child in early reminiscing, however, is perhaps best demonstrated through an intensive longitudinal study in our lab from a much earlier age than previously investigated (see Farrant & Reese, 2000, for complete details). Researchers visited 58 primary caregivers (all mothers) and their children (30 males, 28 females) in their own homes at 19, 25, 32, and 40 months of age. Fifty-two of the mothers described their children as European-New Zealanders, five of the mothers described their children as Maori New Zealanders, and one mother described her child as an Asian-New Zealander. The sample was, on average, of middle socioeconomic status, although a full range of fathers' occupational status was represented (Elley &

Irving, 1976). At each age, a variety of assessments took place, but at all data-points, mothers were asked to engage in a conversation about past events with their children. Two shared events were discussed at 19 months, and three shared events at subsequent datapoints. Events were preselected to be unique, significant, and spanning no more than a day. Examples of events discussed included farm visits, rugby games, and camping trips. Events had occurred an average of 1.5 months prior to the conversation, and were primarily positive in tone (89.4%). Conversations were videotaped, audiotaped, and transcribed verbatim. All maternal and child utterances were coded reliably (kappas ranged from .83 to .86; see Farrant & Reese, 2000, for complete details), but a few utterance types emerged as critical in the development of reminiscing. A critical maternal code was "memory-question elaborations" (MQEL) in which the mother asked or provided new information that had not been pre-viously discussed. For example, the mother and child were discussing a treas-ure dig at the beach and the mother asked, "What did the treasure look like?" Critical child codes included "memory elaborations" (ME), which refer to new information that is provided by the child. For example, during the con-versation about the treasure dig, the mother said, "We went digging in the sand" and the child replied, "Ummm, and that was when um the yellow spade broke." Finally, children's "placeholders" (PL) occurred when a child took an appropriate turn within the conversation but did not provide any content ("Mmm"; "I don't know"; "You tell me"). Placeholders were coded function-ally by transcribing the child's behavior from videotape onto the transcripts; a placeholder could only occur when the child was paying attention to the mother. Thus, children's memory elaborations tapped into their memory performance, whereas children's placeholders measured their participation in the conversation. Means per event for each code were calculated for each dyad at all datapoints. Table 2.1 shows the average occurrence of these codes across time.

Finally, at each datapoint, researchers assessed children's language. At 19 and 25 months, the MacArthur Communicative Development Inventory (CDI; Fenson et al., 1993) was used, whereas at 32 and 40 months, the Pea-body Picture Vocabulary Test III (PPVT III; Dunn & Dunn, 1997) and the Expressive Vocabulary Test (EVT; Williams, 1997) were administered. Total vocabulary was the final language measure at each datapoint (standard scores were available only for the last two datapoints). Table 2.1 displays the average language scores at each datapoint.

Our main interest was in the structure of mothers' and children's reminisc-ing over this time period. Recall that we were examining the development of reminiscing from an earlier age than previously studied, with a larger sample

TABLE 2.1
Mean Frequencies per Event (and sd) of Contributions to Mother–Child
Conversations and Mean Language Scores (and sd) for Children

Mother–Child Variables	*Timepoints*							
	19 Months		*25 Months*		*32 Months*		*40 Months*	
MQ-ELAB	1.96	(1.70)	3.69	(2.18)	4.90	(2.26)	4.30	(2.36)
ME	0.35	(.78)	2.15	(2.10)	3.55	(2.65)	4.46	(2.84)
PL	1.31	(1.79)	1.76	(2.19)	2.71	(3.06)	2.39	(2.14)
CDI	105.85	(107.59)	340.27	(173.79)				
PPVT					98.01	(12.22)	99.58	(12.77)
EVT					97.26	(13.01)	104.58	(12.06)

size and a refined coding scheme. In addition, the language measures at each
datapoint allowed us to control for the effect of children's language development on their verbal memory. To assess directionality in reminiscing over
time, we conducted Pearson correlation coefficients between maternal reminiscing style (MQEL) and children's memory (ME) and participation (PL) in
the conversations, controlling for children's language. Thus, children's concurrent language scores were partialled out of all correlations at that datapoint, and their initial language scores were partialled out of all longitudinal
correlations (e.g., 25-month language was controlled for in the relation
between 25-month MQEL and 32-month ME). The results of these correlational analyses are illustrated in Fig. 2.1 (for the full set of correlations, see
Farrant & Reese, 2000). First, note that mothers were fairly consistent in their
use of memory-question elaborations (MQEL) over time, replicating the existence of a moderately stable maternal reminiscing style (e.g., Reese et al.,
1993). Second, in contrast to Reese et al.'s study with preschoolers, these
younger children were already consistent in their use of memory elaborations
(ME) and placeholders (PL) by 25 months of age. Of course, we do not know
if this consistency will be maintained past the 40-month datapoint, the starting point of the Reese et al. study. Perhaps children's memory elaborations
are reorganized in the early preschool period. Third, children's memory responses and participation were concurrently correlated with maternal reminiscing style at each datapoint (vertical lines), confirming the dialectic interplay between mothers' elaborations and children's increased responding (e.g.,
Reese et al., 1993). Most important, however, are the longitudinal correlations
that address issues of directionality. Initially, the conversations appear to be
mother-directed with maternal reminiscing style at 19 months (MQEL) posi-

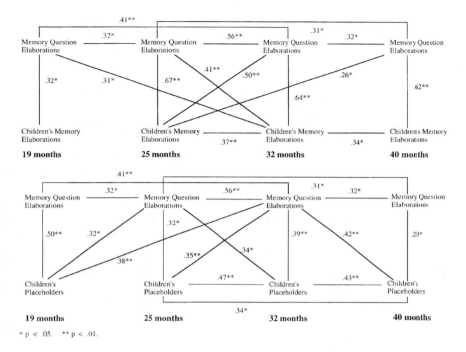

FIG. 2.1. Cross-lagged partial correlations between maternal reminiscing style and children's memory and participation. From Farrant, K., & Reese, E. (2000). Copyright © 2000 by Lawrence Erlbaum Associates, Inc. Reprinted by permission.

tively correlated with children's later memory responding at 32 months (ME). Children's participation at 19 months (PL) was positively correlated with mothers' later reminiscing style, but children's placeholders were not yet stable at this point, lending support to mother-to-child directionality at these ages. From 25 months, the pattern is bidirectional, with children's memory and participation predicting later maternal reminiscing style and vice versa. From 32 months, the pattern once again looks maternally directed, with maternal reminiscing style predicting children's later participation.

We examined the directionality issue further through mediation analyses (Baron & Kenny, 1986; see Farrant & Reese, 2000, for details). We tested the possibility that the apparently direct long-term relations shown in Fig. 2.1 actually reflected indirect paths through the partner's concurrent contribution to the conversation, which then mediated their own later responses. For example, the significant relation between maternal memory question elaborations at 25 months and children's later use of memory elaborations at 32 months might be accounted for by a path through children's 25-month memory elaborations. One long-term relation was unable to be tested for mediation as it did not meet the initial criteria (the correlation between 19-month MQEL and 32-month ME, because 19-month MEs did not correlate with 32-month MEs). For each of the eight remaining significant long-term relations between maternal memory elaborations and children's memory elaborations and placeholders, an alternative indirect path through a concurrent mediator variable was tested through regression analyses. For each regression analysis testing for mediation, the two proposed predictor variables (direct and indirect) were entered simultaneously after controlling for children's concurrent language. A direct variable that ceased to be a significant predictor when entered with the indirect variable, which remained a significant predictor, indicated a mediation path through the indirect variable.

The findings of these mediation analyses are depicted in Fig. 2.2. Note first that of the child-to-mother long-term correlations, children never directly predicted mothers' later reminiscing style. Thus, the effect of children's memory and participation on later maternal reminiscing style was mediated through mothers' concurrent reminiscing style. In predicting children's memory and participation, directionality occurred either through the concurrent child variable or was directly predicted by an earlier maternal variable. For instance, mothers' 25-month MQELs directly predicted children's 32-month MEs. Critically, children's 19-month PLs were also significantly correlated with their 32-month MEs ($r = .46$, $p < .05$). We conducted a conservative test of maternal influence on children's 32-month MEs by entering 25-month maternal MQELs in a regression simultaneously with children's 19-month PLs (controlling for children's language) to predict children's 32-month MEs.

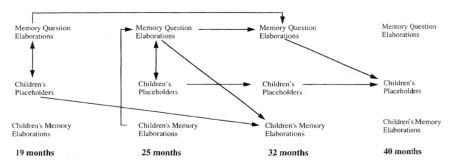

FIG. 2.2.   A mediator model of mother–child memory conversations. From Farrant, K., & Reese, E. (2000). Copyright © 2000 by Lawrence Erlbaum Associates, Inc. Reprinted by permission.

Both maternal reminiscing style ($b = .34$, $p < .05$) and children's earlier participation ($b = .32$, $p < .05$) emerged as significant but independent predictors of children's later memory. Thus, children's memory responding at age 2½ is determined through both their own earlier participation in memory conversations and maternal reminiscing style. If we had not acknowledged the importance of children's participation in the conversations in the form of placeholders, we would not have discovered the critical role that children play in the development of their own reminiscing.

The following example illustrates the interplay between children's participation in the conversations and maternal reminiscing style at the 19-month datapoint. In this conversation, mother and child are discussing a visit to the child's grandfather at the hospital. The child is sitting on the mother's knee throughout the conversation, and is looking at the mother when responding. Maternal memory-question elaborations and children's placeholders are highlighted.

Mother: *Where did we go and see Grandad the other day?*
Child: I don ti.
Mother: Where was Grandad?
Child: Upital.
Mother: Hospital. *And what was he have, what was he getting fixed?*
Child: *Ahh, somefing.*
Mother: Did he have a sore back? He did? *And what did he have at the hospital that you liked? What were you eating at the hospital?*
Child: I nand.
Mother: Bananas?
Child: Nah.
Mother: And some grapes. Did you have some grapes? And a lolly.
Child: *Mmmm.*

The child's clear interest and participation in the conversation, even at an age when she is not capable of producing many memory responses, most likely allows her mother to adopt a more elaborative questioning style.

Clearly mothers and children both contribute to the development of children's reminiscing, even from when children are as young as 1½ years of age. The relationship between mother and child has been developing since before birth, however, and has culminated in the attachment relationship toward the end of the first year of life, well before infants are capable of participating in a conversation about the past. To what degree and in what way does the attachment relationship contribute to the development of reminiscing? To address this question, we first have to review some basic research on the attachment relationship and on the predictive power of attachment for children's later communication and cognition.

INDIVIDUAL DIFFERENCES
IN ATTACHMENT SECURITY

Secure attachment is best conceived of as a balance between the child's proximity to the caregiver and exploration of the environment (Bowlby, 1969/1984). In a secure attachment relationship, the child uses the caregiver as a "secure base" from which to explore the environment (Ainsworth, Blehar, Waters, & Wall, 1978). When this balance is not achieved, resulting in either an excessive reliance on proximity seeking (resistant attachment) or exploration (avoidant attachment), the child is said to be insecurely attached. Cross-cultural studies have revealed that secure attachment is the modal attachment classification across nearly all samples studied, even though the samples varied widely with regard to socioeconomic status and types of preferred caregiving in the culture (van IJzendoorn & Kroonenberg, 1988; van IJzendoorn & Sagi, 1999). Attachment security does vary across cultures, however, with the greatest differences being in the prevalence of different types of insecure attachment (e.g., Grossmann, Grossmann, Spangler, Suess, & Unzner, 1985; Miyake, Chen, & Campos, 1985) and in the meaning attributed to attachment behaviors by caregivers (Harwood et al., 1995). Harwood et al. (1995) distinguished between the adaptation of various attachment behaviors in the phylogenetic sense and in the psychological sense. Phylogenetic adaptation is essentially for survival of the species, whereas psychological adaptation refers to the long-term outcome of different attachment relationships for the child. This distinction reminds us that although a certain attachment strategy may not be beneficial in the long term in one culture, it may well still be an appropriate adaptation psychologically in another culture. Thus, it is possible that an avoidant attachment may be less maladaptive in the long term in a society oriented toward independence, such as North Germany, compared to a society oriented toward interdependence, such as Japan (see Grossman et al., 1985). At present, not enough research has been conducted on the outcomes of insecure attachment relationships in different cultures to argue definitively that insecure attachment is necessarily psychologically maladaptive in all cultures.

OUTCOMES OF ATTACHMENT SECURITY ON
CHILDREN'S COMMUNICATION AND COGNITION

Most research on the outcomes of attachment security has instead been conducted with Western, usually U.S., populations (but see Oppenheim, Sagi, &

Lamb, 1990). We are particularly interested in this chapter in the outcomes of attachment security for children's communication and cognition. Overall, research on the relation between attachment security and general cognition has produced mixed results (Thompson, 1999), but has demonstrated that attachment security is positively related to children's communication skills with caregivers (Bretherton, 1999). The relation between attachment and later cognition and communication may occur mainly through the harmony between securely attached toddlers and their caregivers (e.g., Matas, Arend, & Sroufe, 1978). Meins (1997) conducted an intensive longitudinal study of children's symbolic play, language, problem-solving abilities, and theory of mind as originating from the attachment relationship. Security of attachment positively predicted most skills in interesting ways. For instance, attachment security significantly predicted children's symbolic play, their vocabularies, and their theory of mind development. In turn, attachment security also predicted mothers' readiness to interpret early infant communication attempts as intentional, and mothers' use of sensitive tutoring strategies in problem-solving tasks with their children as preschoolers. The available evidence fits with the hypothesis that the relation between attachment security and children's cognition and communication is mediated through mothers' sensitivity to children's signals, but this hypothesis should be tested directly. As mentioned previously, little cross-cultural evidence is available on the attachment–cognition relationship. In one exception, Kermoian and Leiderman (1986) found that Gusii infants' attachment to child caregivers predicted their scores on the Bayley Scales, whereas their attachment to mothers did not predict cognitive development. In Gusii culture, child caregivers are more likely to talk to, play with, and interact with infants. The maternal role is strictly that of caregiving. Thus, the attachment–cognition relation may be specific to those attachment figures who play a teaching or interactive role in the child's life.

Even less research is available on the relation between attachment security and memory processes per se. Belsky, Spitz, and Crnic (1996) found that insecurely attached boys were more likely to remember negative aspects of the same events compared to securely attached boys. Farrar, Fasig, and Welch-Ross (1997) found relations between attachment status and caregiver–child reminiscing. Insecurely attached daughters talked with greater frequency but in less depth about negative events with their mothers compared to securely attached daughters. We adopted a within-culture approach to this issue by examining individual variability in attachment security in our New Zealand sample as it related to the development of mother–child reminiscing. We predicted that reminiscing would arise in part from the prior attachment relationship between mother and child. Specifically, we predicted that securely attached children would benefit more from their mothers' reminiscing compared to insecurely attached children.

ORIGINS OF MOTHER–CHILD REMINISCING IN THE ATTACHMENT RELATIONSHIP

In addition to the measures already mentioned with our longitudinal sample, we also assessed children's attachment security at 19 months via the Attachment Q-set (AQS; Waters, 1987; see Farrant & Reese, 2002, for full details). The AQS consists of 90 attachment-related behaviors, each listed on a separate card, which mothers or researchers sort on a continuum according to how characteristic the behaviors are of the target child. In our study, mothers completed the sort in the presence of a trained researcher at the first datapoint, after observing their children for the relevant behaviors over the previous week. Children received an attachment security index based on the congruence between the mother's sort and a criterion sort for an ideally secure child (Waters, 1987). In accordance with past research (e.g., Farrar et al., 1997), we then divided dyads into groups with securely and insecurely attached children. The average AQS score for securely attached children ($n = 39$) was .49 and for insecurely attached children ($n = 19$) was .15, with a range of $-.11$ to .67.

Our main question was whether the development of reminiscing revealed in the Farrant and Reese (2000) study would be different for dyads with securely and insecurely attached children, but we also assessed the overall level of elaboration and memory for both dyad types (see Farrant, 1999; Farrant & Reese, 2002). Mothers with securely attached children were, overall, more elaborative in reminiscing than mothers with insecurely attached children, especially immediately after their children had given a placeholder in the conversations. Securely attached children participated more in reminiscing and were more likely to give memory responses compared to insecurely attached children.

We then compared the correlations between maternal reminiscing style and children's memory and participation separately for dyads with secure and insecure children (see Fig. 2.3 and Fig. 2.4). At first glance, it is clear that although the development of reminiscing with securely attached children is richly bidirectional, the development of reminiscing with insecurely attached children is very different. Most notably, long-term relations between mother and child are nearly absent for dyads with insecurely atttached children. The one exception is actually a negative correlation between children's early memory elaborations and mothers' later memory-question elaborations. For dyads with insecurely attached children, mothers responded at 25 months to children's increased memory elaborations by giving them even fewer cues in the form of elaborative questions. Research with typical samples has never before revealed a negative relationship between children's memory elaborations and mothers' elaborations. Fisher-z tests conducted for each pair of correlations across dyad types confirmed many significant differences between the attachment types, as noted in the figures by superscripts. The strongest differences appear to be in (a) maternal consistency, with mothers of securely attached children exhibiting greater consistency across time; and (b) longitudinal relations, with dyads with securely attached children exhibiting greater bidirectionality between maternal reminiscing style and children's memory than dyads with insecurely attached children. Of particular interest is the relation between early maternal reminiscing style and children's later memory elaborations only for the dyads with secure children. Essentially, dyads with

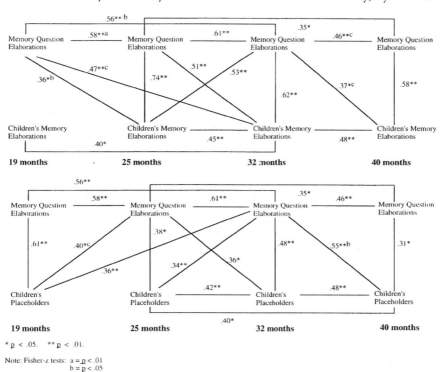

* $p < .05$.   ** $p < .01$.

Note: Fisher-z tests: a = $p < .01$
b = $p < .05$
c = $p < .1$

FIG. 2.3.   Development of reminiscing for dyads with securely attached children.

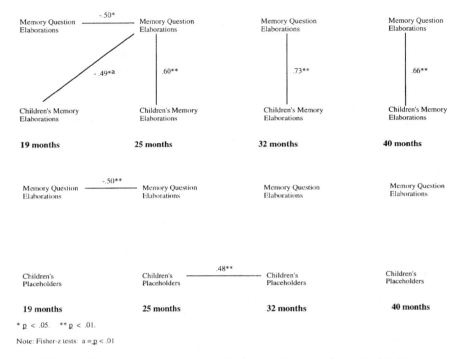

FIG. 2.4.   Development of reminiscing for dyads with insecurely attached children.

securely attached children are engaging in the socialization of reminiscing during this period. Dyads with insecurely attached children appear to respond to each other's reminiscing solely in the immediate conversation, if at all, and do not influence each other positively across time.

Excerpts from conversations of dyads with securely and insecurely attached children illustrate the basic pattern of findings. First, an excerpt from a dyad with a securely attached child discussing a farm visit at the 40-month data-point is lengthy and collaborative. Notice in particular how the mother follows in on information the child gives that the mother has not directly requested.

Mother: What was the farmer's name?
Child: I don't know.
Mother: Can you not remember?
Child: No.
Mother: Do you remember who . . .
Child: (interrupts) I ate all the lollie.
Mother: Yeah, that's it, they had lots of lollies. They did too.
Child: And a farm and a lawnmower, and a big bike.

Mother: (laughs)
Child: Did it?
Mother: Yeah. They had a big four wheeler. And then they had a motorbike that um (pause) they had a lawnmower.
Child: Yeah.
Mother: And you rode around on it.
Child: Yeah.
Mother: Yeah you remembered all that.
Child: And it broke because Amy's being naughty.
Mother: Yeah, but yes it did, didn't it?
Child: Yeah and Amy's been naughty and she broke it.

In contrast, an excerpt from a dyad with an insecurely attached child's conversation about a family fishing trip at the same datapoint is qualitatively different. Even though the child is recalling information, it is not the information the mother wanted. She continues to repeat her own questions even following memory responses from the child.

Mother: And what'd Uncle Mark take with him?
Child: Fish.
Mother: Yeah, but what'd he take with him?
Child: Two fish.
Mother: What'd Uncle Mark take with him on the back of the truck?
Child: Dog.
Mother: It was a boat.

Securely attached children appear to be benefiting more in the long term from their mothers' cueing strategies in the form of MQELs, probably because these maternal utterances are more contingent on the child's own responses. What will be the ultimate impact of this differential socialization on their autobiographical memory and their sense of self? Essentially, securely attached children are being effectively socialized into a reminiscing style. Conceivably, their independent autobiographical memories might eventually be more connected and coherent than those of the insecurely attached children, who are not being effectively socialized into a reminiscing style (see also Fivush, in press). Ultimately, the sense of self for securely attached children might be better integrated with others' views of them. We will be conducting continuing analyses on the content of the securely and insecurely attached children's autobiographical memories, with their mothers and independently, as we see the children at older ages. We will also assess the coherence of the children's self concept at the end of the preschool period to address these questions about the eventual outcome of different reminiscing patterns.

These results are especially significant given the topic of the conversations themselves: past events selected to be meaningful to both participants. Unlike the events in Farrar et al. (1997), in this study the past events selected were potentially positive in tone for both attachment types. We say "potentially" because even though the events outwardly appeared to be positive, occurrences within the event and subjective experiences of the event could well be negative. For example, the event of feeding ducks at the park appears at the outset to be a positive event, at least when compared to a negative event such as attending a funeral. However, the event may have consisted of the mother refusing to give the child any bread because he was noisy on the drive over, and scolding him for getting dirty. These negative aspects of the event could actually be reinforced in later discussions of the past event if the mother focused exclusively on the child's misbehavior. Belsky et al. (1996) demonstrated that insecurely attached children selectively remember the same events in a more negative manner compared to securely attached children. Our present coding scheme did not assess the positive or negative manner in which mothers and children discussed the past events, only the amount of information provided. In future datapoints with the same children, we will be assessing the emotion words used in the conversations as well as how rejecting or accepting mothers are of children's versions of events. We predict that we will find even greater differences between the conversations of dyads with secure and insecure children when we perform these content analyses.

CONCLUSIONS: ATTACHMENT, REMINISCING, AND SELF ACROSS CULTURES

These findings are also interesting in light of cultural differences in reminiscing. Miller et al. (1997) concluded that Chinese mothers discussed past events with their children for different reasons than did European-American mothers. Specifically, Chinese mothers were more likely to use the discussion as a vehicle for recalling and resolving a previous transgression on the part of the child. On the surface, this example may call to mind the conversations of the dyads with insecurely attached children in our study. Miller et al. argued, however, that this form of reminiscing in Chinese culture takes place in the context of a warm, yet firm relationship between mother and child. Therefore, we must take into account the larger attachment relationship when considering cultural differences in form and content of reminiscing. Secure attachment may lead to different forms of reminiscing in different cultures, depending on the value placed on memory in that culture and the preferred forms of reminiscing. We were unable to conduct formal analyses on the conversations of the Maori dyads in our sample ($n = 5$). It is worth noting, however, that all Maori dyads were securely attached with well-above-average Q-set scores ($M = .57$, range from .51 to .66). Yet the average level of maternal elaborations with Maori children dropped precipitously below average for the sample at 32 and 40 months ($Ms = 3.20$ and 1.84 per event, respectively). In turn, Maori children's memory elaborations also dropped below average for the sample at these later datapoints ($Ms = 2.93$ and 2.40 per event, respectively). These very preliminary findings are in line with the reminiscing data reported by Hayne and MacDonald (chapter 5, this volume) with a larger sample of older Maori children. Perhaps secure attachment in Maori culture actually leads to a less elaborative (and more repetitive) caregiver style over time because that is the style that is preferred and adaptive within that culture. Future research could be directed at longitudinal studies of reminiscing as a function of attachment status in Maori and Chinese cultures to confirm these hypotheses.

In terms of the relation between attachment and reminiscing across cultures, at least two alternatives are possible. The first possibility is that the long-term outcome of insecure attachment is culturally variable, and that insecure attachments do not always lead to a less desirable long-term outcome in that culture. For instance, in highly independent cultures, an insecure-avoidant attachment might lead to an earlier capability for independent memory on the part of the child. We would not necessarily expect this earlier independent memory style to be as coherent and integrated, however, as that of a securely attached child. Drawing on our within-culture findings, the second and more likely possibility is that secure attachment leads to the style of reminiscing that is culturally appropriate, and that more effective socialization of reminiscing would always take place with securely attached compared to insecurely attached children. The implications for autobiographical memory and self would then depend on the valued forms of reminiscing in the culture. If it is psychologically adaptive in that culture for children to adopt a less elaborative manner of reminiscing and a sense of self that is interdependent with others, then a secure rather than insecure attachment should lead to that outcome.

REFERENCES

Ainsworth, M. D. S., Blehar, M., Waters, E., & Wall, S. (1978). *Patterns of attachment: A psychological study of the Strange Situation*. Hillsdale, NJ: Lawrence Erlbaum Associates.

Baron, R. M., & Kenny, D. A. (1986). The moderator–mediator variable distinction in social psychological research: Conceptual, strategic, and statistical considerations. *Journal of Personality and Social Psychology, 51*, 1173–1182.

Belsky, J., Spitz, B., & Crnic, K. (1996). Infant attachment security and affective-cognitive information processing at age 3. *Psychological Science, 7,* 111–114.

Bowlby, J. (1984). *Attachment and loss (Vol. 1): Attachment (2nd ed.).* London: Penguin Books. (Original work published 1969)

Bretherton, I. (1999). Internal working models in attachment relationships: A construct revisited. In J. Cassidy & P. R. Shaver (Eds.), *Handbook of attachment: Theory, research, and clinical applications* (pp. 89–111). New York: The Guilford Press.

Dunn, L. M., & Dunn, L. M. (1997). *Peabody Picture Vocabulary Test (3rd ed.).* Circle Pines, MN: American Guidance Service, Inc.

Elley, W. B., & Irving, J. C. (1976). Revised socio-economic index for New Zealand. *New Zealand Journal of Educational Studies, 11,* 25–36.

Engel, S. (1995). *The stories children tell: Making sense of the narratives of childhood.* New York: W. H. Freeman.

Farrant, K. (1999). *A tale of autobiographical memory development: New Zealand style.* Unpublished Ph.D. thesis, University of Otago, Dunedin, New Zealand.

Farrant, K., & Reese, E. (2000). Maternal style and children's participation in reminiscing: Stepping stones in children's autobiographical memory development. *Journal of Cognition and Development, 1*(2), 193–225.

Farrant, K., & Reese, E. (2002). *Attachment security and mother–child reminiscing: Reflections on a shared past.* Manuscript submitted for publication.

Farrar, M. J., Fasig, L. G., & Welch-Ross, M. K. (1997). Attachment and emotion in autobiographical memory development. *Journal of Experimental Child Psychology, 67,* 389–408.

Fenson, L., Dale, P. S., Reznick, J. S., Thal, D., Bates, E., Hartung, J. P., Pethick, S., & Reilly, J. S. (1993). *The MacArthur Communicative Development Inventory: Words and Sentences.* San Diego, CA: Singular Publishing Group, Inc.

Fivush, R. (2001). Owning experience: Developing subjective perspective in autobiographical narratives. In C. Moore & K. Lemmon (Eds.), *The self in time: Developmental perspectives.* Mahwah, NJ: Lawrence Erlbaum Associates.

Fivush, R., & Fromhoff, F. A. (1988). Style and structure in mother–child conversations about the past. *Discourse Processes, 11,* 337–355.

Grossmann, K., Grossmann, K. E., Spangler, G., Suess, G., & Unzner, L. (1985). Maternal sensitivity and newborns' orientation responses as related to quality of attachment in northern Germany. In I. Bretherton & E. Waters (Eds.), Growing points of attachment theory and research. *Monographs of the Society for Research in Child Development, 50,* (1–2, Serial No. 209), 233–256.

Haden, C. A. (1998). Reminiscing with different children: Relating maternal stylistic consistency and sibling similarity in talk about the past. *Developmental Psychology, 34,* 99–114.

Haden, C. A., & Fivush, R. (1996). Contextual variation in maternal conversational styles. *Merrill-Palmer Quarterly, 42,* 200–227.

Haden, C. A., Haine, R. A., & Fivush, R. (1997). Developing narrative structure in parent–child reminiscing across preschool years. *Developmental Psychology, 33,* 295–307.

Harley, K., & Reese, E. (1999). Origins of autobiographical memory. *Developmental Psychology, 35,* 1338–1348.

Harwood, R. L., Miller, J. G., & Irizarry, N. L. (1995). *Culture and attachment: Perceptions of the child in context.* New York: The Guilford Press.

Hudson, J. A. (1990). The emergence of autobiographical memory in mother–child conversation. In R. Fivush & J. Hudson (Eds.), *Knowing and remembering in young children* (pp. 166–196). New York: Cambridge University Press.

Hudson, J. A. (1993). Reminiscing with mothers and others: Autobiographical memory in young two-year-olds. *Journal of Narrative and Life History, 3,* 1–32.

Hyman, I. E., & Faries, J. M. (1992). The functions of autobiographical memory. In M. A. Conway, D. C. Rubin, H. Spinnler, & W. A. Wagenar (Eds.), *Theoretical perspectives on autobiographical memory* (pp. 207–221). Dordrecht, The Netherlands: Kluwer Academic Publishers.

Kermoian, R., & Leiderman, P. H. (1986). Infant attachment to mother and child caretaker in an East African community. *International Journal of Behavioral Development, 9,* 455–469.

McCabe, A., & Peterson, C. (1991). Getting the story: A longitudinal study of parental styles in eliciting narratives and developing narrative skill. In A. McCabe & C. Peterson (Eds.), *Developing narrative structure* (pp. 217–257). Hillsdale, NJ: Lawrence Erlbaum Associates.

Matas, L., Arend, R. A., & Sroufe, L. A. (1978). Continuity of adaptation in the second year: The relationship between quality of attachment and later competence. *Child Development, 49,* 547–556.

Meins, E. (1997). *Security of attachment and the social development of cognition.* Hove: Psychology Press Ltd.

Miller, P. J., Potts, R., Fung, H., Hoogstra, L., & Mintz, J. (1990). Narrative practices and the social construction of self in childhood. *American Ethnologist, 17,* 292–311.

Miller, P. J., Wiley, A. R., Fung, H., & Liang, C. (1997). Personal storytelling as a medium of socialization in Chinese and American families. *Child Development, 68,* 557–568.

Miyake, K., Chen, S. J., & Campos, J. J. (1985). Infant temperament, mother's mode of interaction, and attachment in Japan: An interim report. In I. Bretherton & E. Waters (Eds.), Growing points of attachment theory and research. *Monographs of the Society for Research in Child Development, 50*(1–2, Serial No. 209), 276–297.

Mullen, M. K., & Yi, S. (1995). The cultural context of talk about the past: Implications for the development of autobiographical memory. *Cognitive Development, 40,* 407–419.

Nelson, K. (1993). The psychological and social origins of autobiographical memory. *Psychological Science, 1,* 1–8.

Nelson, K. (1996). *Language in cognitive development: Emergence of the mediated mind.* New York: Cambridge University Press.

Oppenheim, D., Sagi, A., & Lamb, M. E. (1990). Infant–adult attachments on the kibbutz and their relation to socioemotional development four years later. In S. Chess & M. E. Hertzig (Eds.), *Annual progress in child psychiatry and child development, 1989* (pp. 92–106). New York: Brunner/Mazel.

Peterson, C., Jesso, B., & McCabe, A. (1999). Encouraging narratives in preschoolers: An intervention study. *Journal of Child Language, 26,* 49–67.

Reese, E. (2002). A model of the origins of autobiographical memory. In H. Hayne & J. Fagen (Eds.), *Progress in Infancy Research, Volume 2* (pp. 215–260). Mahwah, NJ: Lawrence Erlbaum Associates.

Reese, E., & Brown, N. (2000). Reminiscing and recounting in the preschool years. *Applied Cognitive Psychology, 14,* 1–17.

Reese, E., & Fivush, R. (1993). Parental styles of talking about the past. *Developmental Psychology, 29,* 596–606.

Reese, E., Haden, C. A., & Fivush, R. (1993). Mother–child conversations about the past: Relationships of style and memory over time. *Cognitive Development, 8,* 403–430.

Rogoff, B. (1990). *Apprenticeship in thinking: Cognitive development in social context.* Oxford: Oxford University Press.

Tessler, M., & Nelson, K. (1994). Making memories: The influence of joint encoding on later recall by young children. *Consciousness and Cognition, 3,* 307–326.

Thompson, R. (1999). Early attachment and later development. In J. Cassidy & P. R. Shaver (Eds.), *Handbook of attachment: Theory, research, and clinical applications* (pp. 265–286). New York: The Guilford Press.

Van Ijzendoorn, M. H., & Kroonenberg, P. M. (1988). Cross-cultural patterns of attachment: A meta-analysis of the strange situation. *Child Development, 59,* 147–156.

Van Ijzendoorn, M. H., & Sagi, A. (1999). Cross-cultural patterns of attachment. In J. Cassidy & P. Shaver (Eds.), *Handbook of attachment: Theory, research, and clinical applications* (pp. 713–734). New York: Guilford Press.

Vygotsky, L. S. (1978). *Mind in society.* Cambridge, MA: Harvard University Press.

Waters, E. (1987). *Attachment Behavior Q-set (Version 3.0).* Unpublished instrument, State University of New York at Stony Brook, Department of Psychology.

Williams, K. T. (1997). *Expressive Vocabulary Test.* Circle Pines, MN: American Guidance Service, Inc.

Chapter 3

Joint Encoding and Joint Reminiscing: Implications for Young Children's Understanding and Remembering of Personal Experiences

Catherine A. Haden
Loyola University Chicago

Over the past decade, there has been a dramatic increase in research on the development of autobiographical memory (Nelson & Fivush, 2000; Reese, 2002). Although clearly a complex and multiply determined skill, a growing corpus of work has focused on the effects of early parent–child conversations about the past on children's autobiographical memory (e.g., Fivush, 1991; Haden, Haine, & Fivush, 1997; McCabe & Peterson, 1991; Reese, Haden & Fivush, 1993). The literature indicates the presence of substantial individual differences in the ways in which mothers reminisce (e.g., Engel, 1995; Fivush & Fromhoff, 1988; Haden, 1998; Hudson, 1990; McCabe & Peterson, 1991; Reese, Haden & Fivush, 1993; Welch-Ross, 1997), and longitudinal investigations involving White, middle-class American samples have established that the nature of mothers' talk with their children about past events has a long-term impact on children's developing autobiographical memory skills (McCabe & Peterson, 1991; Reese et al., 1993). Moreover, as detailed in chapters throughout this volume, cross-cultural variations in autobiographical memory have been found (e.g., Markus & Kitayama, 1991; Mullen, 1994), and differences in early parent–child reminiscing may contribute to these cultural differences (e.g., Han, Leichtman, & Wang, 1998; Miller, Wiley, Fung, & Liang, 1997; Mullen & Yi, 1995).

In this chapter, I argue that it is not only the ways events are discussed in retrospect that influences children's autobiographical memory; language-based interactions during events can have a profound impact on how young children come to comprehend and represent those experiences (Fivush, Pipe, Murachver, & Reese, 1997; Nelson, 1996; Ornstein & Haden, 2001). Because memory begins with understanding an event as it is being experienced, it is of major importance to consider how a child makes sense of an event as it takes place. Although understanding can be driven by endogenous forms of knowledge brought to the situation by the child, such as prior knowledge and expectation, exogenous influences, such as parent–child interchanges during a novel experience, can also affect understanding, increasing encoding and subsequent remembering (Haden, Ornstein, Eckerman, & Didow, 2001). Mother–child talk during ongoing events has not been explored as thoroughly as reminiscing about past activities, but it seems likely that conversation as an event unfolds can serve to focus attention on salient aspects of the experience and provide information that may affect a child's interpretation of it. Indeed, conversational interactions that occur during events may facilitate children's understanding of an experience and serve to organize the resulting representation, in turn, affecting its accessibility for later retrieval over long delay intervals—perhaps even a lifetime.

Given this perspective, to understand the development of autobiographical memory skills—and cultural and individual variations in these skills—one must consider the linguistic "milieu" within which the child acts and interacts with others. As Nelson (1993) argued, the emergence of autobiographical memory depends on the ability to encode and represent events in language. In this chapter, I focus on the significant opportunities parent–child conversational interactions about events provide for children to make sense of and remember their experiences. I begin with a treatment of the growing empirical literature on parent–child conversations about previous experiences, emphasizing the impact participating in reminiscing with their caregivers can have on children's developing abilities to recount and represent events. I then consider how language use during an event can facilitate memory, and describe in some detail a longitudinal study my colleagues and I (Haden et al., 2001) conducted to explore linkages between parent–child conversations about ongoing activities and children's subsequent remembering of these experiences. Finally, drawing on the within-culture findings reported here, I suggest that cultural variations in autobiographical memory may be profoundly influenced by differences in the opportunities parent–child conversations about present and past events provide for children to understand themselves and their experiences in their sociocultural world.

PARENT–CHILD REMINISCING

Parents and children begin talking about previously experienced events almost as soon as children start saying their first words, sometime between 12 and 18 months of age (Eisenberg, 1985; Hudson, 1990; Nelson, 1988). However, when they first reminisce together, the parent provides most of the structure and information to the conversation, and the child participates by confirming or repeating what the parent has said. Consider, for example, the following excerpt from a typical past-event conversation between a mother and her 18-month-old child involving discussion of swimming at the hotel pool while on a family vacation:

> **Mother:** We were kicking our feet . . . And do you remember some water was warm and some water was cold?
> **Child:** Yeah.
> **Mother:** 'Cause half the pool was outside and half was inside. And there were bits in the pool where the water was warm and other bits where it was cold. And we moved away from the cold parts fast.
> **Child:** Uh kikikikik (sounds like "kick kick kick")
> **Mother:** And we tried to stay in the warm parts.
> **Child:** Yeah.
> **Mother:** Yes we did.
> **Child:** Mmhm.
> **Mother:** And you practiced kicking. And you even got your face wet . . . Do you remember the best part? I had forgotten. The best part was when daddy and I were both there and you jumped from me to daddy.
> **Child:** Weeeeeee!
> **Mother:** And then back from daddy to me. We jumped and jumped and jumped and jumped and jumped. That was fun, wasn't it?
> **Child:** *Giggles and nods.*
> **Mother:** What happened when we finished swimming?
> **Child:** Um. Ha.

As illustrated here, although in these very early instances of adult–child reminiscing children do not provide much in the way of unique informational content about previously experienced events, they will take appropriate conversational turns, suggesting an interest in engaging in this form of conversational interaction (Farrant & Reese, 2000). Initially, parents heavily scaffold their children's contributions to construct a coherent story. But as children achieve increasing levels of linguistic competence, they begin to initiate past-event conversations and provide information about what occurred. By the time they are 3 to 4 years of age, with practice using narratives to express their personal experiences and to comprehend the experiences of others, children are able not only to carry on sustained discourse about the past, but start to take advantage of language as a representational exchange system (Nelson, 1996). Essentially, at this point, children begin to share and compare knowledge in past-event conversations—to build understanding from what is said—and are no longer tied to their own largely experientially based interpretations of events. Clearly, the shift to language representations involves a long, dynamic process. Nevertheless, it is a critically important development because the ability to integrate new knowledge gained through language with individually constructed knowledge fundamentally changes how children make sense of and internally represent their experiences.

Conversational Styles for Talking About the Past

Given the opportunity that parent–child reminiscing offers for children to come to new understandings of past events, it is significant that there are individual differences among White middle-class American parents in their conversational "styles" for talking about the past (Engel, 1995; Fivush & Fromhoff, 1988; Hudson, 1990; McCabe & Peterson, 1991; Reese & Fivush, 1993; Reese et al., 1993). *High elaborative* parents elicit long, embellished discussions of previously experienced events by frequently asking questions, following in on their children's responses, and providing more and more memory information even when children are not. In contrast, *low elaborative* parents have short past-event conversations during which they provide little descriptive information. They tend to repeat the same question over and over to their children in an attempt to obtain a "correct" memory response, and they are likely to switch topics when children cannot recall.

These reminiscing styles generalize across different types of past events discussed (e.g., excursions and holidays, zoo or museum trips, entertainment outings), and tend to be consistent over several years with the same children (Reese et al., 1993) and across different aged children in the same family (Haden, 1998). Mothers, however, do not appear to adopt a consistent conversational style across disparate contexts, as we (Haden & Fivush, 1996) found when comparing maternal talk across memory and unstructured play situations. Indeed, in our work, mothers using an elaborative style when discussing past events with their children appeared no more or less likely to adopt an elaborative conversational style when talking with their children during free play.

Importantly, there are concurrent and longitudinal differences between children of high and low elaborative mothers in the amount of information that they are able to recall about specific events (e.g., Fivush & Fromhoff, 1988; McCabe & Peterson, 1991; Reese et al., 1993). For example, we (Reese et al., 1993) have shown that maternal elaboration during early conversations with their 40-month-old children was associated positively with children's contribution of memory information in these conversations at 58 and 70 months of age. Moreover, in other research (e.g., Hudson, 1993; McCabe & Peterson, 1991; Peterson & McCabe, 1994), the more elaborative mothers were when their children were 2 years old, the better the children's independent skills for remembering events with an examiner as much as a year and a half later. In these studies, children with high elaborative mothers were better able to respond to questions posed by an examiner and produced longer reports concerning their personal experiences as compared with children with low elaborative mothers. As such, mothers who are highly elaborative early in development clearly facilitate their children's abilities to report on their past experiences in a detailed manner. Moreover, it is argued that as these linguistic skills are learned, children actually come to understand and represent personal experiences in more elaborated ways (Fivush, Haden, & Reese, 1996).

Mental State Understanding

Embellished personal narratives can also provide a rich source of information about mental processes (e.g., Rudek & Haden, 2002; Nelson, 1996; Welch-Ross, Fasig, & Farrar, 1999). Parent–child discussions of past events may include many direct references to intentions, thoughts, beliefs, feelings, and desires, and in this way can enhance children's understanding of why they or others took particular actions, made specific choices, felt certain ways, and so on. Language of mental states can also be used to indicate differences and commonalities between the child's experience and understanding and that of another. Moreover, explicit references to the process of remembering itself and the factors that impact recall that are contained in these conversations may promote general mnemonic understanding.

With these ideas in mind, we (Rudek & Haden, 2002) recently explored mothers' use and children's use of mental state language in conversations about the past. In the context of a longitudinal study, mother–child dyads talked about several past events at two age points, when the children were 2½ and 3½ years old. Recordings of these verbal interchanges were transcribed and scored for the frequency of mental state language. Not surprisingly, given the nature of these conversations, the mental terms most commonly used by mothers and children were *remember, know,* and *think.* On average, mothers included about 20 mental terms in conversations with their children at both the 2½ year and 3½ year age points, which translated to about 23% of their memory-related utterances. The stability in mothers' mental term use contrasted with changes in the children's mental term language that were found during this period. Although only a small percentage of children's utterances contained mental terms, increases were noted over time. The mean number of mental terms used by children at age 2½ was five, corresponding to 1% of their total memory-related utterances, whereas by 3½ children were including close to seven mental terms in these conversations, corresponding to 4% of their utterances.

More interesting, as illustrated in Fig. 3.1, correlational analyses revealed that mother's total mental term use at the 2½-year age point was positively related to children's mental term use a year later. Bidirectionality of effects was apparent as well, with children's total use at 2½ years of age correlating with mothers' later use at the 3½-year-old time point. Regression analyses (which should be considered exploratory given our sample size) conducted to examine these links did not reveal a unique contribution of mothers' term use at 2½ years, over and above children's mental term use at 2½, in predicting children's mental term use 1 year later. Nevertheless, the concurrent and longitudinal relations here are consistent with previous work concerning parent–child mental state language in other settings (e.g., Dunn, Brown, Slomkowski, Tesla, & Youngblad, 1991; Furrow, Moore, Davidge, & Chiasson, 1992; Moore,

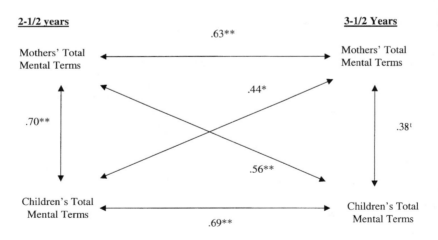

Note: ᵗp < .10, * p < .05, ** p < .01.

FIG. 3.1.   Correlations among mothers' and children's mental term language over time.

Furrow, Chiasson, & Patriquin, 1994). Although further studies are necessary to elucidate the process by which children learn about their own and others' mental worlds, conversations about past events may be an important context in which mental state language and an understanding of mind is fostered.

Narrative Structure

Parent–child conversations about the past also provide children with experience in organizing their memories into coherent narratives. As we have argued (see Fivush & Haden, 1997, for a full discussion), personal narratives to some extent reflect the organization of experiences inherent in the world, but the translation of the event into a "good story" adds layers of comprehensibility above and beyond what is available from direct experience. So although all narratives tell what happened during the event, coherent and meaningful personal stories go beyond this referential information (Labov, 1982; Peterson & McCabe, 1983). Good narratives feature orienting information about when and where the event occurred, and some designation of who was there. Orienting statements may also provide background descriptions and explanations that connect the event being narrated to other related experiences, thus setting it in a larger social and descriptive context. Perhaps more important, personal narratives include evaluative information that conveys why an event was interesting, significant, meaningful, and ultimately, memorable. This information is carried through explicit evaluative statements (*"It was the best time I've ever had."*), as well as by a variety of evaluative devices that intensify (*"It was soooo cold."*), emphasize (*"It never stopped."*), modify (*"He splashed every part."*), and provide internal responses (*"I was sad."; "I wanted to go on the monkey bars."*).

Research suggests that by practicing these forms for telling personal narratives in conversations with their parents, children do indeed learn to remember events in more organized and personally meaningful ways (Fivush, 1991; Peterson, 1990; Peterson & McCabe, 1992, 1994). Consider, for example, a longitudinal analysis we (Haden, Haine, & Fivush, 1997) conducted of mother–child, father–child, and examiner–child conversations about the past when children were 40 and 70 months of age. Individual differences were evident among parents in their use of narrative structures, although mothers and fathers increased similarly in their use of orientations, referentials, and evaluations over time. Children also showed clear developmental changes in the amount of narrative structure they were providing across the preschool years (Fivush, Haden, & Adam, 1995). They increasingly included actions, descriptions, orientations, and evaluations in narratives with their mothers and fathers and in independent stories told to an examiner. Most notable, however, were longitudinal linkages found between parents' use and children's use of narrative structure. We discovered that children's own early skills to include evaluative information in independent personal narratives strongly predicted their later use of these narrative devices. But we also found that mothers' (but not fathers') use of evaluative narrative devices when children were 40 months *uniquely* predicted children's use of evaluations in independent narratives at 70 months. That is, over and above the children's own early use, mothers who emphasized evaluations when reminiscing with their children at 40 months of age had children who were emphasizing evaluations in their independent narratives with an examiner at 70 months of age. In addition, consistent with previous research (e.g., Fivush, 1991; Peterson & McCabe, 1992, 1994), there was some suggestion in these data that mothers who made many orienting comments when reminiscing with their children at 40 months of age had children who were incorporating a great deal of orienting information in their later independent narratives.

Recounting and Representing Past Events

As the research on parent–child reminiscing documents, early conversations about past events have a long-term impact on children's developing skills for remembering. It is not simply the case that children are learning ways to recount their past; rather, these findings have serious implications for children's developing abilities to understand and represent their experiences and themselves. As parents ask questions, and follow in and elaborate on the children's responses, new knowledge can be added to memory beyond that available at the time of initial encoding. Elaborated conversations about previously experienced events can enhance understanding by bringing out meaningful causal and temporal connections between aspects of experience that were previously nonobvious or only partially understood (Nelson, 1996). Moroever, linkages between the event under discussion and the child's prior experiences can be made explicitly and meaningfully in these verbal interchanges, connecting pieces of the child's developing life story. References during reminiscing to thoughts, beliefs, and desires of the child and of other people who participated in the event can facilitate interpretation of others' actions, as well as prompting coordination of different perspectives held by the child and others of the event.

At a more general level, the theoretical argument has been made that as children learn culturally conventionalized narrative forms for recounting their past experiences in these conversational interactions, they simultaneously learn new ways of representing those experiences in conformity with these narrative forms (e.g., Fivush & Haden, 1997). Thus, it is not simply the case that some children come to recount their past experiences in more elaborated ways; rather, it is suggested that some children actually come to represent their experiences more elaboratively. Moreover, children of elaborative parents may be implicitly learning that past event conversations are a valued social activity, and may become more interested in engaging in this form of verbal inter-action and may do so more often than children of less elaborative parents. Also, because in the telling of these stories, linkages are made between the event being narrated and the child's prior experiences, and between the child and other people who shared in the experiences, these stories can become a significant source of self-understanding (who I *am* in relation to who I *was*) and understanding of one's relationships with others.

In addition, parent–child conversations about the past provide a significant opportunity for children to gain experience in retrieving information from memory in response to explicit maternal probes and to further explore the use of language for reporting past activities. Moreover, they can contain some very explicit references to the process of remembering. As such, through these conversational interactions, children may acquire some general principles about the retrieval and reporting of events (Fivush et al., 1996; Ornstein & Haden, 2001). Children learn what is interesting and important to tell in a personal story, and most intriguingly, this may lead them to attend to partic-ular aspects of events as they are being experienced. Indeed, it may be the case that children who engage with their parents in elaborated past talk actually come to encode experiences in a very richly detailed manner. It is to the process of encoding that I now turn.

PARENT–CHILD CONVERSATIONAL INTERACTIONS AS EVENTS UNFOLD

The ways that events are talked about as they are being experienced can play a crucial role in how young children come to understand and represent their experience (Haden et al., 2001; Fivush et al., 1997; Nelson & Fivush, 2000). Initial support of this claim comes from the ground-breaking work by Tessler and Nelson (1994) in which a small sample of 3-year-old children were observed as they visited a museum with their mothers. When an examiner interviewed the children about 1 week later, only the objects and activities that were jointly talked about by both the mother and child during the event were recalled. Similarly, in a second study, mothers and their 4-year-old children were tape-recorded during a picture-taking walk through an unfamiliar neighborhood. Once again, children did not recall anything about their experiences that had been mentioned only by the mother or only by the child; what they recalled had been jointly discussed as the event unfolded. Additionally, Tessler and Nelson found that mothers who frequently connected aspects of the ongoing event to previous experiences had children who later recalled more of the pictures they had taken, and remembered more about the walk, in contrast to children of mothers who did not adopt this narrative style during the encoding of the event. As demonstrated in this study, then, adult–child discussion during ongoing events can focus children's attention and supplement understanding in a way that impacts the content and structure of their later event recall.

Linking Joint Encoding and Recall

My colleagues and I (Haden et al., 2001) recently conducted an exploration of the linkages between mother–child narrative interaction during specified events and children's subsequent memory for these experiences. In this longitudinal study of children from 2½ to 3½ years of age, we observed a sample of White, middle-class mother–child dyads as they engaged in a specially constructed, interesting, and enjoyable event at three time points across the year. Within the confines of a room in the family's home, mothers and children were invited to take part in a camping trip at 30 months, a birdwatching adventure at 36 months, and the "opening" of an ice cream store at 42 months. To summarize the nature of these events, the camping activity began with the mothers and children loading up backpacks with various food items (e.g., hamburgers, hot dogs, sodas) to take with them on their trip. They then hiked to a fishing pond where there was a fishing rod and net to use in catching the fish. After fishing, they continued on to a campsite where there was a sleeping bag, along with a grill, pots, and utensils (e.g., spatula, forks) to use in cooking and eating their food. Similarly, the birdwatching began with the mothers and children selecting from an array of birdwatching equipment (e.g., binoculars, birdcaller) to use in finding the birds. They then followed clues (e.g., feathers, eggs) that led them to the locations of the different birds. Once they had retrieved the birds, they took them to a new place to live: a garden, complete with trees, flowers, birdhouses, and different bird foods (e.g., seeds, worms). At the start of the ice cream shop event, the mothers and children used various tools (e.g., a hammer, nails) to construct the store by attaching signs, a canopy, and shelves. Next, they filled the shop with different kinds of Play-Doh ice cream, toppings (e.g., sprinkles, gummy bears), dishes, and cones.

Finally, as the mothers and children hosted their "grand opening," they donned aprons, set the tables, and made ice cream treats for their first customers: a toy dog and stuffed bear.

In this way, each of these events involved a number of component features (e.g., in the camping event: backpacks, fish; in the birdwatching activity: worms, owl; in the ice cream shop event: hammer, ice cream). And because these interactions were videotaped, we had an exact record of how each mother–child pair nonverbally and verbally interacted with each feature as the event unfolded. Armed with this information, it was possible to link mother–child talk during the events to assessments of the children's memory. The children's recall was elicited by an examiner at 1-day and 3-week delay intervals using a standardized memory interview. The interview was hierarchically structured, beginning with very general open-ended probes (e.g., for the camping event: *"Tell me about the camping trip you had with your mom."*), followed by more specific open-ended probes (e.g., *"What kind of food did you pack up?"*), and, finally, yes–no type probes (e.g., *"Did you pack hot dogs?"*). In addition, within a week of the events, each mother tape-recorded a conversation in which she asked her child to recall the camping, birdwatching, and ice cream shop activities. Following the procedure used in previous work on mother–child reminiscing (e.g., Reese et al., 1993), the mothers in this study were asked simply to talk with their children about these events as they naturally would when discussing past experiences.

Because of our interest in linking children's event recall to interaction during the same activity, a critical first step in the analyses was to characterize mother–child behaviors directed toward specific features of each event. To do so, we developed a coding system to reliably score the videotaped records in terms of mother and child nonverbal and verbal behaviors directed toward specific features of each event. Nonverbal behaviors included pointing to a feature, touching a feature (e.g., patting, tossing, dumping), manipulating a feature (e.g., manually exploring, showing), and functionally using a feature (e.g., pretending to eat the hamburger). Verbal behaviors included calling attention to a feature, requesting the name of a feature, naming a feature, or offering elaborative detail about a feature (e.g., *"The fire's hot."*). As such, for each feature we recorded whether or not it had been engaged nonverbally and/ or verbally during the event in at least one of a variety of ways by one or both of the participants.

In addition, for each feature, it was determined if the nonverbal and verbal behaviors were displayed by the mother and child jointly, the mother only, or the child only. To illustrate this approach, consider the following example taken from the camping event:

Mother: Look. It's a fish! (*Mother Verbal*—fish)
action: Mother moves the big fish as if swimming. (*Mother Non-verbal*—fish)

Child: Catch the big fish. (*Child Verbal*—fish)
action: Child "catches" the big fish. (*Child Nonverbal*—fish)

As reflected here, when both the mother and child nonverbally interacted with the same feature, *Joint Nonverbal* was recorded for that feature. When both the mother and child talked about the same feature, *Joint Verbal* was scored for that feature. As such, the feature "fish" in the example received a *Joint Nonverbal–Joint Verbal* code. If, for example, both participants had in some way handled the fish, but only the mother had verbalized about the fish, then *Joint Nonverbal–Mother Verbal* would have been assigned for this feature. If both the mother and child displayed some form of nonverbal behavior involving the fish, but neither of them had talked about the fish, then *Joint Nonverbal–No Verbal* would have been coded for this feature. By coding in this manner, for each family we could determine within each nonverbal behavior type (Joint, Mother-Only, Child-Only, No Nonverbal) the number of features that were talked about by the mother and child both (Joint Verbal), the mother only (Mother-Only Verbal), or the child only (Child-Only Verbal) during the event. Because the mother–child dyads varied in the ways in which the events were coconstructed, across families any given feature could be coded in multiple ways.

Table 3.1 summarizes the results of this approach to characterizing mother–child engagement with the features of the three events. As can be seen, for each type of nonverbal behavior (mother–child joint, mother-only, child-only, no), we tallied the extent to which each of the four patterns of verbal engagement (mother–child joint, mother-only, child-only, no) was observed. Inspection of the table indicates that the largest category of features was those that were jointly engaged nonverbally by the mother and child (Joint Nonverbal engagement). Mothers and children touched, manipulated, and/or function-ally used approximately 70% (or 17.77) of the total features engaged during the camping activity, 63% (or 15.25) of the total features engaged during bird-watching, and 78% (or 25.11) of the total features engaged during the ice cream store event. Moreover, it is apparent in the table that within each non-verbal behavior type, the majority of features were either jointly talked about by the mother and child, or were talked about only by the mother. For instance, an average of 8.48 features of the camping event were jointly talked about and jointly handled (Joint Nonverbal–Joint Verbal). Another 6.81 fea-tures were jointly handled by the mother and child but verbalized about only by the mother (Joint Nonverbal–Mother Only Verbal).

TABLE 3.1
Mean Number of Features Engaged Nonverbally and Verbally
During the Events

	Event					
Engagement	Camping (30 mos.)		Birdwatching (36 mos.)		Ice Cream Shop (42 mos.)	
Joint Nonverbal						
Joint Verbal	8.48	(3.17)	8.48	(3.89)	13.10	(4.24)
Mother-Only Verbal	6.81	(2.87)	5.81	(3.63)	8.29	(3.89)
Child-Only Verbal	0.38	(0.74)	0.10	(0.30)	1.05	(1.43)
No Verbal	2.10	(1.61)	0.86	(0.85)	2.67	(2.01)
Total	17.77		15.25		25.11	
Mother Nonverbal						
Joint Verbal	0.81	(1.03)	1.52	(1.36)	0.95	(1.02)
Mother-Only Verbal	1.33	(1.46)	1.62	(1.77)	1.29	(1.06)
Child-Only Verbal	0.05	(0.22)	—		0.05	(0.22)
No Verbal	1.00	(1.05)	0.95	(0.97)	0.81	(1.03)
Total	3.19		4.09		3.10	
Child Nonverbal						
Joint Verbal	1.19	(1.89)	2.38	(2.54)	2.05	(1.86)
Mother-Only Verbal	1.24	(0.89)	1.10	(1.76)	0.90	(1.22)
Child-Only Verbal	0.05	(0.22)	0.14	(0.36)	0.14	(0.36)
No Verbal	0.43	(0.87)	0.48	(0.81)	0.57	(0.87)
Total	2.91		4.10		3.66	
No Nonverbal						
Joint Verbal	0.67	(0.97)	0.24	(0.54)	0.05	(0.22)
Mother-Only Verbal	0.86	(0.91)	0.43	(0.60)	0.14	(0.36)
Child-Only Verbal	—		—		—	
Total	1.53		0.67		0.19	
Total Present Features	25.40	(1.86)	24.11	(1.18)	32.06	(2.11)

Note. Standard deviations are in parentheses. From Haden et al. (2001). Reprinted with permission of Society for Research in Child Development.

With the goal of linking mother–child interaction to children's event memory, analyses were conducted to examine how these patterns of engagement with the events related to the children's recall. Because the majority of features that were interacted with during the events were jointly handled by both the mother and the child, these analyses focused on this subset of features that had been jointly engaged nonverbally as the event unfolded. Differences in recall of these jointly handled features were then examined as a function of the

1-Day Recall

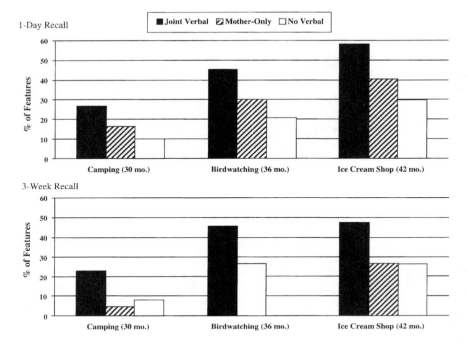

FIG. 3.2. Percentage of features of the camping, birdwatching, and ice cream store events recalled in response to open-ended questions at the 1-day and 3-week delay intervals, as a function of type of talk directed toward jointly handled features. From Haden et al. (2001). Adapted with permission of Society for Research in Child Development.

type of talk directed toward these features during the events (e.g., joint-verbal, mother-verbal, no verbal).

Figure 3.2 summarizes the results of these analyses for the 1-day (upper panel) and 3-week (lower panel) interviews with the researcher. For each event, we plotted the percentage of features recalled of those that were jointly handled and jointly discussed (dark solid bars), jointly handled and talked about only by the mother (striped bars), and jointly handled and not discussed (white bars). It is worth noting that memory for features that were jointly engaged nonverbally but talked about only by the child (Joint Nonverbal–Child Only Verbal) is not illustrated because only a small subset of features fit into this category. This figure depicts a dramatic effect of joint talk during the event on the information children were able to provide in response to general, open-ended questions posed by the interviewer. As illustrated here, those features of the camping, birdwatching, and ice cream events that were jointly handled and jointly discussed by the mother and child were better recalled than features that were jointly handled but talked about only by the mother, which, in turn, were better recalled than those features not discussed. This pattern was observed in interviews with an examiner at both delay intervals for each of the activities, with some indication of a drop in recall over the 3-week delay for features that had been jointly handled but discussed during the event only by the mother. Interestingly enough, as shown in Fig. 3.3, we found essentially the same pattern when we examined the children's recall of the activities in conversations with their mothers about 1 week after the experiences.

In comparison to the examiners, mothers asked relatively fewer open-ended questions, and certainly, the children's recall was lower, particularly for the birdwatching and ice-cream store experiences. Nonetheless, mother- and examiner-prompted recall was highly correlated. And features that had been jointly discussed were best remembered in memory conversations with the mothers as well.

Finally, it is important consider specific conversational techniques that are used during ongoing events that may be most strongly related to recall. As a first step in this effort, we (Ornstein, Haden, Coffman, Cissell, & Greco, 2001) focused on mothers' open-ended feature questions that were directed to particular components of the event as it unfolded, such as *"What are the binoculars used for?" "What should we put on the grill?"* or *"Why do you think there are footprints on this path?"* From our perspective, open-ended feature questions, in contrast to more general open-ended questions (e.g., *"What should we do*

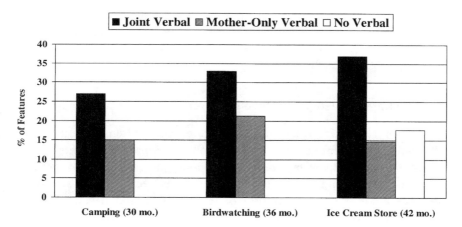

FIG. 3.3.   Percentage of features recalled in response to open-ended questions in the mother–child interviews within 1 week of the event.

TABLE 3.2
Proportions of Features Recalled as a Function of Whether the Mother's
Open-Ended Feature Question About Each Feature During the Event
Had or Had Not Been Followed by Children's Responses

	Mother's Open-Ended Feature Questions	
	Responded To by Child	Not Responded To by Child
Camping (30 months)		
1-day delay	.31	.14
3-week delay	.21	.10
Ice cream store (42 months)		
1-day delay	.51	.37
3-week delay	.42	.30

next?"), may be especially important in terms of directing a child's attention to key features of the experience and facilitating his or her understanding.

In these exploratory analyses, we compared mothers' open-ended features questions that *had* and *had not* been followed by children's responses. Thus, in essence, we compared joint discussion to mother-only talk about specific features of the events, but we did so using a very fine-grained approach by examining open-ended questions posed by the mothers that were and were not coupled with children's responses. As can be seen in Table 3.2, in which we summarize this analysis for the camping (30 months) and ice cream store (42 months) events, features about which questions have been posed and responses generated were better recalled than features about which mothers' questions did not result in children's responses. These results are encouraging, because they illustrate a series of analyses that may offer leverage on the issue of what forms of discussion during events are most strongly predictive of children's subsequent recall.

Constructing Understanding During an Event

In summary, the data presented here indicate that children as young as 2½ years old show mnemonic benefits from conversations about events as they are unfolding. Joint talk between mothers and children during an event is associated quite strongly with children's open-ended recall as much as 3 weeks later. These findings, as well as those of Tessler and Nelson (1994), reinforce the view that mother–child interaction as an event unfolds can serve to focus children's attention on salient aspects of an experience and enhance understanding of it. For example, by asking an open-ended question about component features of an ongoing event, a mother may focus her child's attention on aspects of the situation that are particularly interesting or important. If this questioning is followed by the child's verbal elaboration, a more enriched representation of the event may be established. Further, in the course of narrating events in the here-and-now, some parents make explicit the meaningful links between aspects of an ongoing activity and the child's prior experiences, and follow in and praise the child's nonverbal and verbal behaviors. In this way, mothers and children who are experiencing an event together may come to construct the event in a way that makes it more accessible in the future. Moreover, children who practice talking with their parents this way as events unfold may come not only to remember more about their experiences but may also come to construct an interconnected set of memories that are rich with personal meaning.

Of course, the amount of help from parents that children may need in interpreting a situation can vary considerably as a function of the event that is being remembered. In the relatively novel camping, birdwatching, and ice cream shop activities, joint maternal–child attention in two modalities, linguistic and manipulative, seemed necessary for optimal remembering. In more familiar situations, however, this may not be necessary, as the child's prior knowledge may be sufficient for encoding and remembering. In general, one might expect that there would be a developmental progression in children's understanding of their experiences such that with increases in age, they become able to attend to salient features more on their own, with less maternal structuring of the event. But another possibility is that as children become better at sharing experiences through language, these conversations become increasingly embellished and elaborated, with mothers and children jointly constructing richly detailed and increasingly meaningful stories. Longer term longitudinal studies are necessary to determine how mother–child interactional patterns may change as function of the child's increasing knowledge and linguistic skills, and the implications for subsequent remembering. Nevertheless, together with conversations that often occur after an event, conversations as events unfold may be critical to the process by which children make sense of their personal experiences and construct a coherent sense of self.

FINAL THOUGHTS: JOINT ENCODING, JOINT REMINISCING, CULTURE AND SELF

In this chapter, I stressed that parent–child conversation about present and past events can affect understanding, increasing encoding and subsequent remembering. To be sure, it is consistent with the sociocultural perspective on development (Rogoff, 1990; Vygotsky, 1978; Wertsch, 1985) to think that like middle-class American children, children in other cultures build their understanding of their experiences in joint communication with more knowledgeable others as they participate in culturally valued activities. Thus, although here I focused on individual differences within a cultural group, it also seems likely that cultural variations in autobiographical memory are deeply influenced by cross-cultural differences in the ways parents help children to make sense of events as they are ongoing and after they have occurred. As a growing body of evidence now documents, reminiscing appears to be a culturally variable activity, with parents in diverse cultures found to emphasize different aspects of a child's experience, to use different communicative styles, and to cite different reasons for talking about the past (e.g., Hayne & MacDonald, chapter 5, this volume; Leichtman, Wang, & Pillemer, chapter 4, this volume). An important question to raise in future developmental research is: Do cultural differences in remembering also reflect differences in the ways parents and children jointly encode experiences? Indeed, whereas both joint encoding and joint remembering are likely to be evident across disparate cultures, the goals and means of these communications can be expected to vary to a considerable extent.

I close by emphasizing the idea that by participating in conversations during and after events, children come to coordinate their own experiences and knowledge with that of others in their social and cultural world. When language emerges as a representational exchange system, parents and children begin to truly make sense to each other and share their experiences (Nelson, 1996). As such, joint encoding and joint reminiscing can be critical to the construction of a self-narrative or life history that will at least in part reflect variation in the ways communities and cultures socially share understanding and experience.

ACKNOWLEDGMENTS

Preparation of this chapter was supported in part by HD37114 from the National Institutes of Health and a Faculty Leave Award from Loyola University Chicago.

REFERENCES

Dunn, J., Brown, J., Slomkowski, C., Tesla, C., & Youngblade, L. (1991). Young children's understanding of other people's feelings and beliefs: Individual differences and their antecedents. *Child Development, 62,* 1352–1366.

Eisenberg, A. R. (1985). Learning to describe past experience in conversation. *Discourse Processes, 8,* 177–204.

Engel, S. (1995). *The stories children tell: Making sense of the narratives of childhood.* New York: W. H. Freeman.

Farrant, K., & Reese, E. (2000). Maternal style and children's participation in reminiscing: Stepping stones in children's autobiographical memory development. *Journal of Cognition and Development, 1,* 193–225.

Fivush, R. (1991). The social construction of personal narratives. *Merrill-Palmer Quarterly, 37,* 59–81.

Fivush, R., & Fromhoff, F. A. (1988). Style and structure in mother–child conversations about the past. *Discover Processes, 11,* 337–355.

Fivush, R., & Haden, C. A. (1997). Narrating and representing experience: Preschoolers' developing autobiographical recounts. In P. van den Broek, P. J. Bauer, & T. Bourg (Eds.), *Developmental spans in event comprehension and representation: Bridging fictional and actual events* (pp. 169–198). Hillsdale, NJ: Lawrence Erlbaum Associates.

Fivush, R., Haden, C. A., & Adam, S. (1995). Structure and coherence of preschoolers' personal narratives over time: Implications for childhood amnesia. *Journal of Experimental Child Psychology, 60,* 32–56.

Fivush, R., Haden, C. A., & Reese, E. (1996). Remembering, recounting and reminiscing: The development of autobiographical memory in social context. In D. C. Rubin (Ed.), *Remembering our past: Studies of autobiographical memory* (pp. 341–359). New York: Cambridge University Press.

Fivush, R., Pipe, M.-E., Murachver, T., & Reese, E. (1997). Events spoken and unspoken: Implications of language and memory development for the recovered memory debate. In M. Conway (Ed.), *Recovered memories and false memories* (pp. 34–62). New York: Oxford University Press.

Furrow, D., Moore, C., Davidge, J., & Chiasson, L. (1992). Mental terms in mothers' and children's speech: Similarities and relationships. *Journal of Child Language, 19,* 617–631.

Haden, C. A. (1998). Reminiscing with different children: Relating maternal stylistic consistency and sibling similarity in talk about the past. *Developmental Psychology, 34,* 99–114.

Haden, C. A., & Fivush, R. (1996). Consistency and change in maternal conversational styles in different contexts. *Merrill-Palmer Quarterly, 42,* 24–51.

Haden, C. A., Haine, R. A., & Fivush, R. (1997). Developing narrative structure in parent–child reminiscing across the preschool years. *Developmental Psychology, 33,* 295–307.

Haden, C. A., Ornstein, P. A., Eckerman, C. O., & Didow, S. M. (2001). Mother–child conversational interactions as events unfold: Linkages to subsequent remembering. *Child Development, 72,* 1016–1031.

Han, J. J., Leichtman, M. D., & Wang, Q. (1998). Autobiographical memory in Korean, Chinese, and American children. *Developmental Psychology, 34,* 701–713.

Hudson, J. A. (1990). The emergence of autobiographic memory in mother–child conversations. In R. Fivush & J. A. Hudson (Eds.), *Knowing and remembering in young children* (pp. 166–196). New York: Cambridge University Press.

Hudson, J. A. (1993). Reminiscing with mothers and others: Autobiographical memory in young two-year-olds. *Journal of Narrative and Life History, 3,* 1–32.

Labov, U. (1982). Speech actions and reactions in personal narrative. In D. Tannen (Ed.), *Analyzing discourse: Text and talk* (pp. 219–247). Washington, DC: Georgetown University Press.

Markus, H. R., & Kitayama, S. (1991). Culture and self: Implications for cognition, emotion and motivation. *Psychological Review, 98,* 224–253.

McCabe, A., & Peterson, C. (1991). Getting the story: A longitudinal study of parental styles in eliciting narratives and developing narrative skill. In A. McCabe & C. Peterson (Eds.), *Developing narrative structure* (pp. 217–257). Hillsdale, NJ: Lawrence Erlbaum Associates.

Miller, P. J., Wiley, A. R., Fung, H., & Liang, C. (1997). Personal storytelling as a medium of socialization in Chinese and American families. *Child Development, 68,* 557–568.

Moore, C., Furrow, D., Chiasson, L., & Patriquin, M. (1994). Developmental relationships between production and comprehension of mental terms. *First Language, 14,* 1–17.

Mullen, M. K. (1994). Earliest recollections of childhood: A demographic analysis. *Cognition, 52,* 55–79.

Mullen, M. K., & Yi, S. (1995). The cultural context of talk about the past: Implications for the development of autobiographical memory. *Cognitive Development, 40,* 407–419.

Nelson, K. (1988). The ontogeny of memory for real events. In U. Neisser & E. Winograd (Eds.), *Remembering reconsidered: Ecological and traditional approaches to the study of memory* (pp. 244–276). New York: Cambridge University Press.

Nelson, K. (1993). The psychological and social origins of autobiographical memory. *Psychological Science, 4,* 7–14.

Nelson, K. (1996). *Language in cognitive development: Emergence of the mediated mind.* Cambridge, England: Cambridge University Press.

Nelson, K., & Fivush, R. (2000). Socialization of memory. In E. Tulving & F. Craik (Eds.), *Handbook of memory* (pp. 283–295). New York: Oxford University Press.

Ornstein, P. A., & Haden, C. A. (2001). The development of memory: Towards an understanding of children's testimony. In M. L. Eisen, G. S. Goodman, & J. A. Quas (Eds.), *Memory and suggestibility in the forensic interview* (pp. 29–61). Mahwah, NJ: Lawrence Erlbaum Associates.

Ornstein, P. A., Haden, C. A., Coffman, J., Cissell, A., & Greco, M. (2001, April). Mother–child conversations about the present and the past: Linkages to children's recall. In D. DeMarie & P. A. Ornstein (symposium cochairs) *Remembering over time: Longitudinal studies of children's memory.* Paper presented at the meetings of the Society for Research in Child Development, Minneapolis, Minnesota.

Peterson, C. (1990). The who, when, and where of early narratives. *Journal of Child Language, 17,* 433–455.

Peterson, C., & McCabe, A. (1983). *Developmental psycholinguistics: Three ways of looking at a child's narrative.* New York: Plenum.

Peterson, C., & McCabe, A. (1992). Parental styles of narrative elicitation: Effect on children's narrative structure and content. *First Language, 12,* 299–321.

Peterson, C., & McCabe, A. (1994). A social interactionist account of developing decontextualized narrative skill. *Developmental Psychology, 30,* 937–948.

Reese, E. (2002). Social factors in the development of autobiographical memory: The state of the art. *Social Development, 11,* 124–142.

Reese, E., & Fivush, R. (1993). Parental styles of talking about the past. *Developmental Psychology, 29,* 596–606.

Reese, E., Haden, C. A., & Fivush, R. (1993). Mother–child conversations about the past: Relationships of style and memory over time. *Cognitive Development, 8,* 403–430.

Rogoff, B. (1990). *Apprenticeship in thinking: Cognitive development in social context.* Oxford: Oxford University Press.

Rudek, D. J., & Haden, C. A. (2002). *Mothers' and preschoolers' mental state language during reminiscing over time.* Manuscript submitted for publication.

Tessler, M., & Nelson, K. (1994). Making memories: The influence of joint encoding on later recall. *Consciousness and Cognition, 3,* 307–326.

Vygotsky, L. S. (1978). *Mind in society.* Cambridge, MA: Harvard University Press.

Welch-Ross, M. K. (1997). Mother–child participation in conversations about the past: Relations to preschoolers' theory of mind. *Developmental Psychology, 33,* 618–629.

Welch-Ross, M. K., Fasig, L. G., & Farrar, M. J. (1999). Predictors of preschoolers' self-knowledge: References to emotion and mental states in mother–child conversations about past events. *Cognitive Development, 14,* 401–422.

Wertsch, J. (1985). *Vygotsky and the social formation of mind.* Cambridge, MA: Harvard University Press.

II

Cross-Cultural Variation
in Narrative Environments
and Self-Construal

Cultural Variations in Interdependence and Autobiographical Memory: Lessons from Korea, China, India, and the United States

Michelle D. Leichtman
University of New Hampshire

Qi Wang
Cornell University

David B. Pillemer
Wellesley College

Research over the past two decades has documented powerful effects of culture on human performance across a sweeping array of social and cognitive tasks. For example, how people process stimuli, reason about the causes of events, and describe themselves varies as a function of the culture in which they live (Fiske, Kitayama, Markus, & Nisbett, 1998; Triandis, 1989).

This chapter focuses on one fascinating aspect of this growing portrait of cross-cultural influences, namely emergent differences in autobiographical memory. Our goal is to review recent empirical work that indicates significant differences in the content and style of autobiographical memories of people raised in different cultures. The central question we pose is how the social environment in which a child grows up influences the establishment and maintenance of long-term event memories. What cross-cultural variations in autobiographical memory exist during childhood and adulthood, and what mechanisms are likely to be responsible for them?

One particularly useful distinction in this regard is the difference between independently and interdependently oriented social environments. This distinction, which refers in part to environments that encourage different degrees of focus on the self versus other people, appears to predict several important aspects of what and how children remember. Thus, throughout our discussion, we return to this paradigm for conceptualizing cross-cultural findings.

ORGANIZATION OF THE CHAPTER

This chapter focuses on recent studies conducted in China, Korea, India, and the United States. The studies illustrate how both the quantity and quality of long-term event memories are shaped by the degree to which children's early environments stress independence versus interdependence. To frame the discussion, we first note relevant ways in which the value systems in independent and interdependent cultures differ. Next, we review research showing differences in long-term autobiographical memory among adults in these two kinds of cultures. Then, we describe mechanisms that mediate cultural influences on autobiographical memory and present relevant developmental data. Among a variety of potential mechanisms, we emphasize the role of cross-cultural differences in narrative styles, self-construal, development of emotion situation knowledge, and beliefs about the personal past.

DIFFERENCES IN CULTURAL VALUES

The concepts of interdependence and independence of orientation are closely associated with two overarching approaches to socialization: collectivism and individualism, respectively. Collectivist societies exist in East Asia, Africa, Latin America, and southern Europe. Although diverse in many aspects, these cultures share a relatively extensive focus on interpersonal connectedness, social obligation, and conformity. Collectivist cultures place a high value on common goals, group harmony, and shared identities. They encourage behaviors that allow individuals to fit in seamlessly and get along well with others (Markus & Kitayama, 1998; Pillemer, 1998; Triandis, 1989).

In contrast, individualistic societies exist in North America, western Europe, and Australia. These societies emphasize qualities associated with individuality, self-expression, and personal uniqueness (Fiske et al., 1998; Markus & Kitayama, 1991; Wang & Leichtman, 2000). In broad terms, they promote self-actualization, individuation, and autonomy. In contrast to collectivist societies, individualistic cultures favor the goals of the individual over those of the collective group, and reward individuals for asserting themselves and distinguishing themselves from others (Pillemer, 1998; Triandis, 1989). As Markus and Kitayama (1991) noted, the greatest nightmare in a collectivist culture such as Japan is to be excluded, whereas the greatest nightmare in an individualistic culture is not to be noticed.

Importantly, within any given culture, the degree to which an individual's thinking and behavior reflects the societal values associated with collectivism or individualism can vary extensively. Thus, the degree to which a person's orientation is interdependent or independent is largely but not wholly a function of culture. Likewise, among those societies that are typically considered to be either interdependent or independent, considerable variation exists in the strength of the orientation and the ways in which it is played out. Nonetheless, it is useful to speak about these divergent cultural orientations in general terms, because systematic differences in behavior and thought are associated with them (Trafimow, Triandis, & Goto, 1991; Wang, Leichtman, & White, 1998; Wink, 1997).

The differences between values in interdependent and independent cultures may affect performance on autobiographical memory tasks in a variety of ways. In general, creating a unique, detailed, and accessible store of autobiographical memories is more useful in the context of independent cultures, where establishing one's personal identity is a preeminent social goal. Research on factors that affect autobiographical remembering, such as cultural differences in narrative environments and beliefs about memory, supports this perspective. Before turning to these factors, we examine what is known about cultural differences in personal event memories themselves.

CULTURAL DIFFERENCES
IN AUTOBIOGRAPHICAL MEMORY

Several recent studies suggest that there are cultural variations in the date of adults' earliest memories and in the qualitative characteristics of their autobiographical reports.

Investigators have long been aware that most adults can recall relatively few memories of the earliest years of childhood (Pillemer & White, 1989; Rubin, 1982). Freud's European patients had difficulty retrieving memories from before they were 6 to 8 years old (Freud, 1920/1953). Systematic investigations conducted in the United States have documented that, on average, adults are unable to consciously remember events they experienced before about 3 years of age (Kihlstrom & Harackiewicz, 1982; Pillemer & White, 1989; Sheingold & Tenney, 1982). For example, an early study by Waldfogel (1948) indicated that college students had difficulty reporting memories of events that occurred before age 3, but reported many that occurred after age 5. Confirming this pattern, Wetzler and Sweeney's (1986) analysis of Rubin's (1982) data showed greater deficits in memory for events occurring before age 3 than later in childhood.

Mullen (1994) looked at early autobiographical memories as a function of culture. In a series of questionnaire studies, Mullen found that, on average, the earliest memories reported by a mixed group of Asians and Asian-Americans were approximately 6 months later than those of Caucasian-Americans. Subsequent comparison of the age of earliest memories of native Koreans and Caucasian-Americans revealed an even larger difference of 16.7 months in the same direction (Mullen, 1994).

Wang, Leichtman, and White (1998) asked 255 high school and college students living in Beijing, China to write down and date their earliest memory and then to provide 3 additional childhood memories. The results indicated that, on average, Chinese adults' earliest remembered experience occurred at 3 years 9 months, several months later than typical findings for U.S. populations. Confirming this pattern, Wang (2001a) directly contrasted Chinese and U.S. college samples and found that the average age of earliest memory for the Chinese students was 6 months later than for the Americans.

Sankaranarayanan and Leichtman (2000) focused on a sample of 26 Indian adults living in a remote village and 24 living in urban Bangalore. A trained interviewer raised in the same region as the participants conducted interviews in the regional language. The interviewer asked participants a series of scripted questions about autobiographical memory, beginning with an open-ended question asking whether they recalled any events from childhood. Only 12% of participants in the rural sample and 30% of participants in the urban sample reported a specific event memory from childhood during the interview. Most participants in both samples did not know their own birthdates and could not date their memories. However, of six urban participants who stated their age at the time of recollected events, age estimates ranged between 6 and 11 years, considerably later than similar estimates in studies with U.S. participants.

In addition to dating their earliest memories later, evidence suggests that individuals raised in interdependent societies recount detailed personal event memories less frequently than do their North American counterparts. Several investigators have requested autobiographical memories, in either oral or written form, and have then coded responses as either specific or general.

According to Pillemer, Rhinehart, & White's (1986) coding scheme, specific event memories refer to one-point-in-time events (e.g., "the day my father fell into the well"), as opposed to routines or scripted activities (e.g., "going to school").

Researchers have noted that in the United States, people vary in the degree to which they provide specific memories in response to prompts (Pillemer, 1998; Thorne & Klohnen, 1993). For example, McCabe, Capron, & Peterson (1991) asked young adults to recount several memories of childhood and adolescence, explicitly noting that each memory must be of a clearly visualized specific experience. Despite repeated probes, approximately 20% of the memories they obtained were general in nature. Some participants found this memory task easy, whereas others found it difficult. Likewise, Singer & Salovey (1993) found substantial individual differences when they solicited autobiographical memories from American adults and rated them along a similar dimension (e.g., "single" vs. "summary" memory narratives).

Although substantial individual variation exists, it is commonplace in the United States for adults to think in terms of specific life episodes and to be able to recall them when prompted. For example, in Sankaranarayanan and Leichtman's (2000) study, both Indians and a control group of American adults were asked to provide memories of childhood and these were coded as specific or general. Almost all of the American adults provided a specific memory. In contrast, the majority of participants in both urban and rural Indian samples provided only general memories, even when pressed for specific episodes. Wang (2001a) reported a similar effect in a study in which both American and Chinese college students were prompted to provide their earliest childhood memories. The American participants provided more voluminous, detailed memories of one-moment-in-time events, whereas the Chinese participants provided briefer, more skeletal reports that focused on general, routine occurrences.

In summary, adults who have grown up in independent cultures tend to recount earlier, lengthier and more detailed childhood memories than do adults who have grown up in interdependent cultures. In addition, several studies have noted that North Americans' memories tend to be more self-focused than East Asians' memories (Mullen, 1994; Wang, 2001a). These different characteristics of autobiographical memory accord with differences in the general values of independent versus interdependent cultures.

But what do we know about the mechanisms through which cultural values influence autobiographical memory reports? And at what point in development do cultural differences in autobiographical memory reports appear? We turn to these questions next.

MECHANISMS THROUGH WHICH CULTURE
INFLUENCES AUTOBIOGRAPHICAL MEMORY

Narrative Environments

Studies of cognitive development have highlighted the close relationship between the narrative environment and autobiographical memory (Bruner,
1990; Fivush, 1997; Nelson, 1996). During the early years of a child's life, personal memories become encoded and subsequently accessible for verbal recall
through a process of "co-construction" between the child and the parents
(Nelson, 1996). As children acquire linguistic fluency, they talk with significant adults about both ongoing events and the personal past, and they make
independent contributions by 3 or 4 years of age (Fivush & Hamond, 1990;
Nelson, 1992). In these conversations, adults model the dominant narrative
structure of the society around them, and children learn to discuss events in
ways that others will understand. Early conversations with adults are instrumental in helping children make sense of recent and ongoing autobiographical episodes, and this in turn has the potential to influence the form and content of children's long-term autobiographical memories.

Contemporary research examined memory talk between American parents
and their children. In particular, research revealed two markedly different
styles of parents' talk about the past (Fivush & Fromhoff, 1988; Pillemer, 1998;
Reese, Haden & Fivush, 1993). While investigators used various terms to describe the distinction between these styles (e.g., elaborative/high-elaborative
vs. pragmatic/repetitive/low-elaborative), the findings paint a consistent picture of two kinds of mothers in conversation. High-elaborative mothers often
speak with their children about the past, provide voluminous descriptive
information about experiences, and frequently prompt children to provide
similarly embellished narratives. Even when immature language prohibits
children from contributing much substantive information to conversations,
these mothers persist undaunted in focusing on the details of past experience.
Conversely, low-elaborative mothers talk relatively little about past events and
provide fewer details during past-centered discussions. When these mothers
ask their children about past events, they tend to pose pointed questions with
single correct and incorrect answers (Fivush & Fromhoff, 1988; Reese, Haden,
& Fivush, 1993).

How does parents' use of low- versus high-elaborative styles vary between
interdependent and independent cultures? Further, what differences are evident in other features of parent–child conversations, not directly captured in

the low- versus high-elaborative dichotomy? A number of studies have identified cultural differences in parent–child conversational patterns (e.g., Choi,
1992; Mullen & Yi, 1995; Wang, Leichtman & Davies, 2000).

Naturalistic observations of fourteen 4-year-old children living in a goat-
herding society in rural India provided an apt illustration (Leichtman &
Bhogle, 2000). Children and their families were filmed in the morning and
evening at home. The following excerpt, translated from the local Kanada
language, is typical of parent–child conversations during these observations.
The exchange took place while 4-year-old Krishna shared a meal with his
mother and Santosha and Kitta, his older and younger siblings.

Mother:	Eat quickly. Santosha, want more buttermilk?
Santosha:	No.
Krishna:	I'll eat *ragi* balls and grow quickly.
Mother:	Santosha is older, but he doesn't know anything. Want some salt? Santosha has wiped his mouth. Go and do the same. Kitta, eat quickly. Want buttermilk?
Kitta:	I don't want rice with it. I'll eat it tomorrow.
Mother:	Bend your head and eat. Call Kitta. Come, baby, don't cry. Kitta, have you had a bath?
Kitta:	Yes.
Mother:	Will you go to school?
Krishna:	Don't you eat *ragi* balls? It gives you strength.
Mother:	Wash your hands. Bend and wash. Don't dirty your clothes. Wipe your mouth and hands. Will you go to school? Finished eating? How much did you eat? Did you drink coconut water?
Krishna:	We ate an awful lot.
Mother:	The towel is wet. Who wet it?
Krishna:	Come into the room, I'll lock you up.
Mother:	No, doesn't the baby also have to eat? What will they give you in school?
Krishna:	Sweets, sweet rice, *uppittu*.
Mother:	Is it filling?
Krishna:	No, they give us very little.

This dialogue illustrates a number of features that are typical of parent–
child discussion in cultures with an interdependent social orientation (Han,
Leichtman, & Wang, 1998; Markus & Kitayama, 1991, 1998; Wang et al.,
2000). These features are consistent with a low-elaborative conversational
style, and further with the interdependent emphasis on hierarchy, good social
relations, and proper behavior. In the Indian transcripts, adults spoke to children most often to correct behavior or to encourage children to undertake
particular actions, such as in the directives to eat quickly and to wash up.

Whether adults were engaging in joint activities with children (for example, eating with children or bathing them) or supervising their play, they normally made few elaborative comments about the ongoing events aside from instructions to the children. Adults' questions were most often designed to elicit yes/no answers or single correct pieces of information (e.g., "Want some salt?" "Who wet it?"). Rarely did these questions appear to be for the purpose of following up on the child's leads or probing the child's thoughts. Instead, they were designed to satisfy the adult's need for information, or to ensure that the child had learned a rule or memorized by rote. Furthermore, references to the past or the future were relatively sparse, and those that occurred were brief and pointed (e.g., "What will they give you in school?"). In summary, the dialogues focused on the present and emphasized cooperation, adaptation of behavior to accomplish tasks and to accommodate other people.

In contrast to the Indian example, research indicates that parental conversation styles in the U.S. tend to be relatively more elaborative than those in interdependent cultures. American children at home may talk extensively with adults during shared activities, and adults often ask open-ended questions that require embellishment as opposed to yes/no answers (Haden, Haine, & Fivush, 1997; Leichtman, Pillemer, Wang, Koreishi, & Han, 2000). Further, American parent–child dyads frequently discuss past events, both shared and unshared. These discussions often encourage children to focus on themselves and their feelings about the past, and reinforce the importance of remembering details of their own personal histories (Fivush & Fromhoff, 1988; Leichtman et al., 2000; Tessler & Nelson, 1994). Discussions between adults and children in independent cultures emphasize collegial interchange rather than hierarchy, such that adults may follow the child's lead in conversation rather than insisting on the child's adhering to their agenda.

An example of American mother–child discussion comes from data collected for Leichtman et al.'s (2000) study. The 5-year-old child and her mother discussed what happened during nursery school when they were apart.

Mother: Did anything special happen today?
Child: Um, Martha came to visit with Maisy.
Mother: Oh, my goodness. What was that like?
Child: It was fun. She put it (the baby, Maisy) on a blanket. And we were sitting in a circle so it wouldn't be so crowded for Maisy.
Mother: Oh, yeah. To give her some space, huh? And what did Maisy do?
Child: She lied down on the blanket in the room and we all looked at her.
Mother: Oh.
Child: And Martha gave us each to hold something. The only teacher was holding something was Sue. And all the kids all . . . Aneesha held the

baby thermometer. I hold . . . um . . . the baby's cap when she gets sun
in her eyes.

Mother: Those are all things that the baby needs? Everybody held something
that the baby needs?

Child: Mmmhmm. Even Sue.

Mother: Wow. So everybody was helping. The baby needs a lot of things, huh?

Child: Yeah. She had sixteen things.

Mother: Sixteen things. What did you hold?

Child: The baby's cap.

Mother: The cap to keep the sun out of her eyes. Oh, that's important.

Three noteworthy studies support a contrast between independent and
interdependent parental conversation styles. Mullen and Yi (1995) examined
naturally occurring conversation between Korean or American mothers and
their 40-month-old children. They analyzed tape recordings of one entire day
of ongoing dialogue between mothers and their children. The results indicated that during each hour mothers and children spent together, Americans
referred to an average of three times more past event episodes than Koreans.
The study did not indicate the total amount of talk between dyads, as it was
focused solely on talk about past events. Thus, it is not clear whether American children were exposed to more conversation generally, but they were certainly exposed to more conversation about the past. Further, analyses of the
contents of past-event talk indicated that American mothers talked more than
Koreans about the child's feelings and thoughts, other people's feelings and
thoughts, and the child's personal attributes, whereas Korean mothers talked
more about social norms.

Choi (1992) studied Canadian and Korean mothers and children. In an
analysis of the types of questions mothers posed, Choi found that Korean
mothers did not often seek new information, but instead prompted children
to confirm their understanding of information that the mothers had introduced. Korean mothers did not encourage children to introduce their own
ideas into the conversation and often made statements unrelated to children's
previous utterances, expecting children to follow their leads. In contrast,
Canadian mothers more often followed up and elaborated on children's utterances, encouraged children to contribute ideas, and took partnership, rather
than leadership roles, in conversation.

Wang, Leichtman, & Davies (2000) asked American and Chinese mothers
to talk with their 3-year-old children at home about two past events and a
story. In both types of conversations, American mothers showed a more elaborative style, more often posing open-ended "wh" questions and elaborating
on children's responses. American mothers also focused significantly more

often on children's opinions and predilictions. In contrast, Chinese mothers used a low-elaborative conversational style, frequently posing and repeating factual questions and rarely allowing children's statements to change the direction of the conversation.

Taken together, these studies indicate that children raised in interdependent versus independent cultures are exposed from an early age to distinctive narrative environments that reflect different general values as well as contrasting ideas about the meaning of personal memories. In interdependent cultures, these conversations serve primarily to reinforce key social values, such as moral behavior, connectedness, and responsibility toward others, and they also reinforce the hierarchy between parent and child. In contrast, in independent cultures a primary role of conversations with parents is to help children organize their personal histories in ways that distinguish them as autonomous individuals (Pillemer, 1998; Wang et al., 2000).

Given that the narrative environments in which children grow up vary across cultures, how might these differences affect what children themselves remember about events? In several investigations conducted in the United States, children of high-elaborative mothers have themselves provided longer, more detailed, and more descriptive memory narratives than children of low-elaborative mothers (Haden, Haine, & Fivush, 1997; Hudson, 1990; McCabe & Peterson, 1991).

In addition to differences in style, children's memorial reports show differences in content as a function of their conversations with adults (Fivush, 1991; Hudson, 1990; Reese, Haden, & Fivush, 1993). For example, Tessler and Nelson (1994) tape-recorded dialogues between mothers and children as they walked through a museum together. When researchers interviewed the children 1 week later, they were able to recall exclusively those museum exhibits they had talked about with their mothers. Similarly, Haden, Didow, Ornstein, and Eckerman (1997) interviewed 30- to 42-month-old children about a series of planned events they had experienced with their parents. The children displayed excellent recall of information that was discussed during the events, and poor recall of information that was not discussed. These findings suggest that children whose parents discuss many aspects of ongoing events retain more details of the events than do other children.

Parents also have the potential to influence the content of children's memories through their postevent conversations. Leichtman et al. (2000) documented this effect in a study of 4- to 5-year-olds. The children experienced a surprise event in their preschool classroom—the visit of their former teacher and her new baby. A series of scripted activities occurred during the visit. On the same day, mothers interviewed their own children individually about the event. Mothers were not present during the event and were told to question their children in whatever way they wished. Three weeks later, children were interviewed by a researcher who had not been present during the event and who had no information about the content of the parent–child interviews. The researcher asked each child the same set of nine questions about the event.

The results indicated that mothers' conversational style predicted the amount of information children provided during the mother–child interview. The degree to which mothers used an elaborative style of questioning (e.g., prompting children for details with open-ended and yes/no questions and using contextual and evaluative statements in the interviews) predicted the number of sentences children produced, the number of correct details they remembered, and the number of descriptive terms they used to explain their memories. These responses in the original interview in turn predicted children's responses during the researcher–child interview 3 weeks later. Children whose mothers had conducted more elaborative interviews, and who in turn provided them with richer answers, remembered more accurate details regarding the event after the 3-week delay. Furthermore, children's recall of the specific objects present during the event was influenced by their conversations with their mothers. Eighty-three percent of the items that children recalled during the researcher–child interview had also been discussed with their mothers. Thus, even when parents are naïve to the details of an event their child has experienced, their conversation can draw out details from the child. Rehearsal in this context is associated with an increased likelihood that the child will later recall talked-about aspects of personal experience.

At what point in development do children's memory narratives begin to reflect cross-cultural variations in parents' narrative styles? To address this question, Han, Leichtman, and Wang (1998) conducted a comparative study of Korean, Chinese, and American 4- and 6-year-olds. Researchers interviewed 50 children in each country in their native languages, asking the same series of free-recall questions about recent personally experienced events (e.g., questions about what the child did at bedtime the day before, and about a recent event that was fun).

The findings revealed numerous differences among the three cultural groups, following a pattern reflective of the interdependent/independent distinction. Measured in number of words, American and Chinese children provided voluminous reports of past events, whereas Korean children provided only brief reports. However, American children used more words per proposition (defined as any subject–verb construction) than both Korean and Chinese children. This indicated that American children used comparatively long and complex units of expression, suggesting a detailed, descriptive style of talking about the past. Qualitatively, American children usually provided rich, fleshed-out descriptions of one or two single activities (e.g., a long description of taking a bath, including a detailed description of bathtub activities, objects present, and dialogue), whereas both Korean and Chinese children provided skeletal descriptions of multiple events (e.g., "watched television, took a bath, brushed my teeth"). The major difference between autobiographical narratives of the two Asian groups was that Chinese children talked about a greater number of activities than Korean children.

Consistent with predicted contrasts between interdependent and independent cultures, American children's autobiographical narratives contained more descriptives (i.e., adjectives, adverbs, modifiers), more terms expressing personal preferences (e.g., "I really wanted the red bag"), more personal judgments and opinions (e.g., "The game was boring"), and more personal thoughts or cognitions (e.g., "I forgot about that") than those of children from Korea and China. Americans also provided many more memories that qualified as specific, referring to one-point-in-time episodes as opposed to routines. Finally, when the ratio of children's references to other people versus themselves was calculated, the results demonstrated that American children made comparatively more self references than children from either Asian country.

In terms of developmental trends, children in all cultures increased their narrative volume, elaboration, and description of personal preferences and cognitions with age. However, by age 4 the American children provided narratives that were specific and elaborate, whereas younger Korean and Chinese children's narratives were relatively general and sparse. By the time the Asian children were 6 years old, their narratives were characterized by a degree of specificity similar to that of the American 4-year-olds.

Han et al.'s (1998) study suggested that children's memories may be encoded from an early age in a manner consistent with the dominant narrative style modeled by adults. To confirm this prediction, Wang, Leichtman, & Davies (2000) took a closer look at the relationship between parents' conversational styles in China and the United States and children's autobiographical memories. Chinese and American mother–child dyads discussed memories of shared past events in whatever style was natural for them, and also made up stories together to go along with a picture book the researchers provided. In addition to between-group differences among mothers that we noted earlier (e.g., American mothers were more high-elaborative and child-focused), differences between children in the two cultural groups were apparent. American children provided more information when talking about past events than did

Chinese children, and unlike Chinese children, they tended to provide elaborative responses to mothers' questions. Further, contingency analyses evaluating the relationship between mothers' and childrens' narrative styles indicated a close correspondence between these in both cultural groups. Thus, mothers within each culture who were relatively more elaborative had children who provided more embellished memory and story narratives.

Apart from the stylistic differences that we have discussed, Wang & Leichtman (2000) surmised that there might be cross-cultural differences in the thematic content of children's memories. This work explored whether Chinese and American children's personal narratives would reflect preoccupations with different themes, consistent with contrasts between collectivist and individualistic cultural values. Researchers asked 6-year-olds to tell stories prompted by pictures and standard verbal leads, and then prompted children to recount seven emotional memories. Memory prompts took the following form: "Now tell me one time when you felt really disgusted (ashamed, scared, angry, guilty, happy, sad)."

Content analyses explored the social, emotional, and cognitive characteristics of the story and memory narratives children provided. The findings for both stories and memories indicated distinct differences between American and Chinese samples, consistent with differences in independence/interdependence. For example, Chinese children's stories and memories showed a greater orientation toward social engagement. This was indexed by the number of characters present in the stories, incidents of group action and cooperation, instances of the protagonist (or child herself, in the memories) helping or being helped by others, and instances in which a relationship continued after a disruption. Furthermore, Chinese children's stories and memories showed greater concern with moral correctness, indexed by didactic statements and references to proper behavior and moral character. They also showed greater concern with authority, indexed by number of authority figures, instances of conformity to authority, instances of authority approval, and instances of authority punishment. Compared with Americans, Chinese children showed a less autonomous orientation, indexed by mentions of personal needs and preferences, dislikes and avoidance, evaluations and judgments, and instances in which a character retained personal control in the face of authority. These data provide compelling evidence that even in childhood, the content of Chinese and Americans' memories reflect differences in cultural values and narrative styles.

In summary, research on children's memory narratives indicates that cross-cultural differences appear as early as the preschool years. The evidence to date suggests that these early differences reflect variations in the manner in which adults converse with children about the past. Stylistic and thematic differences between children in interdependent and independent cultures are consistent with overarching values of collectivistic and individualistic societies. Thus, it appears that early conversations are an important route through which culture-specific values are infused into children's autobiographies.

Self-Construal

A central difference between interdependent and independent social orientations is the degree to which individuals are encouraged to focus on themselves as opposed to other people (Markus & Kitayama, 1991). Mullen & Yi (1995) suggested that Korean children were learning from parents that:

> each person has a collection of roles within the social network and that there are behavioral expectations associated with these roles. The sense of self comes from performing these roles. There may be less need to differentiate oneself in terms of these roles, and thus less need for an elaborated autobiographical narrative. (p. 417)

In contrast, they noted that American children were

> being taught that each person has a collection of individual attributes that makes them unique, and that it is important to discover and give expression to this individuality. The construction of accounts of one's experience is an important avenue towards achieving this goal. (p. 417)

Wang, Leichtman, & White (1998) wished to evaluate more directly the proposed relationship between self-construal and autobiographical memory. If self-construal and memory are causally linked, they should covary systematically within a culture, not just between cultures. The one-child policy, in place in China since 1979, provided a unique opportunity to test this prediction. Observers have noted that the "4-2-1 syndrome" in Chinese only-child families, whereby four grandparents and two parents focus completely on one child, may create an environment that departs considerably from traditional Chinese collectivist values (Lee, 1992). Some reports characterize Chinese only children, popularly described as "little emperors," as more self-centered, willful, and egocentric, and less disciplined, obedient, and other-oriented than children from larger families (Fan, 1994; Jiao, Ji, & Jing, 1986; Wang, Cao, Hao, Cao, Dai, & Qu, 1983). These differences amount to a less traditionally interdependent orientation among only children. Wang et al. (1998) examined how the extent to which children are encouraged to focus on themselves during childhood is reflected in their autobiographical memories much later in life.

The sample consisted of 255 young Chinese adults, 99 of them only children. Participants completed two written questionnaires in Chinese. The first, a version of Kuhn and McPartland's (1954) Twenty Statements Test (TST), elicited self-descriptions by asking participants to complete 10 sentences phrased "I am ____." The second questionnaire asked participants to describe and date their earliest memory and three other childhood memories. The results confirmed expectations of differences between only- and sibling-child groups.

Most TST responses fell into two scoring categories: private versus collective self-descriptions. These categories have been used to indicate how self-related information is differentially organized in memory across individuals (Bochner, 1994). *Private* self-descriptions focus on personal traits, states, or behaviors (e.g., "I am intelligent"), whereas *collective* self-descriptions focus on group membership (e.g., "I am a Buddhist.") (Greenwald & Pratkanis, 1984; Triandis, 1989). Past work has shown that participants from independently oriented cultures provide overwhelmingly private self-descriptions, whereas participants from interdependently oriented cultures provide more collective self-descriptions (Bochner, 1994; Trafimow, Triandis, & Goto, 1991). Such differences probably stem from the fact that people from independent cultures focus on their own feelings, values, and goals, and have highly organized and readily accessible sets of information about the private self in memory. In contrast, participants from interdependent cultures focus more on the values and goals of the group, and have ready access to information regarding the collective self (Markus & Kitayama, 1991; Triandis, 1989).

This same contrast that researchers observed between cultures was apparent in Wang et al.'s (1998) analysis of Chinese only- and sibling-child participants. Only-child participants reported more private self-descriptions and fewer collective self-descriptions than sibling-child participants. The findings support the notion that children from the two family structures may organize self-relevant information differently, despite the fact that they are part of the same larger cultural milieu.

With respect to the organization of autobiography, only-child participants reported earliest memories that dated from the time they were 39 months old, on average, whereas siblings reported earliest memories from almost 9 months later. The nature of the reported memories also differed between groups: only-child participants reported fewer memories focusing on social interactions, fewer memories focusing on family, more memories focusing on personal experiences and feelings, and more memories focusing solely on themselves. In addition, only-child participants reported a greater number of specific memories—that is, referring to one-point-in-time events—than their sibling counterparts. Finally, only-child participants' memories contained a lower ratio of other–self mentions, indicating a relatively greater focus on their own past thoughts and activities. Across the sample as a whole, participants' scores on the self-description questionnaire predicted several autobiographical memory variables. Private self-description scores were positively related to narrative length, mentions of the self, and memory specificity, whereas collective self-description scores were negatively related to each of these memory measures.

Using similar methods, Wang (2001a) examined autobiographical memories and self-description scores of a large sample of American and Chinese college students. The results revealed culture effects for both sets of variables, in the direction predicted by differences in social orientation. American participants' TST scores indicated proportionately more "private" and fewer "collective" self-descriptions than their Chinese counterparts, and their autobiographical memories were earlier, more elaborate, more self-focused, and more likely to be specific. Across the sample as a whole, TST scores indicating more "private" self-descriptions were associated with more specific and self-focused autobiographical memories.

Childhood environments appear to affect both the extent and organization of self-related information, and the structure and content of autobiographical memories. The direction of the relationship between the measures of self-construal and memory in these studies is not clear, and may indeed be bidirectional. On the one hand, "When children learn that their own thoughts, desires and feelings are of paramount importance across many situations, they may be inspired to attend to, collect, organize and revisit events associated with their personal histories" (Wang et al., 1998, p. 99). In this sense, self-construal contributes to cultural differences in autobiographical memory. On the other hand, an abundance of early, highly specific, self-focused autobiographical memories may provide the foundation for a private and autonomous sense of self (Wang et al., 1998). The intimate relationship between autobiographical memory and the self may be described best as synergistic (Tessler & Nelson, 1994; Wang, 2001a; Wang et al., 1998).

Emotion Situation Knowledge

Like differences in narrative environments and self-construals, cultural differences in individuals' understanding of emotion have implications for autobiographical remembering. Emotion situation knowledge—understanding which emotions are appropriate reactions to particular situations—is an important precursor to effective remembering of personal events. Mastery of emotion situation knowledge assists individuals in grasping the personal significance of particular events within the social context in which they live. The significance of an event, in turn, affects every step in the memory process: how the event is encoded, organized, and eventually retrieved from the store of autobiographical event memories. For this reason, it is important to consider how the development of emotion situation knowledge varies across cultures, the social practices that lead to such variation, and the potential correlation between emotion situation knowledge and characteristics of autobiographical memory (Wang, 2001b).

Indeed, research indicates that emotional situation knowledge may vary significantly across cultures (Lewis, 1989; Zahn-Waxler, Friedman, Cole, Mizuta, & Hiruma, 1996), such that individuals from different cultures often provide discrepant descriptions of the appropriate or modal emotional reaction to an event. The developmental trajectory of acquiring emotion situation knowledge also appears to vary (Wang, in press), with children in independent cultures acquiring such knowledge relatively early. Because emotion situation knowledge allows children to understand the personal relevance of events and to organize memories according to clearly identifiable emotional labels (Conway & Bekerian, 1987), early acquisition of emotion situation knowledge may confer an advantage for the retrieval of specific autobiographical episodes. Consistent with this possibility, cultural differences in the timing of emotion situation knowledge acquisition correspond with differences in the nature and timing of autobiographical memories of childhood.

Wang (in press) asked 3- to 6-year-old Chinese and American children to identify the emotion of the protagonist in 20 brief stories. Protagonists were children of the same race and gender as participants. Children chose among faces depicting happy, sad, scared, or angry emotions, and then used a specially designed scale to rate intensity of emotion. Mothers and a second group of adults read the same stories and rated the protagonists' emotions on the same dimensions as their children had done.

Results indicated that American preschool children had a greater understanding of emotion situation knowledge than their Chinese peers, based on the overall number of children's responses that accorded with adult judgments. American children's understanding of the "proper" emotions associated with particular situations also improved more with age than did Chinese children's understanding, particularly in the case of negative emotions. There also were cross-cultural differences in intensity ratings, such that both American adults and children gave higher intensity ratings than their Chinese counterparts. Both cultural groups rated negative emotions as less intense than positive emotions, but this was especially true for Chinese participants.

These results accord with differences in the focus on emotion expected in interdependent and independent cultures. In individualistic societies, the extensive discussion about personal experiences that takes place within the family includes examination of the child's own emotional reactions. Such examination is part of building the individual identity that is so valued in the West, and is likely to increase young children's emotion situation knowledge. In contrast, in collectivist cultures, the child's own emotional reactions may be de-emphasized in the service of group harmony. Thus, American children had a better grasp of appropriate emotional reactions and made more rapid progress in understanding protagonists' emotions during the critical 3- to 6-year-old period. Whereas American children showed an advantage in emotional understanding, Chinese children may be better at decoding how others are feeling (Wang, in press); this accords with past results in which Chinese children have been more concerned with and better at recognizing story characters' emotions (e.g., Borke, 1973; Wang & Leichtman, 2000). The greater relative distance between positive and negative emotion ratings for Chinese participants is consistent with the view that negative emotion is dangerous because of its potential to disrupt social relationships.

Wang (2001b) looked at family narrative practices in China and the United States that might foster differences in the development of emotion situation knowledge. Mothers recorded, in their homes, natural conversations with their children about four shared events that had occurred during the past month. The mothers chose one each of events that had made the children feel happy, sad, scared, and angry. The conversations were coded for emotional and social content. Chinese and American mothers spoke with equal frequency about the emotions of their children and other people. This was not surprising because mothers had been instructed to talk with their children about events in which the children felt particular emotions. Importantly, however, American mothers provided more explanations for the causes of emotions. American dyads were also more likely to discuss events in which children's emotional reactions were a consequence of nonsocial objects or events, whereas Chinese dyads discussed events in which other people either caused or shared the child's emotions. Chinese mothers were more likely than Americans to provide an emotional resolution following angry events, whereas American mothers were more likely to reassure their children following fearful events. These differences are consistent with Chinese mothers promoting group harmony, and American mothers discouraging fearfulness, which is not adaptive in individualistic cultures (Kagan, 1984).

Thus, differences in narrative practices may contribute to cultural variation in children's mastery of emotion situation knowledge (Wang, in press). This in turn may contribute to the differences in autobiographical memories. Once children have acquired emotion situation knowledge, they can fully understand the personal significance of events and organize them efficiently for later retrieval.

Beliefs About the Personal Past

Children's narrative environments, their understanding of emotions, and their self-construals appear to contribute to the ways in which they remember autobiographical events as adults. Another factor constitutes an even more direct expression of cultural values: the explicit beliefs that people hold about autobiographical memory. Different value systems associated with interdependent and independent social orientations give rise to different beliefs about the meaning of the personal past. Normative differences in belief may affect, both directly and indirectly, individuals' ability to recall autobiographical events and the style in which memories of these events are expressed.

In Sankaranarayanan and Leichtman's (2000) data, when rural Indian adults were asked to provide personal memories from childhood and the recent past, they often appeared puzzled or even annoyed at the request. Their spontaneous comments indicated that they thought the questions were irrelevant and that such memories were unimportant. Participants commented: "What is the meaning of the past?" "The past is just as the future." "Why would one want to remember such things?"

This view of personal memories contrasts starkly with the normative perceptions of individuals from independent cultures. It is not uncommon for Americans to feel that personal memories are a critical part of their identity and to wonder what they would be without them. Americans in Sankaranarayanan and Leichtman's case study never challenged questions about the personal past, and many said that they often thought and talked about the personal past. The view that personal memories are important has also been evident in discussions of Alzheimer's disease. Patients are described as becoming "a completely different person" once they reach advanced stages of the disease. The loss of identity that may be associated with Alzheimer's disease is doubtless connected with the autobiographical symptoms of sporadic memory loss and the inability to recollect an organized personal history (Pierce, 2000).

This divergence in cultural viewpoints is most apparent in the domain of autobiographical expression. As Pillemer (1998) described, in individualistic cultures people typically are willing or even eager to talk about their own life experiences and are intrigued by the intimate histories of others. In the United States, published autobiographies abound and are consistently on bestseller lists. Popular television shows and movies also suggest a zeal for individual life stories, often presented from an autobiographical perspective (e.g., Lifetime's *An Intimate Portrait*, A & E's *Biography*). This focus on auto-biography is connected to the high value placed on being a unique and inde-pendent person in independently oriented cultures (Gergen & Gergen, 1993; Pillemer, 1998).

In contrast, autobiography has not met with equal enthusiasm in interde-pendently oriented cultures. In traditional Asian cultures, autobiography as such has been rare, at least in part because it has been considered egotistical for a scholar to write a book about the self (Kim, 1990; Pillemer, 1998). Thus, the Chinese writer Jade Snow Wong wrote her own autobiography in the third person. She explained that writing in the first person would appear immodest from the perspective of Chinese propriety, even though she was writing in English (Pillemer, 1998; Wong, 1945). She also noted that in Chinese prose and poetry, "I" almost never appears (Wong, 1945).

Shared cultural beliefs about the meaning of personal memory are reflected in the construction of individual autobiographies. Such beliefs are intimately linked to differences in narrative styles discussed throughout this chapter. If parents believe that personal memories are to be treasured and that discussion about the past is an adaptive tool for becoming an ideal member of society, it follows that they will engage eagerly in memory talk with their children. Through such talk, the value of possessing a unique individual identity is both expressed and reinforced. As noted, these conversations in turn encourage children to focus and elaborate on their own personal memories, enhancing eventual access to such memories and shaping their contents.

CONCLUDING CAVEATS

Autobiographical memory may serve different functions in societies that hold different views of the self and the ideal social world. In individualistic Western cultures, personal memories serve as a forum for solidifying relationships, in addition to confirming the unique attributes of the individual. In contrast, interdependent Eastern cultures that discourage excessive focus on and talk about the self rely on other methods of valuing the individual and ensuring that social bonding takes place. In such cultures, empathy based on implicit understanding and shared points of view that are communicated nonverbally may take the place of explicit dialogue about the personal past (Pillemer, 1998; Wang, 2001b). Cultural values affect how people talk with their children about the past, organize information about the self, understand emotion, and consider the importance of personal memory. These factors contribute to differences in autobiographical memory among adults.

Much of the memory data we reported relies on self-report. How else, after all, can one begin to understand the narratives that individuals produce about their own past experiences? A question arises whether the cultural differences obtained are confined to participants' reports of their memories, or whether they actually reflect differences in underlying memory representations. Although it is clear that cultural differences exist at the level of narrative expression, we would like to underscore our belief that the effects extend to the level of representation. The repeated, detailed reconstruction of events in narrative and thought that occurs in individualistic cultures is likely to create a different autobiographical perspective and organizational structure from the more seldom, sparse, and didactic reconstructions that occur in collectivist cultures. This prediction is supported by cultural differences in the degree of access that adults have to early memories and the accompanying differences in their self-construals and early narrative environments that we reported.

An important additional caveat is that cultural differences in autobiographical memory cannot be equated with sex differences, despite the fact that gender researchers have described women as more interdependently oriented than men. Woman have been labeled as interdependent because they are more focused than men on relationships, interpersonal harmony, and taking care of others (Cross & Madson, 1997; Gilligan, 1982). In this sense, one might expect the characteristic differences in autobiographical memory between interdependent and independent cultural groups also to apply to women and men. However, both anecdotal and research evidence suggest that this is not the case. Contrary to patterns of cultural difference, women appear to more strongly value and more clearly recall personal event memories than do men (Ely & McCabe, 1993; Gergen & Gergen, 1993; Herlitz, Nilsson, & Backman, 1997; Pillemer, 1998). In addition, in studies that included multiple cultures, the patterns of gender and cultural differences are often inconsistent (e.g., Han, Leichtman, & Wang, 1998; Wang, Leichtman, & Davies, 2000). For example, Wang (2001a) found marked differences between Chinese and Americans in self-description and autobiographical memory measures, but no gender differences in the American sample and counterintuitive gender differences in the Chinese sample (i.e., Chinese women appeared to be more "independently oriented" than Chinese men on some measures). Such findings underscore the point that self-construals in the realms of gender and culture are not parallel (Markus, Mullally, & Kitayama, 1997; Miller, 1994)

Finally, relationships among the mechanisms we identified as contributing to cross-cultural differences in memory have yet to be fully specified. For example, we noted that self-construal and autobiographical memory probably act synergistically, each helping to determine the other over time. Likewise, the narrative environment in which a child grows up reinforces cultural beliefs about memory, shapes the child's autobiographical reports, and communicates emotion situation knowledge. At the same time, for each individual child, this environment is itself being shaped by the child's contributions. No single linear model captures these effects.

The production and maintenance of autobiographical memories over the lifecourse is a complex process that takes place within biological, psychological, and environmental contexts. We focused on factors in the sociocultural environment, but we recognize that memory is a product of multiple levels of contextual influence.

REFERENCES

Bochner, S. (1994). Cross-cultural differences in the self concept. *Journal of Cross-Cultural Psychology, 25, 2*, 273–283.

Borke, H. (1973). The development of empathy in Chinese and American children between three and six years of age: A cross-cultural study. *Developmental Psychology, 9*, 102–108.

Bruner, J. (1990). *Acts of meaning*. Cambridge, MA: Harvard University Press.

Choi, S. H. (1992). Communicative socialization processes: Korea and Canada. In S. Iwasaki, Y. Kashima, & K. Leung (Eds.), *Innovations in cross-cultural psychology* (pp. 103–122). Amsterdam: Swets & Zeitlinger.

Conway, M., & Bekerian, D. A. (1987). Situational knowledge and emotions. *Cognition and Emotion, 1*(2), 145–191.

Cross, S. E., & Madson, L. (1997). Models of the self: Self-construals and gender. *Psychological Bulletin, 122*, 5–37.

Ely, R., & McCabe, A. (1993). Remembered voices. *Journal of Child Language, 20*, 671–696.

Fan, C. (1994). A comparative study of personality characteristics between only and nononly children in primary schools in Xian. *Psychological Science, 17*(2), 70–74 (in Chinese).

Fiske, A. P., Kitayama, S., Markus, H. R., & Nisbett, R. E. (1998). The cultural matrix of social psychology. In D. T. Gilbert, S. T. Fiske, & G. Lindzey (Eds.), *The handbook of social psychology* (Vol. 2; 4th ed.; pp. 915–981). Boston, MA: McGraw Hill.

Fivush, R. (1991). The social construction of personal narratives. *Merrill-Palmer Quarterly, 37*, 59–81.

Fivush, R. (1997). Narrating and representing experience: Preschoolers' developing autobiographical accounts. In P. W. Van Den Broek & P. J. Bauer (Eds.), *Developmental spans in event comprehension and representation: Bridging fictional and actual events* (pp. 169–198). Mahwah, NJ: Lawrence Erlbaum Associates.

Fivush, R., & Fromhoff, F. A. (1988). Style and structure in mother–child conversations about the past. *Discourse Processes, 11*, 337–355.

Fivush, R., & Hamond, N. R. (1990). Autobiographical memory across the preschool years: Toward reconceptualizing childhood amnesia. In R. Fivush & J. Hudson (Eds.), *Knowing and remembering in young children* (pp. 223–248). New York: Cambridge University Press.

Freud, S. (1953). *A general introduction to psychoanalysis*. New York: Simon and Schuster. (Original work published 1920)

Gergen, M. M., & Gergen, K. J. (1993). Narratives of the gendered body in popular autobiography. In R. Josselson & A. Lieblich (Eds.), *The narrative study of lives, Vol. 1* (pp. 191–218), Newbury Park, CA: Sage.

Gilligan, C. (1982). In a different voice: Psychological theory and women's development. Cambridge, MA: Harvard University Press.

Greenwald, A. G., & Pratkanis, A. R. (1984). The self. In R. S. Wyer & T. K. Srull (Eds.), *Handbook of social cognition* (Vol. 3, pp. 129–178). Hillsdale, NJ: Lawrence Erlbaum Associates.

Haden, C. A., Didow, S. M., Ornstein, P. A., & Eckerman, C. O. (1997, April). Mother–child talk about the here and now: Linkages to subsequent remembering. In E. Reese (Chair), *Adult–child talk about the past: Theory and Practice*. Symposium conducted at The Biennial Meeting of the Society for Research in Child Development, Washington, DC.

Haden, C. A., Haine, R. A., & Fivush, R. (1997). Developing narrative structure in parent–child reminiscing across the preschool years. *Developmental Psychology, 33*, 295–307.

Han, J. J., Leichtman, M. D., & Wang, Q. (1998). Autobiographical memory in Korean, Chinese and American children. *Developmental Psychology, 34*(4), 701–713.

Herlitz, A., Nilsson, L.-G., & Backman, L. (1997). Gender differences in episodic memory. *Memory and Cognition, 25*, 801–811.

Hudson, J. (1990). The emergence of autobiographical memory in mother–child conversation. In R. Fivush & J. Hudson (Eds.), *Knowing and remembering in young children* (pp. 166–196). New York: Cambridge University Press.

Jiao, S., Ji, G., & Jing, Q. (1986). Comparative study of behavior qualities of only children and sibling children. *Child Development, 57*, 357–361.

Kagan, J. (1984). *The nature of the child*. New York: Basic Books.

Kihlstrom, J. F., & Harackiewicz, J. M. (1982). The earliest recollection: A new survey. *Journal of Personality, 50*, 134–148.

Kim, E. H. (1990). Defining Asian American realities through literature. In A. R. Jan-Mohamed & D. Lloyd (Eds.), *The nature and content of minority discourse* (pp. 146–170). New York: Oxford University Press.

Kuhn, M. H., & McPartland, T. S. (1954). An empirical investigation of self-attitudes. *American Sociological Review, 19*, 68–76.

Lee, L. C. (1992). Day care in the People's Republic of China. In M. E. Lamb & K. Sternberg (Eds.), *Child care in context: Cross cultural perspectives* (pp. 355–392). Hillsdale, NJ: Lawrence Erlbaum Associates.

Leichtman, M. D., & Bhogle, S. (2000). *Childhood memory in rural India: A case study of 14 4-year-olds*. Unpublished raw data.

Leichtman, M. D., Pillemer, D. B., Wang, Q., Koreishi, A., & Han, J. J. (2000). When Baby Maisy came to school: Mother's interview styles and preschoolers' event memories. *Cognitive Development, 15*, 1–16.

Lewis, M. (1989). Cultural differences in children's knowledge of emotional scripts. In C. Saarni & P. L. Harris (Eds.), *Children's understanding of emotion* (pp. 350–374). New York: Cambridge University Press.

Markus, H. R., & Kitayama, S. (1991). Culture and the self: Implications for cognition, emotion & motivation. *Psychological Review, 98*(2), 224–253.

Markus, H. R., & Kitayama, S. (1998). The cultural psychology of personality. *Journal of cross-cultural psychology, 29*(1), 63–87.

Markus, H. R., Mullally, P. R., & Kitayama, S. (1997). Selfways: Diversity in modes of cultural participation. In U. Neisser & D. A. Jopling (Eds.), *The conceptual self in context: Culture, experience, self-understanding. The Emory symposia in cognition* (pp. 13–61). New York: Cambridge University Press.

McCabe, A., Capron, E., & Peterson, C. (1991). The voice of experience: The recall of early childhood and adolescent memories by young adults. In A. McCabe & C. Peterson (Eds.), *Developing narrative structure* (pp. 137–173). Hillsdale, NJ: Lawrence Erlbaum Associates.

McCabe, A., & Peterson, C. (1991). Getting the story: A longitudinal study of parental styles in eliciting narratives and developing narrative skill. In A. McCabe & C. Peterson (Eds.), *Developing narrative structure* (pp. 217–253). Hillsdale, NJ: Lawrence Erlbaum Associates.

Miller, J. G. (1994). Cultural diversity in the morality of caring: Individually oriented versus duty-based interpersonal moral codes. *Cross-cultural Research: The Journal of Comparative Social Science, 28,* 3–39.

Mullen, M. K. (1994). Earliest recollections of childhood: A demographic analysis. *Cognition, 52*(1), 55–79.

Mullen, M. K., & Yi, S. (1995). The cultural context of talk about the past: Implications for the development of autobiographical memory. *Cognitive Development, 10,* 407–419.

Nelson, K. (1992). Emergence of autobiographical memory at age 4. *Human Development, 35,* 172–177.

Nelson, K. (1996). *Language in cognitive development: The emergence of the mediated mind.* New York: Cambridge University Press.

Pierce, C. P. (2000). *Hard to forget: An Alzheimer's story.* New York: Random House.

Pillemer, D. B. (1998). *Momentous events, vivid memories.* Cambridge, MA: Harvard University Press.

Pillemer, D. B., Rhinehart, E. D., & White, S. H. (1986). Memories of life transitions: The first year in college. *Human Learning, 5,* 109–123.

Pillemer, D. B., & White, S. H. (1989). Childhood events recalled by children and adults. In H. W. Reese (Ed.), *Advances in child development and behavior* (Vol. 21, pp. 297–340). Orlando, FL: Academic Press.

Reese, E., Haden, C., & Fivush, R. (1993). Mother–child conversations about the past: Relationships of style and memory over time. *Cognitive Development, 8,* 403–430.

Rubin, D. C. (1982). On the retention function for autobiographical memory. *Journal of Verbal Learning and Verbal Behavior, 21,* 21–38.

Sankaranarayanan, A., & Leichtman, M. (2000). *Adults' recollections of childhood in urban and rural India and the United States.* Unpublished data.

Sheingold, K., & Tenney, Y. J. (1982). Memory for a salient childhood event. In U. Neisser (Ed.), *Memory observed* (pp. 201–212). San Francisco: Freeman.

Singer, J. A., & Salovey, P. (1993). *The remembered self: Emotion and memory in personality.* New York: The Free Press.

Tessler, M., & Nelson, K. (1994). Making memories: the influence of joint encoding on later recall by young children. *Consciousness and Cognition, 3,* 307–326.

Thorne, A., & Klohnen, E. (1993). Interpersonal memories as maps for personality consistency. In D. C. Funder, R. D. Parke, C. Tomlinson-Keasey, & K. Widaman (Eds.), *Studying lives through time* (pp. 223–253). Washington, DC: American Psychological Association.

Trafimow, D., Triandis, H. C., & Goto, S. G. (1991). Some tests of the distinction between the private and collective self. *Journal of Personality and Social Psychology, 60*(5), 649–655.

Triandis, H. C. (1989). The self and social behavior in differing cultural contexts. *Psychological Review, 96,* 506–520.

Waldfogel, S. (1948). The frequency and affective character of childhood memories. *Psychological Monographs, 62,* Whole No. 291.

Wang, Q. (2001a). Culture effects on adults' earliest childhood recollection and self-description: Implications for the relation between memory and the self. *Journal of Personality and Social Psychology, 81*(2), 220–233.

Wang, Q. (2001b). "Did you have fun?": American and Chinese mother–child conversations about shared emotional experiences. *Cognitive Development, 16,* 693–715.

Wang, Q. (in press). Emotion situation knowledge in American and Chinese preschool children and adults. *Cognition & Emotion.*

Wang, Q., & Leichtman, M. D. (2000). Same beginnings, different stories: A comparison of American and Chinese children's narratives. *Child Development, 71*(5), 1329–1346.

Wang, Q., Leichtman, M. D., & Davies, K. I. (2000). Sharing memories and telling stories: American and Chinese mothers and their 3-year-olds. *Memory, 8*(3), 159–177.

Wang, Q., Leichtman, M. D., & White, S. H. (1998). Childhood memory and self description in young Chinese adults: The impact of growing up an only child. *Cognition, 69*(1), 73–103.

Wang, Z. W., Cao, D. H., Hao, Y., Cao, R. Q., Dai, W. Y., & Qu, S. Q. (1983). A preliminary study of education of only children. *Academic Journal of Shenyang Education Institute, 2,* 11–15.

Wetzler, S. E., & Sweeney, J. A. (1986). Childhood amnesia: An empirical demonstration. In D. C. Rubin (Ed.), *Autobiographical memory* (pp. 191–221). New York: Cambridge University Press.

Wink, P. (1997). Beyond ethnic differences: Contextualizing the influence of ethnicity on individualism and collectivism. *Journal of Social Issues, 53,* 329–350.

Wong, J.S. (1945). *Fifth Chinese daughter.* New York: Harper & Row.

Zahn-Waxler, C., Friedman, R. J., Cole, P. M, Mizuta, I., & Hiruma, N. (1996). Japanese and United States preschool children's responses to conflict and distress. *Child Development, 67*(5), 2462–2477.

Chapter 5

The Socialization of Autobiographical Memory in Children and Adults: The Roles of Culture and Gender

Harlene Hayne
Shelley MacDonald
University of Otago,
Dunedin, New Zealand

When adults are asked to report their earliest childhood memories, most can recall nothing about events that occurred prior to their 3rd or 4th birthday. Although the average age of earliest recollection is fairly consistent across studies, at least two individual differences in the age of earliest memory have been reported. First, there is some evidence that the age of earliest memory may vary as a function of an individual's gender. Although gender differences are not always observed (Kilhlstrom & Harackiewicz, 1982; Rubin, Schulkind, & Rahhal, 1999), when they do occur, women typically report earlier memories than men (Dudycha & Dudycha, 1941; Schachtel, 1947; Waldfogel, 1948). Second, there is some evidence that the age of earliest memory may also vary as a function of an individual's cultural background. Mullen (1994), for example, found that Caucasian-American adults report earlier memories than Korean-American adults.

How can we account for these individual differences in adults' earliest memories? Unlike other forms of episodic memory, autobiographical memory is considered to be a social construction, originating through experience but elaborated and maintained through social interaction with others. Nelson (1990, 1993) argued that the social construction of autobiographical memory begins in childhood and takes place, at least in part, in the context of parent–

child conversations about the past. From this perspective, cross-cultural or gender differences in the structure and content of these early conversations are thought to play a pivotal role in individual differences in adults' earliest recollections of childhood.

THE NEW ZEALAND CONTEXT

New Zealand provides a unique opportunity to examine the social construction of autobiographical memory. In contrast to the American notion of a cultural "melting pot," New Zealand strives to maintain a bicultural society. Individuals from two distinct cultural backgrounds live together in the same communities, but they are actively encouraged to maintain their own sense of cultural identity. The indigenous people of New Zealand are referred to as the Maori; they have lived in New Zealand for more than 1,000 years. It has been argued that the Maori culture is among "the finest oral historical traditions in the world" (Biggs, 1970, p. 198). This oral tradition consists of myth, legend, and history and is passed from one generation to the next in the form of narrative, poetry, song, and genealogical recital.

Approximately 150 years ago, European settlers from a variety of Northern European countries including England, Scotland, and Ireland began to settle in New Zealand. The term *Pakeha* was used by the Maori to refer to these Caucasian settlers. Although the correct translation of the term continues to be debated, the word Pakeha is used today to refer to "a person who is not of Maori ancestry, especially a white person" (Hanks, Long, & Urdang, 1983, p. 1055). In this chapter, we use the term Pakeha to refer to the Caucasian-New Zealand adults.

The goal of this research was to examine cross-cultural and gender differences in autobiographical memory within this New Zealand context (MacDonald, Uesiliana, & Hayne, 2000). Richly descriptive accounts of the past play an important role in all aspects of traditional Maori culture (Dewes, 1975; King, 1975). The *haka* (war dances/challenges), *waiata* (songs), *tauparapara* (chants), *pepeha* (proverbs), myths, legends, *whakapapa* (genealogy), and *tikanga* (customs) are shared with each new generation by telling stories about the past (Karetu, 1975). Beginning in early childhood, individuals are socialized into their tribal history. Throughout their lives, they are immersed in discussions about both the recent and the distant past. It is possible that exposure to these rich and elaborate stories about tribal and family history might be reflected in a rich and elaborate personal history as well.

In this chapter, we examine the potential contributions of culture and gender to the emergence and long-term maintenance of autobiographical memory within New Zealand's bicultural context. The empirical research described here addresses two questions. First, what is the impact of culture and gender on the age and content of adults' earliest memories of childhood? Second, do the foundations of these cross-cultural and gender differences begin to emerge in the social context of parent–child conversations about the past?

ADULTS' EARLIEST CHILDHOOD MEMORIES

Given the importance of the past in traditional Maori culture, we predicted that Maori adults might report memories that were earlier or more detailed than those reported by Pakeha adults who, like the Amercian Caucasian adults, trace their cultural roots to Europe. To address this issue, participants were recruited from the student population of the University of Otago in Dunedin, New Zealand (for complete details, see MacDonald et al., 2000). Thirty-two participants were Pakeha (M age = 20.50 years, SE = .49 years) and 32 were Maori (M age = 24.22 years, SE = 1.10 years). There were 16 females and 16 males within each cultural group. Participants were asked to provide a written account of their earliest personal memory and to indicate their age at the time of the event (in years and months).

Age of Earliest Memory

Figure 5.1 shows the mean age of earliest memory expressed in months as a function of culture and gender. The data shown in Fig. 5.1 illustrate three important findings. First, within each cultural group, the age of earliest memories reported by females (M = 37.5 months, SE = 2.6) was similar to that reported by males (M = 38.0 months, SE = 2.5). Second, consistent with prior research using Caucasian-American samples, the average age of earliest memory for the Pakeha participants fell between 3 and 4 years (M = 42.88 months, SE = 2.96). This finding is highly consistent with nearly five decades of research on childhood amnesia. That is, whether adults are asked to identify their single earliest memory (Dudycha & Dudycha, 1933; Kihlstrom & Harackiewicz, 1982), to list all the memories they can recall prior to a particular age (Waldfogel, 1948), or to describe previously documented target experiences (Sheingold & Tenney, 1982; Usher & Neisser, 1993), the vast majority

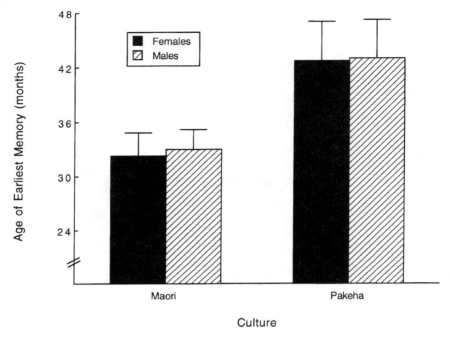

FIG. 5.1.   The mean age in months (+1 *SE*) of adults' earliest memory as a
function of gender and culture.

of their first memories are for events that occurred when they were between 3
and 4 years of age.

Finally, consistent with our original prediction, the average age of earliest
memory for the Maori participants was significantly younger (M = 32.62
months, SE = 1.66) than the average age of earliest memory for the Pakeha
adults. In fact, of the Maori participants, 46.9% reported memories for events
that occurred prior to their 3rd birthday (Pakeha participants = 28.1%). Furthermore, only one Maori participant reported a memory for an event that
occurred after her 4th birthday (Pakeha participants = 11).

Content of Earliest Memory

To evaluate the amount of information participants' provided about their earliest childhood memories, their written descriptions were coded for content
using a scheme similar to that used to evaluate the content of children's autobiographical memories (Butler, Gross, & Hayne, 1995; Fivush, Gray, & Fromhoff, 1987; MacDonald & Hayne, 1996). Participants were assigned points for

providing information about who was present, what happened, where the event took place, and how they felt at the time. Participants were assigned additional points for descriptive information about people and objects that were part of the memory, as well as descriptive information about the context in which the event took place (e.g., the weather, time of year, time of day).

The total amount of information contained in participants' written descriptions of their memories is shown in Fig. 5.2 as a function of both gender and culture. Overall, there was no difference in the amount of information reported by Pakeha ($M = 14.09$, $SE = 1.11$) and Maori ($M = 12.09$, $SE = 1.35$) adults. Across both cultures, however, we did find that the narrative descriptions provided by females ($M = 15.69$, $SE = 1.39$) contained more total information than the narrative descriptions provided by males ($M = 10.50$, $SE = .87$). In general, females tended to provide more richly descriptive accounts of their earliest memory. Across both cultures, the narrative accounts provided by females contained more total information than those provided by males. Female participants described not only the central event, but they also provided additional details about the setting, the people who were present, and how they felt at the time the event occurred. For example, one female participant wrote:

> I was staying with my whanau [family] in Hastings and we would play outside with our cousins at our Nanny's house. The most significant event at that time was my Nanny's tangi [funeral], which was why we were up there. I remember sleeping in the wharenui [meeting house] and how big it seemed and the brown and green maihi [carved eaves] out the front of the whare whakairo [traditional carved house] and crying beside the grave where my Nanny was being put in. I remember the brown fence at the pa [compound], the gravestones and my cousin with a broken arm in a cast. I remember the blue walls in my Nanny's toilet and a 2 cent piece in the toilet. I remember me and my cousin got caught kissing and one night at my Nanny's house we had a pillow fight and were singing the song "Summer of '63—Oh What a Night." (Maori female, 23 years old, describing an experience that occurred at 36 months of age).

To put this memory in context, it is important to understand the funereal process in Maori culture. A typical Maori funeral (*tangi*) is held at the tribal gathering place (*marae*) and usually takes place over a period of 3 days. The body lies in state in an open casket within the meeting house (*wharenui*). Family and friends maintain a constant vigil over the body, which is never left alone, even overnight. Mourners sleep in the wharenui alongside the body or in tents that are pitched on the marae. Throughout the tangi, family and friends share their memories about the deceased. Children are actively included; the tangi provides the opportunity for children to interact with their extended family and to be exposed to their family's oral history (*whakapapa*). Furthermore, despite the extremely sad nature of the event, children are encouraged to enjoy the company of their family. As such, a Maori tangi is similar to any other family gathering that takes place over several days.

In the earliest childhood memory just described, a Maori female imbeds her description of her grandmother's tangi within the context of other events that occurred during the funereal period. She provides important setting information and detailed descriptions of a number of items that are relevant to her story. In contrast, the descriptions provided by males were generally more terse. For example, one Maori male participant also described a memory involving his grandmother's funeral that had occurred when he was the same age as the female participant:

> Going to see my grandmother's body after she had died, lived in Hapuku north of Kaikoura, she had turned different colours, I think she must have had jaundice. (Maori male, 21 years old, describing an experience that occurred at 36 months of age).

In this example, the male participant limits his description of the event to the appearance of his grandmother's body and he provides no additional information about other events that occurred during the tangi. Although both of those examples were drawn from the Maori sample, gender differences in the amount of information reported were also observed in the Pakeha sample. At present, it is impossible to know whether these gender differences in the amount of information provided by males and females of both cultures reflect actual differences in the nature of their underlying memory representation for the event or differences in the way in which the memory is expressed. What is clear, however, is that males and females from both cultural groups differ in the stories that they tell about themselves.

Taken together, the present findings highlight the relevance of gender and culture in adults' earliest autobiographical memories. First, there were cross-cultural differences in the *age* of adults' earliest childhood memories. Adults from a culture with a strong emphasis on the importance of the past reported earlier memories than adults from a culture without this emphasis. Second, there were gender differences in the *content* of participants' earliest memories. Across both cultures, the narrative accounts provided by women contained more information than those provided by men.

What are the possible developmental origins of these individual differences in the age and content of adults' earliest recollections? As described earlier, conversations about the past during childhood are thought to influence the

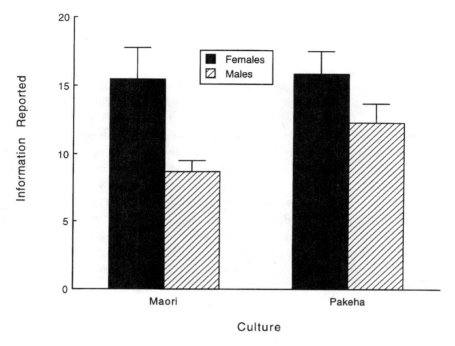

FIG. 5.2.   The mean amount of information (+1 *SE*) included in the adults' written descriptions of their earliest memories as a function of gender and culture.

emergence and long-term maintenance of autobiographical memory (Nelson, 1990, 1993). In general, these conversations are thought to make three important contributions to memory development. First, through conversations about mutually experienced events, children learn how to recount their memories to others. That is, through memory conversations they begin to master the skills necessary to tell a "good story" (Eisenberg, 1985; Fivush, 1991; Hudson, 1990; Reese, Haden, & Fivush, 1993). Second, conversations about the past may influence the way in which other events are subsequently encoded, retrieved, and expressed. That is, the way in which events are discussed within a family may shape the content of a child's emerging autobiography (Fivush, 1991; Fivush & Fromhoff, 1988; Hudson, 1990; Reese & Fivush, 1993; Reese et al., 1993). Third, sometime during the preschool years, children develop the ability to reinstate their memories through conversations about the past with others. Talking about the past, therefore, strengthens the durability of the memory for that event and improves the child's ability to recall the event in the future (Hudson, 1990; Nelson, 1993).

PARENT-CHILD CONVERSATIONS
ABOUT THE PAST

Current empirical research on the development of autobiographical memory examined how the way in which parents talk about the past with their children influences the children's ability to talk about the past. In general, parents tend to exhibit one of two distinct narrative styles when they are asked to reminisce with their children about mutually experienced events. The first style has been referred to as elaborative (Fivush & Fromhoff, 1988), high-elaborative (Hudson, 1990, 1993; Reese et al., 1993), or reminiscent (Engel, 1995). The narrative accounts provided by parents who exhibit this style are characterized by richly descriptive accounts of past events. It has been argued that, in the context of conversations about the past, high-elaborative parents teach their children the social function of memory. By including highly descriptive information in their own past event narratives, high-elaborative parents foster the development of their children's story-telling skills (Fivush, 1993; Fivush & Reese, 1992).

The second style has been referred to as repetitive (Fivush & Fromhoff, 1988; McCabe & Peterson, 1991), low-elaborative (Hudson, 1990, 1993; Reese et al., 1993), or practical (Engel, 1995). The narrative accounts provided by parents who exhibit this style include few details and are characterized by short, repetitive questions. It has been argued that, in the context of conversations about the past, low-elaborative parents teach their children the more pragmatic functions of memory (Reese et al., 1993). By emphasizing the importance of retention per se, low-elaborative parents foster the development of practical memory skills similar to those required for the retention of facts.

There is now considerable evidence that individual differences in parental narrative style shape individual differences in children's ability to talk about the past (Fivush, 1991; Fivush & Fromhoff, 1988; Hudson, 1990; McCabe & Peterson, 1991; Peterson & McCabe, 1994; Reese & Farrant, chapter 2, this volume; Reese & Fivush, 1993; Reese et al., 1993). In general, children whose parents exhibit a highly elaborative style contribute more unique information to conversations about the past than children with less elaborative parents. This relation has been shown to occur both within conversations and across conversations that are separated over months, or even years.

Given that parental narrative style has been shown to influence children's ability to talk about the past, the next question to address is what factors lead parents to adopt one style over the other? One factor that may contribute to individual differences in parental narrative style is the gender of their child. Prior research with Caucasian-American families, for example, has shown that both mothers and fathers exhibit a more elaborative style when discussing shared past events with their daughters than with their sons (Reese & Fivush, 1993). In turn, girls provide longer and more detailed accounts of their own past experiences (see also Han, Leichtman, & Wang, 1998). It has been argued that, through conversations about the past, parents teach their daughters the social value of reminiscence. Over repeated conversations, this value is gradually internalized, and girls begin to tell more detailed stories of their own personal experiences (Reese & Fivush, 1993). Given these findings, there has been some suggestion that gender differences in the age and contents of adults' earliest memories may have their roots in parent–child conversations about the past (MacDonald et al., 2000).

A second factor that may contribute to individual differences in parental narrative style is culture. Several studies have shown that there are cross-cultural differences in the *value* that is placed on past-event narrative and that these differences are reflected in the content and complexity of children's descriptions of their own past experiences (Heath, 1982; Markus & Kitayama, 1991; Miller, Potts, Fung, Hoogstra, & Mintz, 1990; Miller, Wiley, Fung, & Liang, 1997; Scollon & Scollon, 1981; Snow, 1983; Wells, 1985). Miller and her colleagues, for example, studied personal story telling in a working class community in South Baltimore. Their studies showed that personal story telling is highly valued in this community. From a young age, children are exposed to a verbal environment in which talk about the past is actively encouraged. By the age of 2½, these children are extremely proficient at describing their personal past experiences (Miller & Moore, 1989; Miller & Sperry, 1987, 1988).

Other studies have shown that there are cross-cultural differences in the *content* of past-event narratives directed at children. Chinese parents, for example, are more likely to discuss the child's past experiences in terms of explicit rule violations than are African-American or working-class Caucasian-American parents (Heath, 1983; Miller & Moore, 1989; Miller et al., 1990). Furthermore, children from White, middle-income, and working-class communities are encouraged to discuss past experiences in terms of factual information and the literal truth (Heath, 1982, 1983; Scollon & Scollon, 1981; Snow, 1983; Wells, 1985), whereas parents in Chinese and low-income African-American communities are more accepting of fictional embellishments when encouraging children to discuss their personal experiences (Miller et al., 1990).

Finally, there are also cross-cultural differences in the *frequency* with which parents spontaneously initiate conversations about the past with their children. Mullen and Yi (1995) recorded naturally occurring conversations about

the past between Korean and Caucasian mothers and their 3-year-old children. Caucasian mother–child dyads talked about the past three times more
often than did Korean mother–child dyads. In addition, the central focus of
these past-event conversations also differed across cultures. Caucasian mothers were more likely to focus on the child as the central character in the events
under discussion, and they were more likely to include and ask for affective
information when discussing past events. Presumably, what adults choose to
discuss with their children reflects, at least in part, the dominant values of
their culture. In this way, conversations about the past provide an opportunity
for socialization within both the family and the community at large.

Taken together, the studies just described suggest that the way adults
approach narratives about the past and what they choose to talk about is
shaped by their general cultural practices and values as well as by characteristics unique to a particular child. In turn, children use these conversations
about the past as a model as they begin to talk about their own personal
experiences. As such, cross-cultural and gender differences in children's early
narrative environment may play a pivotal role in cross-cultural and gender
differences in the early chapters of their autobiography.

PARENT–CHILD CONVERSATIONS
ABOUT THE PAST IN NEW ZEALAND

As the next step toward understanding the developmental origins of cross-
cultural differences in autobiographical memory, we recently began a prospective analysis of parent–child conversations about the past in families from
different cultural backgrounds. Our initial focus was on conversations between children and their *mothers*. There were both practical and theoretical
reasons for this choice. From a practical perspective, mothers are often more
available to participate in research of this kind and most of the prior work with
American participants has been restricted to mothers (but see Reese & Fivush,
1993). From a theoretical perspective, however, we were particularly interested
in the role that mothers might play in the socialization of Maori children.
Within traditional Maori culture, for example, women are the predominant
caregivers and women play a prominent role in the maintenance and trans-
mission of tribal history. The results of our original study with adults suggested that Maori mothers may play a particularly important role in the socialization of their children's autobiographical memory. Of the Maori adults in
our sample who had only one Maori parent, individuals with a Maori mother
reported earlier memories than individuals with a Maori father.

At present, 38 mother–child dyads have participated in our ongoing study. Dyads were recruited from public birth records, Te Kohanga Reo (Maori language preschools), Kura Kaupapa (Maori language schools or classrooms), and by word of mouth in Dunedin, New Zealand. Eighteen of the children were Maori and 20 were Pakeha. Approximately half of the children in each cultural group were 3 to 4 years old (M age = 3.85 years, SE = .12) and half were 7 to 8 years old (M age = 7.97 years, SE = .12). All children were from middle-class backgrounds. On average, the mothers were high school graduates (range = 4th form [U.S. grade 8] to postgraduate study).

The procedure used to record conversations about the past was similar to that used by Fivush, Reese, and Haden in their prior research with Caucasian-American (Reese & Fivush, 1993; Reese et al., 1993) and New Zealand (Farrant & Reese, 2000; Harley & Reese, 1999; Reese & Farrant, chapter 2, this volume) families. Each mother–child dyad was visited twice in their own home by a culturally similar, female experimenter. During the first visit, the experimenter asked the mother to select several unique past events in which the mother and child had both participated. Mothers were asked to select three events from the recent past (i.e., up to 1 month ago) and three distant events (i.e., more than 6 months ago).

The experimenter was not present during the taping of the conversations. Instead, mothers were provided with a tape recorder and were allowed to record their conversations at their own convenience over the subsequent week. Mothers were instructed to talk to their children as they normally would when talking about things that had happened in the past and to record approximately 30 minutes of conversation in total. The experimenter returned a week later to collect the tape. During this second visit, mothers were also asked to recall their own earliest childhood memories using the procedure described earlier.

Age of Mothers' Earliest Memory

Consistent with our earlier findings, Maori mothers (M = 33.24 months, SE = 3.48) reported earlier memories than the Pakeha mothers (M = 45.78 months, SE = 3.51). Furthermore, the mean age of earliest memory reported by the Maori and Pakeha mothers in this study was highly similar to that reported by women from the same cultural groups in our prior study with adults.

Maternal Narrative Style

Audiotapes of the mother–child conversations about the past were transcribed verbatim and the transcripts were coded using an expanded version of the structural coding scheme originally used by Reese et al. (1993). For the purpose of this chapter, we selected three maternal variables (elaborations, repetitions, and evaluations) and three child variables (elaborations, repetitions, and evaluations) for analysis. These variables have been the primary predictors used in prior research on parent–child conversations about the past (Reese et al., 1993; Reese & Farrant, chapter 2, this volume). In the present sample, these three variables captured 91% of the total contributions mothers made to the conversations and 80% of the total contributions made by children. The coding scheme for these variables is shown in the appendix. Interrater reliability for this scheme using the present sample was uniformly high (maternal codes: kappa = .88; child codes: kappa = .90).

Consistent with prior research, there were differences in the way in which mothers talked to their children about the past. Some mothers described the larger context of the target event and provided descriptive details about the particular objects and people present. On the other hand, some mothers focused on a more limited aspect of the event and repeatedly asked the same questions, apparently in an attempt to elicit a particular response. The average number of maternal elaborations, repetitions, and evaluations are shown in Fig. 5.3 as a function of culture. As shown in Fig. 5.3, there were cross-cultural differences in the mothers' contributions to these conversations about the past: Pakeha mothers used more elaborations than Maori mothers, and Maori mothers used more repetitions than Pakeha mothers. There was no cross-cultural difference in mothers' use of evaluations.

To further evaluate stylistic differences between mothers, we assigned each mother to one of two categories, *low-elaborative* or *high-elaborative*, based on the mean frequency of their elaborations. Within each age group, mothers were categorized using a median split of their elaboration scores (Reese et al., 1993). In the 3- to 4-year-old age group, 11 mothers were assigned to the low-elaborative category and 9 mothers were assigned to the high-elaborative category (median number of elaborations = 15). In the 7- to 8-year-old age group, 9 mothers were assigned to the low-elaborative category and 9 mothers were assigned to the high-elaborative category (median number of elaborations = 22.34).

Next, we examined the number of Maori and Pakeha mothers who were assigned to each category. In the 3- to 4-year-old age group, there were 7 Maori mothers and 4 Pakeha mothers in the low-elaborative category and 3 Maori mothers and 6 Pakeha mothers in the high-elaborative category. In the 7- to 8-year-old age group, there were 6 Maori mothers and 3 Pakeha mothers in the low-elaborative category and 2 Maori mothers and 7 Pakeha mothers in the high-elaborative category. Taken together, the present findings

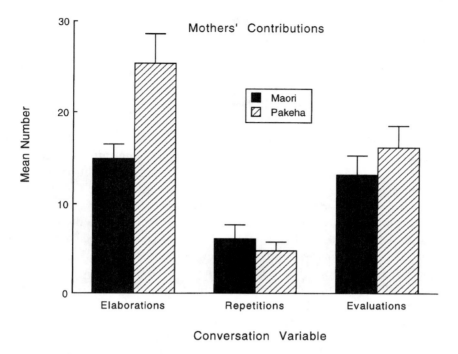

FIG. 5.3.   The mean number (+1 *SE*) of elaborations, repetitions, and evaluations that mothers made as a function of culture.

indicate that Maori mothers used a less elaborative narrative style when discussing the past with their children than Pakeha mothers, $X^2(1) = 3.88, p < .05$.

Although our implicit assumption was that we would find a cross-cultural
difference in maternal narrative style, the direction of the difference we found
initially surprised us. Given that Maori adults reported earlier autobiographical memories than Pakeha adults, we assumed that Maori mothers would
exhibit a more elaborative narrative style when talking to their children about
the past. In prior research on the development of autobiographical memory,
the underlying assumption has been that a more elaborative narrative style
not only leads to richer memories (Fivush & Fromhoff, 1988), but to earlier
memories as well (MacDonald et al., 2000; Mullen, 1994). The results of the
present study, however, provide no support for this view. Rather, if adults' earliest autobiographical memories are influenced by the nature of parent–child
conversations about the past, then, on the basis of the present findings, we
would conclude that repetition within (and across) conversations may be one
way in which these early memories are strengthened and preserved over time.
This interpretation is consistent with the view that conversations about the

past allow children the opportunity for reinstatement that contributes to the long-term maintenance of autobiographical memories (Nelson, 1993).

The more repetitive narrative style exhibited by the Maori mothers in our sample is consistent with cross-cultural studies of adult narrative style in other contexts. McNaughton and his colleagues examined story-book reading between parents and children in New Zealand families (e.g., McNaughton, Ka'ai, & Wolfgramm, 1993). As in conversations about the past, parents also exhibit distinctive styles during these joint book-reading sessions. Some parents attempt to foster the child's understanding of the narrative structure of the storybook. The emphasis in these interactions is on collaboration between the adult and child. Other parents focus on accurate recitation of the text, which leads to the development of an extensive recitation memory. Mc-Naughton (1994) has shown that the first style is most commonly found in middle-class Pakeha families, whereas the second style is more common in Maori families. Similarly, Smith and Swain (1988) showed that a major feature of Te Kohanga Reo (Maori language nests) is a strict emphasis on repetition. Smith and Swain argued that repetition in this context reinforces the rote memory skills required by the Maori oral tradition.

In contrast to prior studies conducted with American samples, we found that the gender of the child had no influence on the mothers' use of elaborations, repetitions, or evaluations. This finding suggests that there may be important cross-cultural differences in the way in which conversations about the past are used to socialize young children. In past research with American families, for example, there have been consistent differences in the way in which parents structure past-event conversations for boys and girls (Fivush & Reese, 1992; Reese & Fivush, 1993; Reese et al., 1993; Sperry & Sperry, 1993). In our research with New Zealand families, however, there were no differences in mothers' narrative style as a function of their child's gender (see also Farrant & Reese, 2000). These findings suggest that parents may not universally place a different emphasis on past-event conversations for boys and girls. Instead, the value placed on reminiscence may vary considerably across cultural groups, both within and between different countries.

Children's Contributions

Children's ability to contribute to conversations about the past in our sample increased as a function of age. Although there was no age-related difference in the number of repetitions or evaluations that children contributed to the conversation, there was an age-related increase in the number of unique pieces of memory information (i..e., elaborations) that they reported (see Fig. 5.4). In

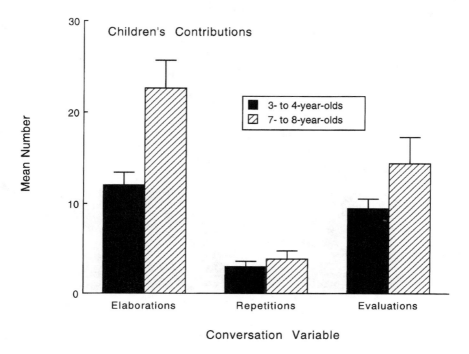

FIG. 5.4.   The mean number (+1 *SE*) of elaborations, repetitions, and evaluations that children made as a function of age.

addition to these age-related differences, there were also cross-cultural differences in children's contributions to these conversations about the past. Although Pakeha children had a tendency to include more elaborations and
evaluations in the conversation than Maori children, this pattern was reversed
for repetitions (see Fig. 5.5).

The Relation Between Maternal Narrative Style and Children's Memory Performance

In past research on parent–child conversations about the past, the way in
which adults structure the conversation influences the contributions children
make. To explore the relation between mothers' narrative style and children's
contributions to the conversations in the present sample, we calculated correlations between maternal elaborations and maternal repetitions and the
corresponding conversation variables for children. These correlations are
shown in Table 5.1. Consistent with past research (Reese et al., 1993), there

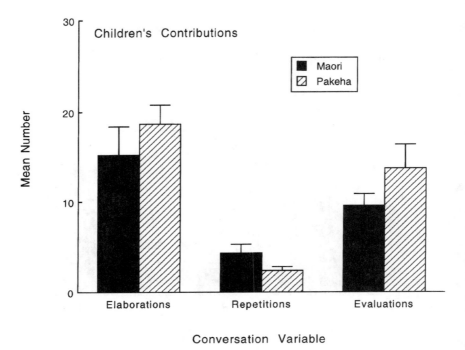

FIG. 5.5.   The mean number (+1 *SE*) of elaborations, repetitions, and evaluations that children made as a function of culture.

was a significant, positive correlation between maternal use of elaborations
and children's elaborations. There was also a significant, positive correlation
between maternal use of repetitions and children's repetitions. The relation
between maternal and child contributions was quite specific. As shown in
Table 5.1, there was no correlation between maternal elaborations and children's repetitions or between maternal repetitions and children's elaborations.

In summary, although there were similarities in the way in which Maori
and Pakeha mothers talked to their children about the past, there were also
some differences in the narrative style adopted by mothers from the two different cultures. These differences were reflected in the way their children contributed to the conversations about the past. That is, Maori mothers adopted
a more repetitive narrative style than Pakeha mothers. In turn, Maori children
used more memory repetitions than Pakeha children in their conversations
about the past. Pakeha mothers, on the other hand, adopted a more elaborative
style than Maori mothers. In turn, Pakeha children used more elaborations
and evaluations than Maori children. These findings are consistent with the

TABLE 5.1
Correlations Between Maternal and Child Conversation Variables

	Child Variables	
Maternal Variables	Elaborations	Repetitions
Elaborations	.59**	—
Repetitions	—	.37*

*p < .05
**p < .0001

view that the way in which children experience talk about the past influences the way in which they begin to talk about the past themselves (e.g., Fivush & Reese, 1992; Heath, 1983; Miller & Moore, 1989; Miller et al., 1990; Mullen & Yi, 1995; Scollon & Scollon, 1981).

CONCLUDING COMMENTS

Taken together, our results suggest that cross-cultural differences in adults' earliest autobiographical memories may have at least some of their developmental origins in adult–child discussions about the past. Beginning at an early age, parents and children construct narratives of mutually experienced events in their lives. These conversations about the past appear to be one way in which Maori and Pakeha children learn the culturally appropriate way of describing their own past experiences. What adults choose to emphasize and the way in which they structure conversations about the past may shape the content and complexity of children's early recollections and may provide a model for children to use as they begin to recount their own personal experiences. As such, these conversations may have an important impact on the formation, development, content, and long-term maintenance of an individual's autobiographical memories.

There is still a lot we do not know about the source of individual differences in adults' earliest childhood memories. In our research, for example, we looked exclusively at narrative style. We have yet to explore potential cross-cultural differences in the content of these early conversations. Our findings with Pakeha and Maori adults suggest that there may be cross-cultural differences in the nature of the events that individuals designate as their earliest memory (MacDonald et al., 2000). We are currently exploring whether similar patterns emerge in the course of conversations about the past during childhood.

To date, our research has focused exclusively on mothers' role in the socialization of autobiographical memory. Although mothers are important social partners for young children, additional family members including fathers, siblings, and grandparents may also play a role in shaping a child's autobiographical memory. In New Zealand, Maori children often grow up in a household that includes not only their parents and siblings, but other members of their extended family as well (MacDonald et al., 2000). As such, the relative contributions of these social partners may vary substantially in Maori and Pakeha families.

Finally, although the construction of autobiographical memory begins in early childhood, it continues throughout our life span. For young children, the socialization of autobiographical memory takes place primarily within the context of the family, but for older children and adolescents, peers may play an important part in the way in which personal past experiences are remembered and relayed to others. The role of expanding social interaction outside the family in the development of autobiographical memory is an important avenue for future research.

ACKNOWLEDGMENTS

The authors would like to thank Julien Gross for helpful comments on an earlier draft of this chapter. Data collection with Maori participants was undertaken in consultation with members of the Ngai Tahu Iwi.

REFERENCES

Biggs, B. (1970). The Maori language past and present. In E. Schwimmer (Ed.), *The Maori people in the 1960's: A symposium* (pp. 65–84). Auckland, NZ: B. & J. Paul.

Butler, S., Gross, J., & Hayne, H. (1995). The effect of drawing on memory performance in young children. *Developmental Psychology, 31,* 597–608.

Dewes, T. (1975). The case for oral arts (55–85). In M. King (Ed.), *Te ao hurihuri, the world moves on: Aspects of Maoritanga.* Wellington, NZ: Hicks Smith & Sons Ltd.

Dudycha, G. J., & Dudycha, M. M. (1941). Childhood memories: A review of the literature. *Psychological Review, 38,* 668–682

Dudycha, G. J., & Dudycha, M. M. (1933). Some factors and characteristics of childhood memories. *Child Development, 4,* 265–278.

Eisenberg, A. (1985). Learning to describe the past. *Discourse Processes, 8,* 177–204.

Engel, S. (1995). *The stories children tell: Making sense of the narratives of childhood.* New York: W. H. Freeman.

Farrant, K., & Reese, E. (2000). Maternal style and children's participation in reminiscing: Stepping stones in children's autobiographical memory development. *Journal of Cognition and Development, 1,* 193–225.

Fivush, R. (1991). The social construction of personal narratives. *Merrill-Palmer Quarterly, 37,* 59–82.

Fivush, R. (1993). Developmental perspectives on autobiographical recall. In G. S. Goodman & B. L. Bottoms (Eds.), *Child victims, child witnesses: Understanding and improving testimony* (pp. 1–24). New York: Guilford Press.

Fivush, R., & Fromhoff, F. A. (1988). Style and structure in mother–child conversations about the past. *Discourse Processes, 11,* 337–355.

Fivush, R., Gray, J. T., & Fromhoff, F. A. (1987). Two-year-olds talk about the past. *Cognitive Development, 2,* 393–409.

Fivush, R., & Reese, E. (1992). The social construction of autobiographical memory. In M. A. Conway, D. C. Rubin, H. Spinnler, & W. A. Wagenaar (Eds.), *Theoretical perspectives on autobiographical memory* (pp. 115–132). The Netherlands: Kluwer Academic Publishers.

Han, J. J., Leichtman, M., & Wang, Q. (1998). Autobiographical memory in Korean, Chinese, and American children. *Developmental Psychology, 34,* 701–713.

Hanks, P., Long, T. H., & Urdang, L. (Eds.). (1983). *Collins Dictionary of the English Language.* London: William Collins Sons & Co. Ltd.

Harley, K., & Reese, E. (1999). Origins of autobiographical memory. *Developmental Psychology, 35,* 1338–1348.

Heath, S. B. (1982). What no bedtime story means: Narrative skills at home and at school. *Language in Society, 11,* 49–76.

Heath, S. B. (1983). *Ways with words: Language, life and work in communities and classrooms.* New York: Cambridge University Press.

Hudson, J. A. (1990). The emergence of autobiographical memory in mother–child conversation. In R. Fivush & J. A. Hudson (Eds.), *Knowing and remembering in young children* (pp. 166–196). New York: Cambridge University Press.

Hudson, J. A. (1993). Reminiscing with mothers and others: Autobiographical memory in young 2-year-olds. *Journal of Narrative and Life History, 3,* 1–32.

Karetu, S. (1975). Language and protocol of the marae (pp. 35–54). In M. King (Ed.), *Te ao hurihuri, the world moves on: Aspects of Maoritanga.* Wellington, NZ: Hicks Smith & Sons Ltd.

Kihlstrom, J. F., & Harackiewicz, J. M. (1982). The earliest recollection: A new survey. *Journal of Personality, 50,* 134–148.

King, M. (1975). *Te ao hurihuri, the world moves on: Aspects of Maoritanga.* Wellington, NZ: Hicks Smith & Sons Ltd.

MacDonald, S., & Hayne, H. (1996). Child-initiated conversations about the past and memory performance by preschoolers. *Cognitive Development, 11,* 421–442.

MacDonald, S., Uesiliana, K., & Hayne, H. (2000). Cross-cultural and gender differences in childhood amnesia. *Memory, 8,* 365–376.

Markus, H. R., & Kitayama, S. (1991). Culture and self: Implications for cognition, emotion, and motivation. *Psychological Review, 98,* 224–253.

McCabe, A., & Peterson, C. (1991). Getting the story: A longitudinal study of parental styles of eliciting narrative and the development of narrative skill. In A. McCabe & C. Peterson (Eds.), *Developing narrative structure* (pp. 217–253). Hillsdale, NJ: Lawrence Erlbaum Associates.

McNaughton, S. (1994). Human development and the reconstruction of culture. In P. V. Geert, L. P. Mos, & W. J. Baker (Eds.), *Annals of theoretical psychology*, (Vol. 10, pp. 311–323). New York: Plenum Press.

McNaughton, S., Ka'ai, T., & Wolfgramm, E. (1993, March). *The perils of scaffolding: Models of tutoring and sociocultural diversity in how families read books to preschoolers.* Paper presented at the Biennial Meeting of the Society for Research and Development, New Orleans.

Miller, P. J., & Moore, B. B. (1989). Narrative conjunctions of caregiver and child: A comparative perspective on socialisation through stories. *Ethos, 17,* 43–64.

Miller, P. J., Potts, R., Fung, H., Hoogstra, L., & Mintz, J. (1990). Narrative practices and the social construction of self in childhood. *American Ethnologist, 17,* 292–311.

Miller, P. J., & Sperry, L. L. (1987). The socialisation of anger and aggression. *Merrill-Palmer Quarterly, 33,* 1–31.

Miller, P. J., & Sperry, L. L. (1988). Early talk about the past: The origins of conversational stories of personal experience. *Journal of Child Language, 15,* 293–315.

Miller, P. J., Wiley, A. R., Fung, H., & Liang, C. (1997). Personal storytelling as a medium of socialisation in Chinese and American families. *Child Development, 68,* 557–568.

Mullen, M. K. (1994). Earliest recollections of childhood: A demographic analysis. *Cognition, 52,* 55–79.

Mullen, M. K., & Yi, S. (1995). The cultural context of talk about the past: Implications for the development of autobiographical memory. *Cognitive Development, 40,* 407–419.

Nelson, K. (1990). Remembering, forgetting, and childhood amnesia. In R. Fivush & J. A. Hudson (Eds.), *Knowing and remembering in young children.* (pp. 301–316). Cambridge: Cambridge University Press.

Nelson, K. (1993). The psychological and social origins of autobiographical memory. *Psychological Science, 4,* 7–14.

Peterson, C., & McCabe, A. (1994). A social interactionist account of developing decontextualized narrative skill. *Developmental Psychology, 30,* 937–948.

Reese, E., & Fivush, R. (1993). Parental styles of talking about the past. *Developmental Psychology, 29,* 596–606.

Reese, E., Haden, C. A., & Fivush, R. (1993). Mother–child conversations about the past: Relationships of style and memory over time. *Cognitive Development, 8,* 403–430.

Rubin, D. C., Schulkind, M. D., & Rahhal, T. A. (1999). A study of gender differences in autobiographical memory: Broken down by age and sex. *Journal of Adult Development, 6,* 61–71.

Schachtel, E. (1947). On memory and childhood amnesia. *Psychiatry, 10,* 1–26.

Scollon, R., & Scollon, S. (1981). *Narrative, literacy, and face in interethnic communication.* Norwood, NJ: Ablex.

Sheingold, K., & Tenney, Y. J. (1982). Memory for a salient childhood event. In U. Neisser (Ed.), *Memory observed* (pp. 201–212). New York: Freeman.

Smith, A. B., & Swain, D. A. (1988). *Childcare in New Zealand.* Wellington, NZ: Allen & Unwin.

Snow, C. (1983). Literacy and language: Relationships during the preschool years. *Harvard Educational Review, 53,* 165–189.

Sperry, L. L., & Sperry, D. E. (1993, April). *The socialisation of narration in African-American toddlers.* Poster presented at the Biennial Meeting of the Society for Research in Child Development, Seattle.

Usher, J. N., & Neisser, U. (1993). Childhood amnesia and the beginnings of memory for four early life events. *Journal of Experimental Psychology: General, 122,* 155–165.

Waldfogel, S. (1948). The frequency and affective character of childhood memories. *Psycholog-ical Monographs, 62,* 1–39.
Wells, G. (1985). *Language development in the preschool years.* New York: Cambridge University Press.

APPENDIX

CODING SCHEME FOR MOTHER/CHILD CONVERSATIONS ABOUT THE PAST

The following coding scheme was based on a scheme originally developed by Reese, Haden, and Fivush (1993).

Mothers' Conversation Codes

1. *Elaborations*

Elaborations structure the conversation by introducing an event, moving to a new aspect of the event or adding more information about a particular aspect of the event under discussion. Elaborations include (a) any question asking the child to provide a piece of new memory information about an event or a particular aspect of an event (e.g., *"what did you have to do with the helicopter?"*), (b) any question requiring the child to confirm or deny a piece of information provided by the mother (e.g., *"Did Daddy come with us?"*), and (c) any statement that provides the child with information about the event under discussion but does not call for a response (e.g., *"There was a great big pig."*).

2. *Repetitions*

Repetitions repeat the content or gist (non-verbatim) of a previous utter-ance, regardless of whether the previous utterance was a statement or ques-tion. For example, a mother may request the same information from the child as in her previous utterance (e.g., *"what did you eat on the train?"* and in her next conversational turn repeats *"what did you eat?"*). In addition, a mother may ask the child to confirm or deny the same information as in the previous utterance (e.g., *"we went in the car with Granny Robin to get the heater"* and in her next conversational turn she asks *"you went in Granny Robin's car didn't you to get the heater?"*). Finally, a mother may make a statement that repeats the exact content or gist of her previous utterance (e.g., *"that prickled him didn't it?"* and in her next conversational turn she repeats *"that prickled him"*).

3. *Evaluations*

Evaluations confirm or negate a child's previous utterance, and often include repetition of the child's previous utterances (e.g., if the child says: *"the sand was black and hot"* and the mother replies *"that's right, it was black."*)

Children's Conversation Codes

1. *Elaborations*

Children's elaborations either move the conversation to a new aspect of the event, or provide new information about the event being discussed (e.g., *"the keas were up at the top"*). Elaborations also include children's genuine memory questions asking the mother to provide memory information (e.g., *"was Dad there, Mum?"*).

2. *Repetitions*

Children's repetitions repeat their own or their mother's previous utterance regarding the event without adding any new information (e.g., *"we had to go on a big plane"* then next turn *"we had to go on a plane"*).

3. *Evaluations*

Children's evaluations confirm or negate a mother's previous utterance (e.g., mother says *"the big dog bit you didn't he?"* and the child responds, *"yes, he bit me"*).

Chapter 6

On the Bilingual's Two Sets of Memories

Robert W. Schrauf
Northwestern University Medical School

David C. Rubin
Duke University

People who grow up in one place and move in early adulthood or later to another country, adopt its customs, and learn its language, offer a unique window into the effects of language and culture on autobiographical memory. Linguistically speaking, such adult immigrants are "sequential" or "late" bilinguals, because they learn one language and then, after childhood and adolescence, learn a second language. Culturally speaking, they are individuals who, having been "enculturated" into the culture of origin from infancy, engage later in life in a subsequent process of "acculturation" into the culture of adoption (Schrauf, 2002). Because both of these changes—second language acquisition and acculturation—are complex psychological processes including cognitive and affective elements, immigration affords a kind of "natural" experiment for viewing the effects of culture change on memory. Culture and language (although confounded) are the "independent variable." The "test group" comprises immigrants with a "dual" language and enculturation. In the "control group" are individuals left in a state of "single" language and enculturation. History has designed the experiment. People emigrate.

From the perspective of autobiographical memory, immigration occasions profound changes. In a crude cognitive sense, there are two of "something" here: two sets of mental organizations and two contexts of encoding and retrieval. Nevertheless, translating the complex experience of immigration—

at the intersection of psyche and culture—into the language of cognitive and psycholinguistic experiment has not been an easy task because the socio-cultural, linguistic, and cognitive factors seem too many and the directions of influence too diffuse. Nevertheless, by devising more sophisticated concepts of language, culture, and memory, it is possible to bring bilingual–bicultural autobiographical memory into focus.

This chapter addresses the issue in five steps. It begins (first) with a description of the bilingual experience of having different senses of the self and of the world in either language. Because identity is tied to one's memory for who one is and what one has done in the past, this leads (second) to an examination of bilingual autobiographical memory done in more formal studies: a consideration of bilingual retrieval of memories in psychotherapy and a review of some current experimental work on bilingual recollection. Giving an adequate account of these findings requires a revision of the notions of language and memory in current research. Therefore (third), a discussion of language moves from the notion of a decontextualized code to the interweaving of language and culture in "linguacultures" (Attinasi & Friedrich, 1995). A consideration of memory retrieval (fourth) suggests a shift from an emphasis on atomistic mnemonic traces to multimodal narrative wholes. These theoretical considerations make it possible to offer a more fruitful approach to bilingual autobiographical memory (fifth) by advocating a linguacultural view of the encoded experience and corresponding language-specific retrieval.

THE EXPERIENCE OF LIVING IN TWO WORLDS

There is a tantalizing array of evidence, from formal and experimental to informal and testimonial, that suggests that becoming bicultural and speaking two languages has the "feel" of living in two worlds and perhaps of being different persons in those worlds. In early experimental work, Ervin (1964) found that French-English bilinguals expressed different cultural themes when responding to TAT prompts in their native French versus their acquired English. She found the same results in sentence completion tests with Japanese-English war brides in the United States: systematic shifts in content were observed with changes in language. She replicated the results again with a 27-year-old Japanese-American telling a story in both languages in response to a picture prompt (Ervin-Tripp, 1973). Grosjean (1982, pp. 282–283) suggested that changes in personality are not language-specific but context-specific; that is, the shift in views or attitudes is due to situation, not language. But if situation or context can trigger the activation of a cultural mind-set proper to the language being used, we may still see bilinguals as persons with resources for constructing multiple identities (Schrauf, 2000a).

Successor to the work of Ervin-Tripp is that of contemporary linguistic anthropologist Kovèn (1998, 2001) who argued that persons who are bilingual from birth possess not only two different languages but a whole array of registers and codes they can use to negotiate contextually appropriate (and strategic) presentations of the self. Kovèn worked in France with French-speaking children of Portuguese immigrants. Her (1998) published examples include transcripts of two women ("Ana" and "Isabel") telling of a "bad experience with a stranger," once in French to a Portuguese-French bilingual, and once in Portuguese to another Portuguese-French bilingual. Relating the exact same story in either language, the women cast themselves as protagonists differently in each language.

> Both Ana and Isabel, in French, speak through a colloquial register that marks them as part of the landscape of urban French youth culture. Indeed, both seem to take on a more critical, irreverent stance in their French tellings and a more deferential, less empowered stance in Portuguese to convey their displeasure with their interlocutors in the narrated events. (Kovèn, 1998, p. 436)

These women use their dual cultural-linguistic resources to reflect different cultural roles in different tellings of their experiences. This is much the same point made by LePage & Tabouret-Keller (1985): speech acts are "acts of identity." They reflect the social identity that the speaker wishes to effect. Although monolinguals may also do this (using the various registers and codes of one language), the bilingual–bicultural individual has distinctly cultural (vs. subcultural) resources for "being" a number of identities.

More informal, testimonial evidence for bilinguals' sense of living in two worlds and having different identities in each comes from Pavlenko (1998) who gathered the autobiographical reflections of a number of individuals who acquired a second language as adults and who became writers in that language. For these individuals, more poignantly, immigration and second language learning brought with them a sense of profound loss of the mother tongue and "mother culture" and their replacement or substitution by the adopted culture. For these authors, the shift in language brought with it a corresponding shift in identity. She quoted the experience of the Russian-English writer Helen Yakobson: "My 'Americanization' took place at all levels of my existence; in one sweep I had lost not only my family and my familiar surroundings, but also my ethnic, cultural, and class identity" (Yakobson, 1994, p. 119).

Equally moving are these reflections from Hoffman's (1989) autobiographical *Lost in Translation:*

All around me the Babel of American voices, hardy midwestern voices, sassy New York voices, quick youthful voices, voices arching under the pressure of various crosscurrents . . . Since I lack a voice of my own, the voices of others invade me as if I were a silent ventriloquist. They ricochet within me, carrying on conversations, lending me their modulations, intonations, rhythms. I do not yet possess them; they possess me. But some of them satisfy a need; some of them stick to my ribs . . . Eventually, the voices enter me; by assuming them, I gradually make them mine." (p. 220)

Pavlenko concluded that these "'language learning' narratives also testify that languages are indeed separate worlds, which cannot be reduced to a simple mentalese expressed in various codes" (Pavlenko, 1998, p. 17).

In sum, bilinguals may show different personality characteristics consistent somehow with the personas they exhibit in either of their languages. The experience of living life in one culture, speaking one language, and then changing wholesale to another culture and learning another language, can be a deeply transformative experience. Although the notions of *self* and *identity* are themselves quite complex, both are certainly tied to autobiographical memory. Philosophers have sewn identity to memory for centuries. For Hume (1739/1978): ". . . memory alone acquaints us with the continuance and extent of this succession of perceptions, 'tis to be considered, upon that account chiefly, as the source of personal identity" (p. 261). For Dennett (1991), the self is the "center of narrative gravity" (p. 418), the selfsame protagonist of a series of remembered stories. Reflecting on notions of personhood in Pakistan, anthropologist Ewing (1990) suggested that the notion of unitary personhood is illusory and that we possess different selves, each with its own *curriculum vitae,* a chain of memories (p. 267) reaching into the past. Might not the bilingual individual have at least two *curricula vitae,* two chains of associations, two sets of memories?

CLINICAL AND EXPERIMENTAL DATA ON BILINGUAL AUTOBIOGRAPHICAL MEMORY

The attempt to deal with such lyrical conceptions in any precisely scientific way is bound to seem pedestrian and tiresome, but the clinical and experimental study of bilingual autobiographical memory does yield interesting results. The following clinical cases were drawn from published reports of psychoanalytic therapists. The experimental studies were carried out in laboratories both in the United States and in Denmark.

Schrauf (2000a) reviewed 24 published case reports of psychoanalytic therapy with bilingual–bicultural clients. Of these 24 cases, 21 were immigrants (having moved to another culture either during childhood or adulthood). Schrauf found five patterns of language shift during therapy. In all of the cases, therapy began in the second language and at moments or for extended periods of time shifted to the first language (Table 6.1). Type 1 described individuals who were seemingly unable to retrieve painful and/or important memories in the second language until some word or phrase in the mother tongue triggered an association. Type 2 described cases in which the language of therapy shifted entirely from the second language to the first, again "enabling" the client to access previously unavailable memory material. Type 3 described several cases in which memories for key past events were indeed recalled in the second language but rendered flat, colorless, and emotionally lifeless. When recalled in the mother tongue, however, such memories assumed the emotional force and detail of the original event. Type 4 described

TABLE 6.1
Language Shifts During Therapy: 24 Clinical Cases
of Psychoanalysis With Bilingual Patients

	Number of Cases	Character of the Language Shift*
Type 1	3	A specific word in L1 triggers a particular memory usually of intense emotional or anxiety producing character which was previously unretrieved in L2
Type 2	6	The global switch in therapeutic language from L2 to L1 facilitates abundant retrieval of memories from L1 associated with childhood/youth which were previously unavailable in L2
Type 3	6	Memories which were previously available in L2 but in abbreviated form, or which were lacking in appropriate emotional accompaniment, are retrieved in detail and with intense emotional involvement when accessed in L1. Alternately, L2 is employed tactically to maintain the stance of detached observer from personal recollections; L2 serves as the language of "experience-distant" as opposed to "experience-near" description
Type 4	8	L2 serves as the linguistic and cultural mediation of current conceptions of the self while simultaneously distancing past identity or the past self which is associated with L1 and the culture of childhood/youth
Type 5	1	Emotional outbursts directed in the present at the therapist take place in L1 which is not spoken at any other time during therapy

Note. *L1 = first language; L2 = second language.
Adapted from: Schrauf, R. W. (2000a).

cases in which recall in either language was felt by the clients to be consistent with their different "identities" in either language. (A fifth type of change in language during therapy, not pertinent here, concerned one individual who switched to the mother tongue when swearing).

Remembering, or "forgetting" in psychoanalytic therapy, is of course an act motivated by both conscious and unconscious dynamics. Choice of language can be a form of resistance, so that the analysand can either avoid or facilitate the possibility of recall (Types 1 & 2) or the analysand might relate a memory in a second language in order to avoid the associations that might render it frightening, disgusting, embarrassing, etc. (Type 3). This latter is "isolation of affect." Or use of a second language might free up an individual to reframe his or her first language memories in the narrative context of a "new" life-story (Type 4). But the other side of strategically "choosing" a language in therapy is that such choice takes for granted that a memory or memories exist in some language-specific (mother-tongue) state that seems durable, pristine, adamantine, and ineluctably interwoven in an associational network of meanings linguistically and culturally connected to the mother-culture. That a bilingual might feel himself or herself capable of self-expression and self-understanding in two culturally distinct ways is not, after all, so surprising. There seems to be a fund of memories (Ewing's curriculum vitae) undergirding either identity. Therapy may act to dislodge and disengage certain memories from the original (e.g., mother-tongue) network to set them in different cultural frames, and indeed this may count as healing, but that they are encoded in a specific linguistic and cultural frame seems undeniable.

The notion that autobiographical memories are encoded and retrieved in specific natural languages has also been tested in a series of experimental studies (Larsen, Schrauf, Fromholt, & Rubin, 2001; Marian & Neisser, 2000; Schrauf & Rubin, 1998, 2000). This research starts from the question: Will memories cued in one language trigger retrievals in that same language? In Schrauf & Rubin (1998), 12 older adult, Spanish-English speakers, who had immigrated to the United States in their late 20s and 30s, were given 50 Spanish cue words to trigger memories on one day and 50 English words on another day. These older bilinguals did *not* show preferential retrieval according to language. That is, memories triggered by Spanish words commemorated events from throughout the life span; memories triggered by English showed the same pattern. However, participants were also asked to indicate if any of the memories seemed to come to them in Spanish during the English sessions (or in English during the Spanish sessions). These "crossover" memories showed dramatic differences. Memories that came in Spanish commemorated events that occurred when the participants were much younger (mean

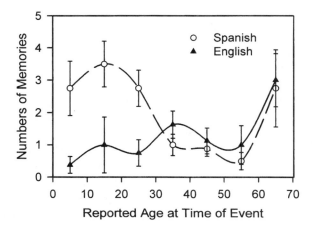

FIG. 6.1. Histogram of autobiographical memories of older
(> 60) Spanish-English immigrants ($n = 8$) who identified
memories given to word cues during Spanish and English sessions as coming to them in Spanish or in English. Error bars
show standard errors.

age = 29.7) than memories in English (mean age = 46.5). This suggested that
bilinguals were reporting memories in the language of the day (Spanish during Spanish sessions, English during English sessions), but that these reports
were *mental translations* of retrievals in the "other" language. In other words,
memories were like other "inner speech" activities (like dreaming or talking to
oneself) and could occur in a specific language and be translated according to
the circumstances of the situation.

To test this distinction between an *external language* of memory performance ("telling the memory") and an *internal language* of memory retrieval
("the language in which it came to me"), Schrauf & Rubin (2000) designed
a second experiment, modeled on the first, in which immigrant Spanish-
English speakers were asked, immediately after retrieving each memory,
whether they thought the memory came to them in either no language (pure
imagery) or in either Spanish or English. Again, Spanish memories commemorated events from earlier in life (mean age at memory = 27.3), whereas English memories were much later (mean age at memory = 50.5; Fig. 6.1).

In a third experiment, Larsen, Schrauf, Fromholt, and Rubin (2002) tested
20 Polish-speaking immigrants who were forced to leave Poland in 1969–
1970. Recruitment into the study divided participants into two groups. Ten
Early Immigrators were on average 24.1 years old at the time of immigration,
and 10 Later Immigrators were 33.6 years old (and 51.4 and 61.4 years of age

respectively at the time of testing). Thus, although all participants had spent the last 30 years in Denmark, the first group was younger at immigration than the second group. Using the measures of inner speech developed in the previous studies, Larsen et al. found that Early Immigrators tended to think, dream, talk to themselves, write notes to themselves, appreciate jokes, and prefer emotional expression more in Danish, whereas Later Immigrators still favored Polish. Again, using the methods of the previous studies, memories were cued in both languages; participants were asked to report the memory in the language of the session; and they indicated in which language "the memory came to them." To test for internal language of retrieval for events in the decades before and after immigration, the data were analyzed by displaying the proportions of memories recalled internally in Polish versus Danish for each decade of life (Fig. 6.2). Both groups showed a higher proportion of retrievals in Polish for the period preceding immigration and a decreased proportion of recalls in Polish for each decade after immigration. Early Immigrators showed a decrease in Polish recalls during their 20s and Later Immigrators showed the decrease in their 30s. This follows the pattern seen with other inner speech behaviors: Early Immigrators recall more memories in Danish, Later Immigrators recall more memories in Polish.

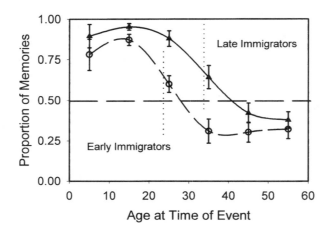

FIG. 6.2. Proportion of autobiographical memories of Polish-Danish immigrants retrieved in Polish. "Early immigrators" immigrated to Denmark from Poland at a mean age of 24 years old; "Late immigrators" immigrated at a mean age of 34 years old. Both curves represent the proportion of memories retrieved in Polish per decade (leaving unpictured the mirror image Danish retrievals). Error bars show standard errors.

Finally, in an experiment not directly related to the internal language of retrieval, Marian and Neisser (2000) used the cuing procedure with younger Russian-English bilinguals (mean age = 20.2) who had immigrated during early adolescence (mean age at immigration = 13.4). Each participant took part in a Russian and an English session in which all communication, except for some of the cue words, was in either Russian or English. Russian-English bilinguals were cued in both Russian and English and asked whether Russian or English "was spoken by, to, or around the participant" (p. 362) at the time of the event. If Russian were spoken at the time of the event, that memory was deemed a "Russian memory." Russian cues presented during Russian sessions elicited more "Russian memories;" English cues presented during English sessions elicited more "English" memories (Experiment 1). This held true even when cues from both languages were presented during "Russian sessions" (or alternately, "English sessions"). That is, in a Russian session during which a person might be expected to be "thinking" in Russian, more Russian memories were recalled, and across sessions Russian words triggered more Russian than English memories (Experiment 2). Marian and Neisser interpreted these results in terms of a language-dependence recall: language at retrieval correlates with the language at encoding.

This study differs from the previous studies in finding language-specific recall to cues in the external language of the report (without considering the internal language of retrieval). This may be attributable to the participants' having fewer years of bicultural experience and corresponding fewer years of experience with the second language. Indeed, it would be interesting to know in what languages these students carried out the other activities of inner speech. Nevertheless, the overall finding is consistent with those of the previous studies: bilinguals seem to retrieve memories in the same language in which they were encoded. These are instances of encoding specificity where the relevant feature is the language of encoding (Tulving & Thompson, 1973).

In sum, bilingual clients in therapy give evidence of possessing certain memories, encoded during youth and childhood, that are only fully retrieved in terms of detail and emotional salience when retrieval takes place in the mother tongue. Experimental studies also suggest that some memories are encoded in a specific language and internally retrieved in that same language, although these memories can be translated to any other language the bilingual speaks. Both these lines of evidence suggest that some memories are durably encoded in particular languages. This is our best scientific approximation of the more colorful testimonials mentioned earlier. Bringing these views together, however, requires considerable revision of approaches to memory, language, and culture than are common in formal inquiry. Minimally, an adequate interpretation of the linguistic data requires, first, a change in our understanding of how language achieves semantic reference and is tied to its contexts of use. That is, we need a more nuanced view of language than the notion that it "provides names for things." Secondly, an adequate understanding of the memory data requires a shift in our understanding of memory as the retrieval of atomistic mnemonic traces to the coactivation of multiple sensory and associational systems in the construction of narrative wholes. That is, we need a view of memory different from the notion of a "getting an item off a (mental) shelf and taking it to the counter (consciousness)." The remainder of this chapter explicates these two theoretical revisions, the first on language, the second on the nature of memory, in order to explain better the phenomenon of bilingual autobiographical memory.

LANGUAGE: FROM DECONTEXTUALIZED CODE TO MEANING HOLISM AND "LINGUACULTURE"

Grammarians and formal linguists usually approach language as a system of phonological, morphological, and syntactic forms with fixed semantic referents in a hypothetically changeless universe of meanings. Methodologically, the native speaker is privileged as the arbiter of what is acceptable and unacceptable, and the linguist is charged with systematizing these insights. This is, of course, the legacy of Saussure's (1959) distinction between *langue* and *parole* and Chomsky's (1965) distinction between "competence" and "performance." Linguists are concerned with the former elements in these pairs (language as a formal system), rather than the latter elements (language in use). That is, their concern is with the abstracted formal properties of phonology, morphology, syntax, and semantic reference and with how these may be combined to make acceptable sentences by the "ideal" speaker. They are much less concerned with individual and necessarily idiosyncratic messages of real speakers.

This way of understanding language underlies much work on the psycholinguistics of bilingualism as well. When a lexical decision task requires that a person review a list of words and distinguish nonsense items from first or second language items, or when the task requires naming a picture in either language or providing a translation of words from one language to another, such tasks rely on the insights of an individual as a native speaker versus his or her insights as a speaker of a second language. And in each of these cases, the emphasis is placed on the individual's knowledge of language as a decontextualized system. Actual usage, the *parole*, language as "performance" (imply-ing individual differences), is not at issue.

This decontextualization of language tends to reduce it to its referential or ostensive function; that is, language is just about *naming* things. This is the Wittgenstein of the *Tractatus-Logico-Philosophicus* (1922/1961). For the early Wittgenstein, language, more particularly "meaning," is a question of hooking up *word*-elements with *world*-elements. Words link up with the world by pic-turing pieces of it. But, as the later Wittgenstein of the *Philosophical Investiga-tions* (1953) was to concede, such a view cannot do justice to the complexity of language. Not all language use has to do with correct naming or accurate reference. Consider, for instance, the person who has been in the habit of call-ing her mother on the phone every Sunday for 20 years and who finds herself having the same conversation every Sunday. This is a "game" that is not about naming things. In his later view, Wittgenstein maintained that people engage in many, different language games, and that people learn the meaning of words by knowing the larger games in which words figure. These latter sorts of language games may, in fact, predominate in daily experience and be only loosely connected to the ostensive function of securing accurate seman-tic reference (e.g., we joke, we fantasize, we tell stories, we navigate, we balance budgets, we do therapy, we mourn, etc.).

Giving an adequate account of language, therefore, requires a fair consider-ation of how multifunctional language is for us. Reference remains one of the essential functions, of course, but hooking up individual words with individ-ual things does not accurately portray how language "refers." Quine (1964) argued that it is not words, nor even propositions, that mirror the world of sense; rather, it is the whole network of interrelated words and propositions. For example, if I say to you: "This is a long chapter. Countless forests have given their lives to make this chapter possible," the sentence has meaning, not because we can sit down together in an analytic fit and demonstrate concrete linkages between each of the terms and real referents (*This* chapter? This very chapter? The pages in front of you? What forests? "Lives" in what sense? And doesn't the quip invoke a whole history of the production of paper out of wood and possibly the contemporary destruction of the Amazon rain forest? But no reference was made to the Amazon rain forest, right?). Reference to the real world is integral to meaning but:

> ...it is only sentences taken collectively—bodies of theory, or our whole going theory of the world—that have or has empirical meaning. Empirical meaning or content is spread across the sentences that together can be tested against experience. (Nelson & Nelson, 2000, p. 34)

This is what contemporary philosophers refer to as *meaning holism*. "Our statements about the external world face the tribunal of sense experience not individually but only as a corporate body" (Quine, 1964, p. 41).

Natural languages are many, of course, and possess this same relationship to the worlds they mirror. That is, different natural languages exhibit referential links to the world as linguistic networks and not in terms of item-to-item correspondences. And that raises the question: Would different natural languages reflect different versions of experience or are they simply alternate "codes" for experience? After all, if languages are merely codes, learning another language is just learning another way of coding the world. This assumes that there is an objective, essentially noncultural world coded slightly differently by different languages. By implication, either the codes are interchangeable, or, more perniciously, "our code" is normative and "our world" is the "real" world. Thus,

> . . . we project the objects of our language, our semiotic world, onto another language. From the start, we erase a field of difference between the two languages. We habitually ignore the fact that *different linguistic and cultural forms of expression have different objects.* By doing so, we create a new field of difference in which the speakers of the other language must be using language differently: deluding themselves (intentionally or habitually) with contradictions, metaphors, symbols, and analogies while we are forthright and literal. And so we translate their language differently than our own: ours is instrumental, referentially flat and transparent, unelaborated and thin; their expressions are poetic, symbolically loaded and deep, thick with meanings, but always referring to our world of objects. (Becker & Mannheim, 1995, p. 238; italics ours)

The "code" metaphor suggests that language only *reflects* the world (again, it "names" things), whereas language in fact has the power to *shape* the world we experience. Insofar as language has the power to shape a world, it suggests that we inhabit different worlds (Goodman, 1978), although this need not imply either the incommensurability of these worlds or the impossibility of translation.

In practical terms, in both reflecting and shaping the world, language does so in real-life speech events involving engaged social actors who use language to accomplish specific ends. This approach to language-in-use is the special province of sociolinguistics (Hudson, 1980) and linguistic anthropology: "the study of language as a cultural resource and of speaking as a cultural practice" (Duranti, 1997, p. 2). Lost in the view of language as a decontextualized system is the way in which meaning is constructed and negotiated in real speech.

Much work in linguistic anthropology in the recent past focused on showing how meaning is deeply dependent on situation or context (Hanks, 1996a,

1996b; Lucy, 1993; Silverstein, 1976, 1979, 1987). This is the notion of *indexicality*, including standard deictic elements (e.g., words like "here, "then," "this," "you,") that obviously depend on context for their interpretation, but extending to many other forms as well (e.g., honorifics in Japanese). Language-in-use derives its meaning from the contexts in which it is used:

> In this view, meaning (of messages, acts, situations) is made possible not only through conventional relationships between signs and their contents—e.g., the word *desk* means a certain type of material object at which people sit and carry out other tasks—but also through signs-activated connections between selected aspects of the on-going situation and aspects of other situations. (Duranti, 1997, p. 37)

Thus, language in any one context points backward to past or laterally to current or forward to future contexts, and meaning is dependent on how these other contexts are invoked or shaped in this present context. Thus, "meaning—even literal sense—derives from the fusion of language form with context" (Hanks, 1996b, p. 232). There are many speech behaviors that enter into the contextual constitution of meaning (Goodwin & Duranti, 1992). Speakers focus their attention, now jointly, now to some new object or context. They continually refocus figure and ground. Speakers continuously provide one another with the necessary "contextualization cues" (Gumperz, 1992, 1996) for the ongoing interpretation of discourse. Speakers presume and invoke background knowledge, both proximal and from distant, other contexts. Speakers "position" one another in speech and do so from particular moral discourses (Harre & van Langenhove, 1999; Schrauf, 2000b). In short, meaning is achieved situationally because language depends on context for its interpretation, because speakers use language to invoke relevant contexts, and because speakers position their own and their interlocutor's "voice." Words have meaning because they have associated with them a whole "discourse history" of contextual associations (Schrauf, 2002).

From a developmental perspective, when children learn a language, they do not learn a decontextualized "code." Rather, they are engaged as active participants by caregivers in context-specific, socially constituted speech events in which cultural knowledge is learned and mediated in subtle and pervasive ways by language. Enculturation and language socialization are integrated and simultaneous processes for children in their own culture and often for immigrants in a second culture. This is the research paradigm of "language socialization" (Ochs, 1988; Schieffelin & Ochs, 1986a, 1986b). The cultural desideratum is that children (and immigrants) come to be competent members of their culture(s). This requires *linguistic competence,* or "the tacit knowledge underlying the grammatical structure of clauses and sentences" (Ochs, 1988, p. 33), *communicative competence,* or the knowledge of how language—for example, specific genres and registers—is used in particular speech situations (Hymes, 1971), and *cultural competence,* or "competence in the ideational realm that constitutes a culture—schemata, scripts, models, frames . . . that are culturally constituted, socially distributed, and personally construed" (Poole, 1994, p. 833). Perhaps the best term for the interwoven linguistic–cultural whole in which a person comes to such competence is *linguaculture* (Attinasi & Friedrich, 1995).

To say that a fluent bilingual immigrant has two interchangeable codes is wholly to miss the point. Further, to say that she inhabits two different "worlds" is not simply lyrical and metaphorical. Rather, her mother tongue is tied to an innumerable concatenation of vividly remembered, half-remembered, and nearly forgotten contexts in which she came to communicative and cultural competence, learning where and when and how to be unconsciously "native." She grew up in a world whose features were distinguished by her linguistic interaction with her contemporaries. The same holds for her life in her second language. In cognitive terms, the fluent immigrant who possesses communicative and cultural competence in both her culture and language of origin as well as the culture of adoption is a person with dual associational networks of meaning or sociocultural worlds (meaning holism). Mother tongue and second language are for her, not codes (although when talking to "foreigners" she is probably capable of reducing them to codes), but *linguacultures.* And, yes, according to both informal testimonials and experimental evidence, she seems to have two of them.

MEMORY: FROM MNEMONIC ATOMS (LEXICAL–CONCEPTUAL PAIRINGS) TO MULTIMODAL NARRATIVE WHOLES

Also necessary for a more accurate view of bilingual autobiographical memory is a revision of what we understand to be the object of memory or, perhaps better, the *memory trace.* Theoretical models of bilingual memory, based generally on psycholinguistic models of speech production (Levelt, 1989), suggest that the bilingual individual possesses dual linguistic facilities (Language One and Language Two) for the recognition and production of appropriate forms at phonological, morphological, and syntactic levels. These forms are represented in a Language One Lexicon and in the Language Two Lexicon and are connected to representations in an underlying, nonlinguistic Conceptual

Store (semantic representations). Additionally, the Lexicons are connected to one another, and this facilitates translation. This is the *Revised Hierarchical Model* (Dufour & Kroll, 1995; Kroll & Sholl, 1992; Kroll & Stewart, 1994; Sholl, Sankaranarayanan, & Kroll, 1995). Alternately, the *Conceptual Features Model* (De Groot, 1992a, 1992b, 1993), inspired by semantic activation and parallel distributed processing paradigms, portrays individual lexemes as having links to series of nodes in conceptual memory. Translation equivalents with very concrete referents (e.g., "rock") might completely share an underlying set of nodes. Others, more abstract and culturally distinct (e.g., "privacy," see Pavlenko, 1999), might activate overlapping but distinct sets of underlying conceptual nodes.

Among the laboratory tasks typically employed to examine bilingual memory, there are priming tasks, lexical decision tasks, Stroop tests, picture naming, word association, word translation, and semantic differential tasks (for a review, see Francis, 1999). These tasks, like the models they are designed to test, focus on lexical–conceptual pairings. Lexical–conceptual pairings are problematic, however, for the study of bilingual autobiographical memory for two reasons. On the one hand, such pairings work from the code metaphor of language and reduce it to its "ostensive function" (albeit intramentally). On the other hand, an autobiographical memory, understood as a sequenced narrative, is far more complex than a assemblage of referents or nodes from a Conceptual Store. Unlike the memory-objects of lexical decision tasks or list-learning, an autobiographical memory is an extremely complex cognitive phenomenon.

Next is an account of the structure of autobiographical memory centering on a treatment of its phenomenological properties with consideration of the neurophysiological underpinnings of these properties. This is the "multi-systems approach" (Rubin, 1998; Rubin & Greenberg, 1998; Rubin, Schrauf, & Greenberg, 2002).

One approach to analyzing autobiographical memories is to describe them according to the multiple phenomenological properties of which they are comprised (Casey, 1987; Johnson, Suenegas, Foley, & Raye, 1988; Robinson & Swanson, 1990). We have explored and identified the key phenomenological properties of recollective experience with both bilinguals (Schrauf & Rubin, 2000) and more extensively with monolinguals (Rubin et al., 2002) and measured the relationships among them.

A first phenomenological property is the rememberer's present consciousness of a prior conscious experience (Wheeler, Stuss, & Tulving, 1997). To tap into this property, individuals were asked to think of a memory and then asked to judge whether they had a sense of reliving the experience they had remembered. Like each of the following properties, this awareness is variable. On one extreme, there might be no sense of reliving ("I just know it happened"); on the other, there might be the sense that the experience is so strong that it is "as if it were happening right now." A philosophical implication of this is the patently obvious notion that if I have a sense of reexperiencing an event, then I am concomitantly convinced that the prior experience is *my* experience and not the experience of some other person (this is Kant's "synthetic unity of apperception"—Kant, 1781/1965). Although this seems obvious, however, the "feel" that an experience is mine grounds the very nature of autobiographical memory (a memory "related to the self"—Brewer, 1986, 1996). Parenthetically, in the case of confabulation, a person may "have a memory" for an event that simply never occurred and yet possess an incorrigible feel that the memory is hers.

Secondly, autobiographical memories have various component processes. Some of these are clearly sensory and have to do with the "feel" of the memory. Memories may have *visual* detail, either "not at all" or "as clearly as if it were happening right now." There may be *auditory* information: sounds, voices (one's own or others). The remember may be distinctly aware of the *setting* in which the event took place; alternately, he or she may be only dimly aware of the physical and spatial circumstances of the event remembered. Sometimes memories come in *words* (propositional renderings of events) or memories contain words (snatches of conversation, self-talk during an event, texts like signs, newspapers, notes). Memories are frequently accompanied by the re-experience of the *emotions* of the original event, other times the feeling is "washed out" of the event. Some memories simply have no attendant feel; the event was mundane and quotidian. Another phenomenological property, not sensory per se, but relevant to the form of the memory, is the *narrative* quality of the memory. Sometimes events surface in memory as narrative wholes, storied sequences complete with plots and resolutions; other times they are isolated or jumbled scenes.

A third class of properties links autobiographical memories to the cognitive and affective processes of the ongoing life story of the remember. Some memories recall *specific,* one-moment-in-time events; others are amalgamations of several similar events and have a *merged* quality. The *importance* of memories varies from "no importance" to "as important as any event in my life." Some memories are frequently thought about or talked about; others are rarely invoked. This is the memory process of *rehearsal.* Finally, memories for events have a particular *age-of-memory* according as they commemorate events that happened long ago and are very old memories or they commemorate events from the last few years and are recent memories.

The component processes and phenomenological properties are mapped onto the neural circuitry that supports them. This is the *multisystems approach* to autobiographical memory. Based on available evidence, the component processes are an integrative memory system (which is classically attributed to the medial temporal lobe and more recently has been expanded to include the frontal lobes), imagery in individual modalities as well as a multimodal spatial imagery system, language, narrative reasoning, and emotions. A full-blown autobiographical memory requires the integrative memory system, at least one modality-specific imagery system (usually visual imagery), and, to varying degrees, spatial imagery, imagery in the other senses, narrative reasoning, and emotions. Thus, insofar as many cerebral systems are collectively and coordinately involved in having an experience and rendering it present in short-term memory, so the same systems are involved in retrieving the experience and making it present again—with more or less attention, imagery, and emotion.

It is instructive to consider just how complex a neural event an autobiographical memory is in contrast to the usual tasks employed in the study of bilingual memory. The time taken to complete a lexical decision task, Stroop test, or picture versus word naming task is on the order of seconds, often milliseconds. Contrariwise, the average undergraduate takes approximately 10 seconds (an older adult 15 to 20 seconds) to retrieve an autobiographical memory to a cue word (Rubin, 1998). The coactivation of multiple brain areas and coordination and sequencing of sensory, linguistic, and emotional information require a considerable amount of "psychological time." Thus, the object of autobiographical retrieval is an extremely complex mental representation.

Interestingly, although reaction time from cue to retrieval is of particular interest both in lexical–conceptual pairing experiments and autobiographical memory experiments alike, an autobiographical memory usually requires considerably more time in the telling. The recall of an event is itself *durative.* That is, it takes time to relate, not simply because the teller might explain the details or the context or the meaning of the memory. It takes time because event-memories are "storied." They have beginnings, middles, ends; they require, in Labovian terms, an orientation in space and time, some "complicating event" that motivates the action, the result, and often some evaluation of the story (a "point"; Labov & Waletzky, 1967). From the simple story "I got the scab from falling off my bike" to the extended story of "When Jennifer and I were going to see the priest about getting married we got into this big fight in the car and she got so mad she nearly drove off the road and we stopped the car and yelled at one another in the church parking lot and finally the priest came out to see what was going on but we were too upset to be embarrassed," *it takes time to remember.* No doubt it also takes time to remember in the lexical retrieval paradigm, but for rather different reasons. Again, the multimodal retrieval of an event memory requires more processing time.

The linguacultural context of the original event is integrally encoded with the event. If the language of encoding is lost, specific aspects of the event tied to the original linguacultural context will be lost because the knowledge needed to retrieve them will be lost. Thus, for instance, loss of the mother tongue would entail losses in memories for childhood events (not total amnesia, but losses in detail and connections in the associative network). This need not affect retrieval of events encoded in the second language, however. A parallel can be drawn to visual-memory-loss amnesia (Rubin & Greenberg, 1998), in which loss of visual memory due to neurological damage causes a loss in all aspects of autobiographical memory because so much of the information needed to access the nonvisual information is visual. In such cases, events experienced after the visual loss can be remembered because they are experienced and encoded without visual information. Events experienced in the second linguaculture are recalled in it and not in the first.

In sum, fundamental differences exist between bilingual memory approached from an experimental and theoretical paradigm that is driven by lexical–conceptual pairings, what are here called *mnemonic atoms,* and a paradigm driven by the retrieval of multimodal (sensory, linguistic, conceptual) autobiographical memories. The latter is more accurately described as a temporally extended, coordinated coactivation of multiple kinds of information. An autobiographical memory is a sequenced narrative whole.

LINGUACULTURAL EXPERIENCE AND
BILINGUAL AUTOBIOGRAPHICAL MEMORY

How do these perorations on the interweaving of language and cultural context (the notion of *linguaculture*) and on autobiographical memory as a multimodal, sequenced retrieval help us to understand the experiences of the Portuguese-French-speaking "Ana" and "Isabel," Pavlenko's displaced authors, the bilingual analysands, and the Spanish-English, Polish-Danish, and Russian-English experimental subjects discussed earlier? Gathering up the threads of the argument, we propose that *encoding* and *retrieval,* the two key structural moments in autobiographical memory, are linguistically marked, if not constitutively linguistic, and that this accounts for language-specific retrieval.

What is *encoded* is an experience, and that experience takes place in some linguaculturally defined space. Epistemologically speaking, there is no objective, nonsemiotic, noncultural world. More precisely, there is no such world *for us*. The world as we know it is precisely that: the world *as we know it*. (This is true even from a neurophysiological perspective: every freshman philosophy student learns that "color isn't out there" but is rather a human visual coding of electromagnetic radiation). More to the point, the world we learn is a thoroughly cultural world. The features we learn to distinguish are the features that our particular speech community has found relevant. The language of this community "hooks onto" the world in some idiosyncratic way as a total network of propositions about the world (this is meaning holism). Further, language not only reflects but also shapes the world (and this is the force of the discussion on indexicality). Language not only depends on context for its meaning but invokes context as well (else we would be filling in details every time we opened our mouths). Any experience, then, if complex in any way, will be marked by the linguacultural context that makes it possible as a meaningful human event.

Think how the following list of activities invoke "context" in American English and the culture of the United States in ways that they would not in Spanish and in Spain: buying a T-bone, getting a pink slip, or hearing Auld Lang Syne. Could these items be translated? Of course they could be translated—there are similar events in both places—but in both places these events are embedded in different linguistic networks of meaning. In Spanish and to the Spaniard, the different phrases would invoke different contexts.

Turning to the bilingual immigrant, then, is a matter of grasping that her experiences do not belong to an objective, nonsemiotic, noncultural world for which she has two entirely interchangeable codes. Rather, her experiences take place in one of two different subjective, already semiotic, cultural contexts, each of which she has appropriated through different processes of language socialization. The encoding of these experiences in memory necessarily includes the encoding of the linguacultural worlds in which and through which they have meaning.

The various sensory and emotional systems interact with more atomistic language processes and narrative systems in ways that affect how an event is encoded and therefore how it will be remembered later. That is, the pattern of activation among these systems at the time the event is experienced will select those aspects of the sensory, emotional, linguistic, and narrative systems that will be most likely to be active at retrieval. Raw, pure, untainted, primitive, sensory, and emotional information, as viewed by a mythical neutral observer, will not be encoded and will not be available for reconstructive retrieval by the narrative system. The information is encoded in a specific cultural context and is subsequently available through associative networks proper to that *mental* linguacultural context.

Retrieval matches these moments in the temporally extended reconstruction of the experience in consciousness, and this "storied," narrative whole is extremely complex. Consider that an autobiographical memory preserves, in different systems, the sights and sounds and settings and emotions of the commemorated event. Consider that it preserves not only words but also a linguistically shaped world, through language, as a layered phonological, morphological, syntactic, and semantic set of resources tied, always idiosyncratically, to the social, microcontext of the encoded event. Consider that it preserves this specific or generic event in the larger sequence of the life story, and in this story interlinked to other linguistically and culturally similar larger and smaller contexts (Schrauf, 1997).

The bilingual immigrant might recall the first day of school from her childhood in Costa Rica and in this mental (and neurophysiological) reconstruction, she activates sights and sounds and settings and emotions and the whole semantic network of linguacultural associations in which and through which her recollection has meaning, and all of this is ineluctably tied to childhood in her homeland. Or she might think of Christmas last year in New Jersey with very different results.

Immigrants of long standing, those who moved from their homelands and took up permanent residence in another culture, those who adopted its ways and became fluent in its language, those like the professional writers whom Pavlenko described (1998), may have a sense of loss as the linguaculture of their homeland recedes from them and becomes less accessible even in memory. In cognitive terms, the reasons for this may be a lack of rehearsal of old memories and a consequent loss of content. From their reflections, it would seem that it is not the loss of this or that memory that they principally mourn but the fading of the network itself. And the fading of the network may amount to the fading of that network of memories that undergird the identity tied to the culture of origin—that particular curriculum vitae of memories. This results in a sense of loss of identity, or a replacement of it by another.

The experience of the analysands in psychoanalytic therapy reflects another dimension: that of bilingual "forgetting." The notion that bilingual clients tend to recall old and powerful memories in detail and with full emotional salience only in the mother-tongue was offered earlier as evidence that these memories are indeed integrally encoded in a stable state in the languages in which they took place. That these memories seem forgotten in the second language suggests two things. From a psychoanalytic perspective, it may suggest that the material is threatening and that a motivated forgetting is taking place. But from a cognitive–linguistic perspective, it may suggest that retrieval is state-dependent (Weingartner, 1978), and, as Schrauf (2000a) suggested, the relevant "state" here may be linguistically shaped "selves." That is, the associative network that has come to define the self of the immigrant may act as a sort of state. Insofar as retrieval is state-dependent, memory is blocked.

Experimental work on bilingual autobiographical memory looks initially as if it shares the experimental paradigm with lexical–conceptual pairings. Memories are triggered with individual cue words in sessions devoted, now to the first, now to the second language. Cue words, and the languages of the sessions, are expected to carry the full weight of the languages (and cultures) from which they are taken. It would be surprising if single words, or a session devoted to one language, would have the ability to cue the "linguaculturally saturated" character of memories that we have already described. But they do. Time and again in this experimental work, the mother-tongue triggers mother-tongue memories, and the second-language, second-language memories, either at face value (Marian & Neisser, 2000) or via the medium of inner speech (Larsen et al., 2002; Schrauf & Rubin, 1998, 2000). As with the clinical data, this suggests that memories are in fact encoded in stable manner in one language and preferentially retrieved in that same language.

Is retrieval language-specific for the bilingual? What counts against this notion is a view of language that treats words as elements of interchangeable code linked to an essentially noncultural world paired with a view of memory that links words from dual bilingual lexicons with nonlinguistic conceptual representations. This theory would not predict anything like the different worlds bilinguals claim to experience, nor the different selves they feel themselves to be. As researchers, we are fortunate that nature has designed an experiment that tests these notions. Immigration presents us with a sample of individuals whose language socialization took place in one culture, and who later in life took up language socialization in another culture. The results of this natural experiment (the anecdotal, testimonial, clinical, and experimental data that we have presented) suggest that neither of the aforementioned views of language and memory tell the whole story. Rather, by sophisticating our understanding of language so that it connotes culturally contextualized language-in-use and our understanding of memory so that it denotes a temporally extended, coordinated, coactivation of multiple kinds of information, we are confident that remembering is, in fact, language-specific for the bilingual. And insofar as memory is language-specific, it makes sense to think of the bilingual immigrant as inhabiting different worlds and having the experience of language-specific selves.

In this sense, then, a bilingual has two "sets," more precisely, two networks, of memories.

ACKNOWLEDGMENTS

Research and writing for this chapter were supported by National Institute of Aging grant #R0-1 AG16340 "Memory, Language, Culture."

REFERENCES

Attinasi, J., & Friedrich, P. (1995). Dialogic breakthrough: Catalysis and synthesis in life-changing dialogue. In D. Tedlock & B. Mannheim (Eds.), *The dialogic emergence of culture* (pp. 32–53). Chicago: Illinois University Press.

Becker, A., & Mannheim, B. (1995). Culture troping: Languages, codes, and texts. In D. Tedlock & B. Mannheim (Eds.), *The dialogic emergence of culture* (pp. 237–252). Chicago: University of Illinois Press.

Brewer, W. F. (1986). What is autobiographical memory? In D. C. Rubin (Ed.), *Autobiographical memory* (pp. 25–49). Cambridge: Cambridge University Press.

Brewer, W. F. (1996). What is recollective memory? In D. C. Rubin (Ed.), *Remembering our past: Studies in autobiographical memory* (pp. 19–66). Cambridge: Cambridge University Press.

Casey, E. S. (1987). *Remembering: A phenomenological study.* Bloomington, IN: Indiana University Press.

Chomsky, N. (1965). *Aspects of the theory of syntax.* Cambridge, MA: MIT Press.

De Groot, A. M. B. (1992a). Bilingual lexical representation: A closer look at conceptual representations. In R. Frost & L. Katz (Eds.), *Orthography, phonology, morphology, and meaning* (pp. 389–412). Amsterdam: Elsevier Science Publishers.

De Groot, A. M. B. (1992b). Determinants of word translations. *Journal of Experimental Psychology: Learning, Memory, and Cognition, 18*(5), 1001–1018.

De Groot, A. M. B. (1993). Word-type effects in bilingual processing tasks: Support for a mixed representational system. In R. Schreuder & B. Weltens (Eds.), *The Bilingual Lexicon* (pp. 27–51). Amsterdam: John Benjamins.

Dennett, D. C. (1991). *Consciousness explained.* Boston: Little, Brown, and Company.

Dufour, R., & Kroll, J. F. (1995). Matching words to concepts in two languages: A test concept of The Concept Mediation Model of Bilingual Memory. *Memory and Cognition, 23*(2), 166–180.

Duranti, A. (1997). *Linguistic anthropology.* Cambridge: Cambridge University Press.

Ervin, S. M. (1964). Language and TAT content in bilinguals. *Journal of Abnormal and Social Psychology, 68,* 500–507.

Ervin-Tripp, S. (1973). Learning and recall in bilinguals. In S. Ervin-Tripp (Ed.), *Language acquisition and communicative choice.* Stanford, CA: Stanford University Press.

Ewing, K. P. (1990). The illusion of wholeness: Culture, self, and the experience of inconsistency. *Ethos, 18*(3), 251–278.

Francis, W. S. (1999). Cognitive integration of language and memory in bilinguals: Semantic representations. *Psychological Bulletin, 125*(2), 193–222.

Goodman, N. (1978). *Ways of worldmaking.* Indianapolis: Hackett.

Goodwin, C., & Duranti, A. (1992). Rethinking context: an introduction, *Rethinking Context: language as interactive phenomenon* (pp. 1–42). Cambridge, UK: Cambridge University Press.

Grosjean, F. (1982). *Life with two languages: An introduction to bilingualism*. Cambridge, MA: Harvard University Press.

Gumperz, J. J. (1992). Contextualization and understanding. In A. Duranti & C. Goodwin (Eds.), *Rethinking context: Language as an interactive phenomenon* (pp. 229–252). New York: Cambridge University Press.

Gumperz, J. J. (1996). The linguistic and cultural relativity of inference. In J. J. Gumperz & S. C. Levinson (Eds.), *Rethinking linguistic relativity* (pp. 374–406). Cambridge, UK: Cambridge University Press.

Hanks, W. F. (1996a). *Language and communicative practices*. Boulder, CO: Westview.

Hanks, W. F. (1996b). Language form and communicative practices. In J. J. Gumperz & S. C. Levinson (Eds.), *Rethinking linguistic relativity* (pp. 232–270). Cambridge, UK: Cambridge University Press.

Harre, R., & van Langenhove, L. (Eds.). (1999). *Positioning theory: Moral contexts of intentional action*. Oxford: Blackwell.

Hoffman, E. (1989). *Lost in translation: A life in a new language*. New York: E. P. Dutton.

Hudson, R. (1980). *Sociolinguistics*. Cambridge: Cambridge University Press.

Hume, D. (1978). *A treatise of human nature*. Oxford: Clarendon Press. (Original work published 1739)

Hymes, D. (1971). *On communicative competence*. Philadelphia: University of Pennsylvania Press.

Johnson, M. K., Suenegas, A. G., Foley, M. A., & Raye, C. L. (1988). Phenomenal characteristics of memories for percieved and imagined autobiographical events. *Journal of Experimental Psychology: General, 117*(4), 371–376.

Kant, I. (1965). *Critique of pure reason* (Norman Kemp Smith, Trans.). (Unabridged edition). New York: Saint Martin's Press. (Original work published 1781)

Kovèn, M. (1998). Two languages in the self/the self in two languages: French-Portuguese bilinguals' verbal enactments and experience of self in narrative discourse. *Ethos, 26*(4), 410–455.

Kovèn, M. (2001). Comparing bilinguals' quoted performances of self and others in tellings of the same experience in two languages. *Language in Society, 30*(4), 513–558.

Kroll, J. F., & Sholl, A. (1992). Lexical and conceptual memory in fluent and nonfluent bilinguals. In R. J. Harris (Ed.), *Cognitive processing in bilinguals* (pp. 191–204). Amsterdam: Elsevier Science Publishers.

Kroll, J. F., & Stewart, E. (1994). Category interference in translation and picture naming: Evidence for asymmetric connection between bilingual memory representations. *Journal of Memory and Language, 33*(2), 149–174.

Labov, W., & Waletzky, J. (1967). Narrative analysis: Oral versions of personal experience. In J. Helm (Ed.), *Essays on the verbal and visual arts: Proceedings of the 1966 annual spring meeting of the American Ethnological Society* (pp. 12–44). Seattle, WA: University of Washington Press.

Larsen, S., Schrauf, R. W., Fromholt, P., & Rubin, D. C. (2002). Inner speech and bilingual autobiographical memory: A Polish-Danish cross-cultural study. *Memory, 10*(7), 45–54.

LePage, R. B., & Tabouret-Keller, A. (1985). *Acts of identity: Creole-based approaches to language and ethnicity*. Cambridge: Cambridge University Press.

Levelt, W. J. M. (1989). *Speaking: From intention to articulation*. Cambridge, MA: MIT Press (Bradford Books).

Lucy, J. A. (Ed.). (1993). *Reflexive language: Reported speech and metapragmatics*. New York: Cambridge University Press.

Marian, V., & Neisser, U. (2000). Language-dependent recall of autobiographical memories. *Journal of Experimental Psychology: General, 129*(3), 361–368.

Nelson, L. H., & Nelson, J. (2000). *On Quine.* Belmont, CA: Wadsworth Thomas Learning.

Ochs, E. (1988). *Culture and language development: Language acquisition and language socialization in a Samoan village.* Cambridge: Cambridge University Press.

Pavlenko, A. (1998). Second language learning by adults: Testimonies of bilingual writers. *Issues in Applied Linguistics, 9*(1), 3–19.

Pavlenko, A. (1999). New approaches to concepts in bilingual memory. *Bilingualism: Language and Cognition, 2*(3), 209–230.

Poole, F. J. P. P. (1994). Socialization, enculturation and the development of personal identity. In T. Ingold (Ed.), *Companion encyclopedia of anthropology* (pp. 831–890). New York: Routledge.

Quine, W. V. O. (1964). *Word and object.* Cambridge, MA: MIT Press.

Robinson, J. A., & Swanson, K. L. (1990). Autobiographical memory: The next phase. *Applied Cognitive Psychology, 4,* 321–335.

Rubin, D. C. (1998). Beginnings of a theory of autobiographical remembering. In C. P. Thompson, D. J. Herrman, D. Bruce, J. D. Read, D. G. Payne, & M. P. Toglia (Eds.), *Autobiographical memory: Theoretical and applied perspectives* (pp. 47–67). Mahwah, NJ: Lawrence Erlbaum Associates.

Rubin, D. C., & Greenberg, D. (1998). Visual memory-deficit amnesia: A distinct amnesic presentation and etiology. *Proceedings of The National Academy of Sciences, 95,* 5413–5416.

Rubin, D. C., Schrauf, R. W., & Greenberg, D. L. (2002). Belief and recollection of autobiographical memories. Manuscript submitted for publication.

Saussure, F. D. (1959). *Course in general linguistics* (W. Baskin, Trans.). New York: Philosophical Library.

Schieffelin, B. B., & Ochs, E. (1986a). Language socialization. *Annual Review of Anthropology, 15,* 163–91.

Schieffelin, B. B., & Ochs, E. (Eds.). (1986b). *Language socialization across cultures.* Cambridge: Cambridge University Press.

Schrauf, R. W. (1997). ¡Costalero quiero ser! Autobiographical memory and the oral life story of a Holy Week brother in southern Spain. *Ethos, 25*(4), 428–453.

Schrauf, R. W. (2000a). Bilingual autobiographical memory: Experimental studies and clinical cases. *Culture & Psychology, 6*(4), 387–417.

Schrauf, R. W. (2000b). Narrative repair of threatened identity. *Narrative Inquiry 10*(1), 127–145.

Schrauf, R. W. (2002). Comparing cultures within subjects: A cognitive account of acculturation as a framework for cross-cultural study. *Anthropological Theory, 2*(1), 101–118.

Schrauf, R. W., & Rubin, D. C. (1998). Bilingual autobiographical memory in older adult immigrants: A test of cognitive explanations of the reminiscence bump and the linguistic encoding of memories. *Journal of Memory and Language, 39*(3), 437–457.

Schrauf, R. W., & Rubin, D. C. (2000). Internal languages of retrieval: The bilingual encoding of memories for the personal past. *Memory and Cognition, 28*(4), 616–623.

Sholl, A., Sankaranarayanan, A., & Kroll, J. F. (1995). Transfer between picture naming and translation: A test of asymmetries in bilingual memory. *Psychological Science, 6*(1), 45–49.

Silverstein, M. (1976). Shifter, linguistic categories, and cultural description. In K. H. Basso & H. A. Selby (Eds.), *Meaning in anthropology* (pp. 11–56). Albuquerque, NM: University of New Mexico Press.

Silverstein, M. (1979). Language structure and linguistic ideology. In P. R. Clyne, W. F. Hanks, & C. L. Hofbauer (Eds.), *The elements: A parasession on linguistic units and levels* (pp. 193–247). Chicago: Chicago Linguistic Society.

Silverstein, M. (1987). The three faces of function: Preliminaries to a psychology of language. In M. Hickmann (Ed.), *Social and functional approaches to language and thought* (pp. 17–38). New York: Academic Press.

Tulving, E., & Thompson, D. M. (1973). Encoding specificity and retrieval processes in episodic memory. *Psychological Review, 80,* 352–373.

Weingartner, H. (1978). Human state-dependent learning. In B. T. Ho, D. W. Richards, & D. C. Chute (Eds.), *Drug discrimination and state-dependent learning* (pp. 361–382). New York: Academic Press.

Wheeler, M. A., Stuss, D. T., & Tulving, E. (1997). Toward a theory of episodic memory: The frontal lobes and autonoetic consciousness. *Psychological Bulletin, 121*(3), 331–354.

Wittgenstein, L. (1961). *Tractatus-Logico-Philsophicus* (O. F. Pears & B. F. McGuinness, Trans.). London: Routledge and Kegan Paul. (Original work published 1922)

Wittgenstein, L. (1953). *Philosophical investigations.* Oxford: Blackwell.

Yakobson, H. (1994). *Crossing borders: From revolutionary Russia to China to America.* Tenafly, NJ: Hermitage.

III

The Construction of Gender and Identity Concepts in Developmental and Situational Contexts

Chapter 7

Creating Gender and Identity
Through Autobiographical Narratives

Robyn Fivush
Emory University

Janine P. Buckner
Seton Hall University

We each author our own life story; in constructing and recounting our past, we are simultaneously constructing and reconstructing our selves. Who we are is very much created through autobiographical narratives. In the words of Rosenwald and Ochberg (1992):

> How individuals recount their histories—what they emphasize and omit, their stance as protagonists or victims, the relationship the story establishes between teller and audience—all shape what individuals can claim of their own lives. Personal stories are not merely a way of telling someone (or oneself) about one's life; they are the means by which identities may be fashioned." (p. 1)

Through examining autobiographical narratives, we gain access to individuals' construction of their own identity. What individuals choose to tell, what information they select to report, provides converging evidence of how individuals conceptualize their selves. But importantly, these narratives are not static entities; autobiographical narratives and self-identity are fluid and dynamic, changing both developmentally as well as situationally. Those aspects of identity that are highlighted in specific retellings of the past reflect those aspects of identity that are deemed important in specific situations, with specific others, for specific goals.

In this chapter, we explore one critical aspect of identity, namely gender. Whereas many theorists have conceptualized gender as a foundational construct, setting the stage for an understanding of self (e.g., Chodorow, 1978; Gilligan, 1982), we argue instead that gender and identity are defined dialectically in the process of interacting with others (e.g., Deaux & Major, 1987). Most important, from a developmental perspective, we argue that both gender and identity must be viewed as evolving concepts that change as a function of the specific developmental tasks individuals face as well as the specific contexts in which particular aspects of gender and identity are privileged over others; there are some developmental and situational contexts in which gender will be foregrounded and differences between females and males maximized, whereas there are other developmental and situational contexts in which gender will be backgrounded, leading to few differences between females and males. From this perspective, gender cannot be conceptualized in terms of the ways in which females and males are different, but rather must be contextualized in terms of situations in which aspects of male and female identity are more or less likely to be highlighted. We first present evidence for this assertion and then try to provide a developmental contextual model for understanding when and why gender may or may not be a critical aspect of identity.

GENDER, IDENTITY, AND AUTOBIOGRAPHY

Scattered throughout the literature on autobiographical memory, a number of studies demonstrate differences in male and female life stories (see Buckner, 2000, and Fivush & Buckner, 2000, for reviews). Stemming from postmodern and feminist theories of gender identity, researchers have focused on explanations of these differences as emanating from the ways in which females and males characterize their relationships to and with others in recounting their past experiences (e.g., Cross & Madson, 1997; Gergen, 1992). Females are hypothesized to be relationally oriented and thus perceive themselves as being situated in a rich web of interconnections with others, and portray themselves as socially and emotionally entwined with those around them. Males, in contrast, are thought to be more autonomous in their orientation, presenting themselves as independent of others, focusing on individual goals and achievements. These differences are often assumed to be rooted in basic developmental experiences (Chodorow, 1978; Gilligan, 1982). According to Chodorow (1978), our first intimate interactions are with our mothers and our identities depend on how we negotiate that relationship. Males must break away from the mother in order to establish a masculine identity; thus they come to view themselves as unconnected, autonomous beings. Females, on the other hand, remain identified with the mother, and thus their identity is based on maintaining connections. This difference is expressed as ways of being in the world, with males continuously carving out a separate space for themselves, apart from others, and females creating interpersonal networks, connected with others.

Indeed, many of the gender differences documented in standard laboratory assessments of autobiographical narratives conform to this distinction. Females tend to tell life stories that focus on people and relationships, as well as the emotions of both themselves and others. Males' narratives are more likely to highlight self and individual achievement, containing fewer references to others or to emotions (Davis, 1990; Merriman & Cross, 1982; Schwartz, 1984; Sehulster, 1996; Thorne, 1995). Based on these kinds of findings, gender has been conceptualized as a stable variable that plays an explanatory role in individual differences in autobiography. Males and females have fundamentally different orientations to the world and, because of this, they construct life stories focused on different aspects of experience and identity (e.g., Gilligan, 1982; Markus & Oyserman, 1989).

Yet we must be cautious in drawing firm conclusions. The ways in which identity develops and the specific issues individuals face at different developmental points can be assumed to play a role in how gender is understood and expressed as part of one's identity. Moreover, telling one's life story to an unfamiliar adult in an experimental context may only allow individuals to express particular aspects of identity. In more varied interactions with a variety of others, individuals may display more nuanced and less rigid definitions of self and gender. From this perspective, gender is not conceptualized as a stable aspect of identity, but rather is viewed as emerging from specific contextual factors. Although individuals clearly remain female or male across situations and development, the way in which gender identity is understood, and how salient gender is as an aspect of identity, will vary both situationally and developmentally. Over the past several years, we have been exploring the ways in which self and gender are expressed in autobiographical narratives in a variety of contexts. As we shall see, the pattern of results presents a far more subtle picture of gender and identity.

DEVELOPMENTAL DIFFERENCES IN AUTOBIOGRAPHICAL NARRATIVES

The first set of studies we describe examines gender differences in autobiographical narratives across childhood. Somewhat surprisingly, as early as age 3, we already see differences in the ways in which girls and boys describe their experiences. In a longitudinal study, we interviewed children four times across the preschool years about novel past experiences (Fivush, Haden, & Adam, 1995). Even at 40 months of age, girls' narratives were longer and more detailed than were boys'. Girls also included more internal state language, commenting on emotions and cognitions, to a greater extent than did boys. Moreover, these differences remained stable through 6 years of age. At age 8, we reinterviewed some of these children and included a new group of same-age peers as well (Buckner & Fivush, 1997). Girls' narratives remained longer and more detailed than boys' narratives at this age. In addition, girls referred to more people and more relationships in their narratives and included more emotional information than did boys. For example, one young girl, when asked to tell about a time that she felt left out or alone, responded (remarks in parentheses are the interviewer's comments and questions):

> Well, I have a best friend at school and her name is Christina, and she has a nice friend that I like a lot. She was just coming over for like two or three months. Her name is Camille and she is from France. And one time I felt really left out because she was only going up to Camille and not me. (Oh really?) I felt left out. (What else about that?) Um, but then we tried to get her to talk to me, and I got to play with them.

In this excerpt, we see that this child is strongly connected to her peers. She begins by introducing her best friend, explicitly marking an important relationship, and goes on to talk about how that relationship was threatened by another child. Moreover, her feelings of loneliness were directly caused by being excluded from social interaction. Interestingly, she ends her narrative by resolving the interpersonal problem caused by the appearance of Camille, with all three of them becoming friends. This is clearly a narrative based in interpersonal connection, and these connections are primary in this child's presentation of self. In contrast, a young boy asked the same question responded:

> My friends at school wouldn't let me play a game since there were too much people. (Oh, tell me about that.) I think it was, ummm, I don't know what the game was since they wouldn't tell me and I think David, yeah, David was in it and Michael. They wouldn't let me play. And some other people. I don't know their names though. But they wouldn't let me play since there were lots of people in it. There were about ten people and that was enough for the game.

Note that in this narrative, the focus is on being excluded from participation in a game, not from social interaction per se. Moreover, although people are mentioned (David, Michael), their relationships to the teller are not explicitly marked. The identity presented here is one of a member of a group to be sure, but it is not a group that engages in social and emotional interactions. The presented self is one based in activities rather than relationships.

Thus, from an early age on, it seems that girls are constructing their past experiences differently than are boys. That girls mention more people, more relationships, and more emotions in their autobiographical narratives suggests that females are more relationally oriented in their presentation of self than are boys, and that this is a fundamental aspect of self-construal even very early in development. Yet, when we turn to college students, a somewhat different picture emerges. Buckner (2000) asked male and female college students to narrate four specific experiences of: (a) feeling connected to other people; (b) achieving a desired goal; (c) being cautious or planful; and (d) feeling stressed out or tense.[1] Only when narrating stressful experiences were gender differences found. For these events, males talked more than females, made more references to self, and mentioned more internal states than did females. For the other three types of experiences, no gender differences were observed, suggesting that male and female college students narrate these experiences similarly, mentioning others, relationships, and emotions at equal rates. Why would we see a decrease in gender differences from middle childhood to young adulthood? Why is gender not a salient aspect of identity, at least as presented in autobiographical narratives, for these college students?

An answer may lie in the developmental tasks that college students face. College is a challenging time, to say the least, especially in terms of identity. Individuals are living away from home for the first time, surrounded by others of similar age and goals, and facing the fundamental developmental challenge of creating a self-identity. As Erikson (1968) so cogently argued, this developmental period is rife with doubts about who one is, what one believes, and how one should live one's life. In essence, it is the developmental period of the "identity crisis." In this study, Buckner (2000) also assessed participants' identity status, using the Ego Identity Scale (EIS; Tan, Kendis, Fine, & Porac, 1977), which measures the extent to which the individual is in identity crisis or has resolved this crisis and formed a committed identity. Although individuals' identity status was not strongly related to the content of their autobiographical narratives, it was found that the majority of these students scored in the middle of the EIS scale, indicating issues concerning identity.

Thus we may see gender and identity weaving together and breaking apart as a function of developmental issues. During the preschool years, as gender is emerging as a stable category (Kohlberg, 1966), children may use gender as an

---

[1] These prompts were derived from Tellegen's Multidimensional Personality Questionnaire (Tellegen & Waller, 1997) for reasons unrelated to this chapter.

important differentiating variable. Certainly, as children develop gender constancy, acknowledging that they are of a particular gender, they also begin to value their own gender and disparage the other gender (Maccoby & Jacklin, 1989). During middle childhood, when gender segregation reaches its peak (Maccoby, 1988), gender may become a critically important feature of identity. Being female or male, and identified as such, may be a core basis of identity during this developmental period. Children are in the process of learning about and defining themselves along culturally prescribed dimensions. At this developmental period, we also see heightened gender stereotypes, with both girls and boys ascribing to clear and rigid conceptualizations of gender (Signorella, Bigler, & Liben, 1993). In early and middle childhood, gender is highly salient and important for one's emerging self-concept.

But as one grows older, becomes involved in cross-gender friendships, becomes cognitively able to conceptualize gender along more complex and overlapping dimensions (Martin, 1993), and especially begins to think about long-term life goals, gender may or may not remain salient across contexts and personal goals. For the college population studied by Buckner (2000), which represents a highly elite private college population, both females and males may be focused on career and professional issues as they begin to question their identity. Thus, for this population, at this developmental point, gender may be backgrounded. In support of this interpretation, virtually all of the narratives produced by both males and females in the Buckner study focused on academic achievement regardless of the specific narrative prompt! Clearly, for these individuals, academic success leading to professional advancement was paramount. It would be illuminating to examine these issues in a less professionally oriented population, one in which different life goals may be salient, such as marriage and family. For these individuals, gender may remain foregrounded.

Thus the argument is not a necessary developmental shift, but a contextual shift, depending on the specific roles that each individual adopts. An implication of this argument is that gender is not a categorical variable per se, but rather a contextual variable; whether and how gender will be displayed in any given autobiographical narrative will depend on those aspects of identity that are most salient at that particular time.

Moreover, gender may be differentially highlighted in different contexts even for the same individual at the same time point. That is, who one is telling one's life to, and why, may influence which aspects of gender will be salient. In particular, we need to consider the goals of reminiscing. In an experimental context, with an unfamiliar interviewer, participants might highlight autonomous aspects of self, but in more meaningful interactions with familiar others, individuals might highlight relationships. Thus we may see in both males and females a more autonomous self presented in some contexts and a more relational self presented in others.

A few studies have documented that the context in which personal experiences are elicited must be considered. For example, Middleton & Edwards (1990) asked groups of participants to recall a movie they had all recently seen, *ET.* When the group was asked to do this with an experimenter present, the participants relayed the movie in chronological order. But when the experimenter left the room before the conversation began, participants did not give a chronological narrative; they focused on their favorite parts of the movie, jumping from scene to scene, expressing their delight or horror at particular occurrences. Similarly, Tenney (1989) tape-recorded phone conversations of new parents telling about the birth of their child to friends and family. With family, the new parents focused on the babies, their height, weight and behavior, whereas with friends, conversations focused on the birth itself, the difficulties of labor, and the medical problems. These studies underscore that autobiographical narratives are not stories set in stone, but reflect the perceived appropriateness of reporting certain kinds of information over others to particular listeners. How might the interpersonal context influence the presentation of a gendered identity?

GENDERED REMINISCING IN A FAMILY CONTEXT

We have been studying autobiographical reminiscing among family members over the past decade and exploring the ways in which gender is displayed in parent–child conversations about the past. Parents begin telling stories about their lives to their infants well before their infants are able to comprehend, let alone participate in these stories (Fiese, Hooker, Kotary, Schwagler, & Rimmer, 1995). Once children are able to participate in these retellings, at about 20 to 24 months of age (Sachs, 1983), past events emerge as topics of conversation about five to seven times an hour (Miller, 1994). Obviously, telling our life stories is a pervasive part of human interaction.

Family reminiscing is especially interesting because in this context, individuals are both constructing their own independent life stories and creating a shared history based on family membership. There are reasons to assume that gender will be both more rigid and more flexible in these conversations. On the one hand, reminiscing about the past is an important avenue for socialization (e.g., Schieffelin & Ochs, 1986), especially of identity (e.g., Fivush,

1994; Miller, 1994). Thus, mothers and fathers may reminisce in stereotypically gendered ways with daughters and sons in order to provide information about culturally appropriate gender roles to their children. On the other hand, parent–child reminiscing is also a critical activity for creating and maintaining interpersonal bonds through the construction of a shared history (Fivush, Haden, & Reese, 1996). Thus parents may focus on interpersonal connections with both boys and girls, and not on autonomy. Moreover, because family reminiscing occurs in an emotionally close familial context, males may be more likely to display aspects of identity, such as relatedness and emotionality, that are perceived to be less acceptable when conversing with less familiar others. In fact, in terms of emotional disclosure, research has demonstrated that males can be as emotionally disclosing as females, but tend to do so only in contexts in which they are interacting with very close intimates (Aukett, Ritchie, & Mill, 1988; Snell, Miller, Belk, Garcia-Falconi, & Hernandez-Sanchez, 1989). Given these various considerations, how might gender be displayed in parent–child conversations about the past?

One way to address this question is to examine the way in which emotion is integrated into parent–child conversations about the past. Emotions are a primary way of connecting with others. Emotional states and reactions bond us to the outside world, and relationships with others are framed and regulated in terms of emotional connections (Campos & Barrett, 1984; Fogel, 1993). A great deal of research has documented that, overall, females discuss emotions more than males, disclose emotional aspects of self more frequently and to a greater variety of people than do males, and report feeling emotions more frequently and more intensely that do males (see Fischer, 2000, for an overview). In all these ways, females use emotions as ways of connecting with others to a greater extent than do males. Would we see these same differences in a familial context?

In a longitudinal study (Adams, Kuebli, Boyle, & Fivush, 1995), mothers and fathers independently conversed about specific novel events with their children when they were 40 months of age, and again when they were 70 months of age. No mention was made of our interest in emotion; parents were simply asked to select special, distinctive events that they had experienced with their child and to discuss these events in as natural a way as possible. Somewhat surprisingly, mothers and fathers did not differ in how much they mentioned emotional aspects of past events. Fathers talked about emotions and elaborated on emotional states and reactions to the same extent as did mothers. However, both mothers and fathers talked about emotions differently with daughters than with sons. Overall, parents talked about emotions more with daughters, and they elaborated on emotional aspects of experience more with daughters than with sons. This was especially true for the emotion of sadness.

As for the children themselves, at 40 months of age, there were no differences between girls and boys in how much they talked about emotions, but by 70 months of age, girls talked about emotions more then three times as frequently as did boys. This pattern suggests that parental differences in emotion talk are not being initially elicited by children's differential ability to understand and/or talk about emotion, but rather that gender differences in emotional talk may emerge, at least partly, due to parental goals for socialization. By talking more about emotion with girls than with boys, parents may be implicitly teaching their daughters that emotions are an integral and important aspect of their experience, whereas boys are not getting this message. Of course, in this study, we did not focus parents on emotion. Thus any talk about emotion was spontaneous. Would we see similar patterns if we explicitly asked parents to discuss emotional experiences?

In order to investigate this question, we asked mothers and fathers to talk about emotional experiences with their 4-year old children (Fivush, Brotman, Buckner, & Goodman, 2000). Specifically, parents were asked to converse with their child about a time their child felt happy, sad, angry, or scared. These four emotions were selected both because these are the basic emotions that children this age talk about most often (Bretherton, Fritz, Zahn-Waxler, & Ridgeway, 1986) and because these were the four emotions that appeared most frequently in spontaneous conversations about past emotions. In this context, similar to previous research on gender differences in emotional talk, mothers talked more about emotions overall than did fathers. So in the context of simply talking about past experiences, mothers and fathers mention emotional aspects equally often. But when specifically focused on emotions per se, mothers are more likely than fathers to integrate emotional states, reactions, and elaborations in their conversations. This difference is illustrated in the following excerpts in which parents discuss a sad event with their child. The first is a mother and daughter conversation (M stands for mother and C stands for child):

M: I remember when you were sad. You were sad when Malika had to leave on Saturday, weren't you?

C: Uh huh.

M: You were very sad. And what happened? Why did you feel sad?

C: Because Malika, Malika say, was having (Unintelligible word).

M: Yes.

C: And then she stood up on my bed and it was my bedroom. She's not allowed to sleep there.

M: Is that why you were sad?
C: Yeah. Now it makes me happy. I also, it makes me sad. But Malika just left.
M: Uh huh.
C: And then I cried.
M: And you cried because . . . .
C: Malika left.
M: Because Malika left? And did that make you sad?
C: And then I cried (makes "aaahhhh" sounds) like that. I cried and cried and cried and cried.
M: I know. I know. I thought you were sad because Malika left. I didn't know you were also sad because Malika slept in your bed.

The event the mother targets that made her daughter sad is clearly a social one: a friend leaving after spending the night. The mother emphatically confirms that the child was sad and asks her to elaborate on why she felt that way. The child agrees she was sad, but claims it was because her friend slept in her bed. After a bit of negotiation, the mother and child agree that the child was sad both because Malika slept in her bed and also because Malika then left. Sadness and crying are mentioned quite frequently throughout the discussion and the whole conversation revolves around describing and explaining the child's emotional reactions. In contrast, here is a father discussing a sad event with his son:

F: Do you remember last night when you took your juice upstairs?
C: Uh huh.
F: What did you do with the juice? When you were going up the steps?
C: I spilled it.
F: You spilled it? Did you get upset?
C: Uh huh. I was just sad.
F: You were sad? What did you do?
C: Went downstairs.
F: Yeah, what did you do when you came downstairs?
C: Get some more.
(10 conversational exchanges about the child getting some soda)
F: You came down. What did you tell me?
C: That I spilled it.
F: Yeah, what kind of face did you have?
C: A sad face.
F: A sad face.
C: Uh huh.
F: What did we do?
C: Clean it up.

In this conversation, the father does not select an interpersonal event that caused the child to be sad, but rather chooses an accident; the child is sad because of a behavioral mishap. Moreover, most of the conversation focuses on what happened, not on how the child felt about it (although this is mentioned). Whereas the mother–daughter conversation is clearly relational and emotional in focus, the father–son conversation revolves around the actions and resolutions of a physical event.

As also seen in these excerpts, we found again that parents talked about emotions differently with daughters than with sons. Both mothers and fathers talked more about emotions overall with daughters than with sons, and especially about the causes of emotions. Again, this was particularly true for the emotion of sadness. That parents talk more about sadness with daughters than with sons is extremely interesting in its own right. Clearly, sadness is stereotypically a female emotion (Fabes & Martin, 1991), and females report feeling sad more frequently, more intensely, and in a wider variety of contexts than do males (Snell et al., 1989; Stapley & Haviland, 1989). The fact that parents talk more about sadness with girls (and overwhelmingly so) suggests that girls may be socialized to feel sad more often, and it has implications for coping with sadness, as well as for the higher incidence of depression among females than males (see Fivush & Buckner, 2000, for a full discussion).

Turning to the children, there were no overall differences in girls and boys talk about emotion in this study, although both girls and boys talked more about the causes of emotions with their mothers than their fathers. Examination of the conversations suggests that this was a direct effect of mothers initiating talk about causes of emotions more than fathers and children responding to these initiations.

We also examined the overall themes of each event discussed. Did parents and children converse about an interpersonal experience, mentioning other people and relationships, or did they converse about an independent event, focusing only on the child? Again, there were no differences between mothers and fathers, but both mothers and fathers placed events in an interpersonal context to a greater extent with daughters than with sons.

Clearly, gender of the child is an important influence on the emotional content of parent–child reminiscing. In both studies, mothers and fathers talked more about emotions with daughters than with sons. Moreover, this cannot be attributed to differences in girls and boys' ability or willingness to engage in these conversations, inasmuch as overall length of conversation was similar, indicating that both daughters and sons were equally engaged. Moreover, there were no differences between girls' and boys' use of emotional language early in development, suggesting that parents were not simply responding to child differences. Rather, it seems that parents themselves are focusing more on emotion with girls than with boys. Furthermore, parents are placing these emotional experiences in a social-interactional context with daughters to a greater extent than with sons. Through their participation in these gendered conversations, girls may be learning more about their emotional experiences, and perhaps more importantly, may be learning that their emotional experiences are more integral and self-defining than are boys.

Yet differences between mothers and fathers are less pervasive. It is only when explicitly focused on emotion that mothers display more emotional language than fathers. Perhaps when simply reminiscing, fathers are implicitly bonding with their children and therefore are as emotionally disclosing as mothers, but when emotion is highlighted, gender may come to the foreground, leading females to increase their emotional language and males to subdue their emotional language, in line with their respective gender identities.

In addition to examining emotion, we have also begun to explore the ways in which people and relationships are discussed in parent–child reminiscing (Buckner & Fivush, in press). We reanalyzed the data from the longitudinal study in which parents reminisced about past experiences with their 40-month-old children, and again when the children were 70 months of age. When the children were 70 months old, we also asked parents to talk with their child about an experience from their own childhood. We were interested in whether there would be differences in the ways in which parents discussed their child's experiences and the ways in which they discussed their own childhood experiences. The parent–child reminiscing context is one of sharing an event together and the parent and child coconstruct the narrative. In contrast, when parents narrate an experience from their own childhood, the experience is not shared, but provides an opportunity for the parents to display their independent identities to their child by focusing on their own experiences.

We examined four aspects of these conversations: references to self, references to others, affiliative talk (talk about relationships, togetherness, emotional connections, and so on), and whether the narrative was social-relational or autonomous in overall theme. When parents were reminiscing with their children about shared experiences, there were few differences between mothers and fathers, only that fathers mentioned themselves more often than mothers did. However, gender of the child again had an effect. With daughters, parents mentioned their child more often, and placed these experiences in a social-relational context to a greater extent than with their sons. The children in this study also showed substantial gender differences. In coconstructing their own experiences with their parents, girls provided more references to both self and others than boys did, and they made more affiliative remarks. Interestingly, both boys and girls made more references to themselves and others in reminiscing with their fathers than with their mothers, a finding that is difficult to interpret (but see Buckner & Fivush, in press, and Reese, Haden, & Fivush, 1996, for discussion). Putting these pieces together, it appears that when coconstructing shared experiences, parents and their preschool daughters tell stories rich with people and how they are related, but parents and preschool boys construct personal narratives that are more autonomously oriented. Similar to talk about emotion, in a close familial context in which parents are discussing their child's experiences, fathers were just as relationally oriented as mothers.

When recounting an experience from their own childhood, mothers and fathers again showed few differences. But both mothers and fathers tended to make more references to others and more affiliative remarks with daughters than with sons. As with the narratives of shared experiences with their child, in discussing their own personal past, parents provided a more relationally oriented narrative to girls than to boys. To illustrate these differences, consider the following two narratives. The first is a parent telling a childhood narrative to her daughter:

> But when I was a little gi-i-rl, and it snowed, we lived in New Jersey, it used to snow some in the winter time. And my dad used to get my brother Tom and my sister Patty to go out and shovel the dri-i-veway. And we, they used to shovel the driveway all in one big stack in one corner of the driveway. And then, if it was the right kind of snow, they used to make me IGLOOS . . . Anyway, on snowy da-ays, I used to say, "Ohhhh, make me an igloo! Make me an igloo!" And then Uncle Michael and I would put on all our snow clothes and we would go out there and just play and play and play in this igloo. . . .

And here is a parent narrating a childhood event to his son:

> I remember catching that fish up on the wall. Mm hmm, I, Daddy had given me a fishing pole for Christmas . . . You know that red one I still have? He gave me that when I was a kid. And we went to a farm near great granddaddy's farm. And Daddy helped me. He put a purple rubber worm on the hook. And it was almost dark. And we were walking around the lake, we were just casting into the lake. And I didn't think I was gonna catch anything. And then, the fish came and saw that purple worm on the bottom and he GRABBED it a-a-nd he JUMPED up out of the water! And I pulled and I screamed ahhhhhh! (laughs) I got it, and I reeled and I reeled and I reeled and I didn't think I was gonna catch it. And I pulled it out of the water and onto the bank and it was the biggest fish I had ever seen alive. . . .

Both narratives are clearly engaging and tell about a childhood event that was great fun, and both clearly place the parent in his or her own family of origin. But the first narrative, told to a daughter, mentions more people and more relationships, and the exciting event concerns the parent interacting with her brother (the child's uncle). The whole point of the narrative is how much fun it was to play with Uncle Michael. The second narrative, told to a son, also places the parent in a family context by referencing his own father (the child's grandfather). But here, the grandfather is not integral to the activity being described. It is the parent alone who reels in the fish. Thus, whether coconstructing their child's experience or narrating an event from their own childhood, mothers and fathers tell more socially oriented, relational stories to daughters than to sons. Furthermore, that parents show these same patterns in both reminiscing contexts suggests that they are not simply responding to gender differences in their children's contributions. If this were the case, we would expect the differences to be attenuated in parents' recounting of their own past when children are not able to contribute.

Overall, this research program demonstrates both the very early emergence of gender differences in children's autobiographical narratives and simultaneously, very few gender differences between adult males and females when reminiscing in a family context. Paradoxically, although there are few differences between mothers and fathers, there are pervasive differences in how parents reminisce with daughters and with sons, which cannot be attributed solely to gender differences among the children themselves. With daughters, parents tell more emotional, social, and relational stories about the past than with sons. How can we interpret these findings and what do they mean for developing relations among gender, identity, and autobiography?

DEVELOPMENTAL AND CONTEXTUAL INFLUENCES ON GENDERED AUTOBIOGRAPHIES

Somewhat surprisingly, we found that many of the gender differences reported in adult autobiographical narratives in previous research emerge as early as the preschool years. When preschool girls tell the stories of their lives, they include more people, more relationships, and (at least by the end of the preschool years) more emotions than do preschool boys. This might suggest that females and males construct very different ways of understanding their experiences, with girls placing their experiences in a more social and relational context, highlighting their connections to others, and boys viewing themselves and their experiences as more separate from, and independent of, others. Yet this conclusion is too facile. As our research has shown, when recounting narratives of achievement, college students show few gender differences, and when reminiscing with their young children, mothers and fathers are remarkably similar. These findings indicate that when males and females are focused on similar tasks or have similar purposes in recounting their past, gender differences are attenuated. However, when specifically asked to discuss emotional aspects of the past, mothers and fathers begin to reminisce in gendered ways. Thus, in contexts in which gender is foregrounded, either developmentally as children's gender concepts are being formed and elaborated, or situationally, as when adult males and females are focused on emotion, gender differences are most likely to emerge. But when gender is backgrounded, as when college students are grappling with issues of professional identity development, or when parents are focused on creating and maintaining bonds with their young children, gender differences in autobiography recede.

Intriguingly, although mothers and fathers show few differences in reminiscing, both mothers and fathers reminisce differently with daughters than with sons, placing past events in a more social, relational, and emotional context with girls than with boys. These patterns indicate that gender cannot be conceptualized as stable differences in the ways in which males and females characterize themselves and their lives, but rather is an emergent property of the specific developmental and situational context. Moreover, gender differences may be just as much a function of one's conversational partner as of one's own gender.

Still, although gender differences are exaggerated or attenuated as a function of context, it must also be emphasized that when gender differences do emerge, they are always in the direction of females reporting more social, relational, and emotional autobiographical narratives. In this sense, then, gender differences are predictable and stable, even if not pervasive. It does seem to be the case that females are more likely than males to tell socially embellished personal narratives in a wider variety of contexts. It may be that males are only able and/or willing to reminisce in socially embellished and emotionally explicit ways in contexts in which they are conversing with intimate others. Indeed, it may even be that males are only willing to relax their stereotypically gendered way of interacting in situations in which there is a clear power differential. Feminist theories of gender and identity emphasize the role of power as a determinant of who is allowed to say what to whom (see Miller & Scholnick, 2000, for a review). More specifically, in reminiscing, males may only feel comfortable relinquishing an independent identity, and emphasizing social and emotional aspects of experience, when conversing with a partner who is clearly in a position of lesser power and in need of nurturance, such as a young child, or in situations where they feel safe being "vulnerable" with an intimate other, where power may be less overt. To date, we have not examined reminiscing in the larger family context, between parents, or parents and older children. It may very well be the case that patterns of reminiscing change as a function of the relationship and developmental stage of the familial participants. Research currently underway in our lab is exploring some of these ideas.

Furthermore, all of the research we discussed in this chapter, and much of the research in the field, has focused on autobiographical narratives within a White, middle-class population. Certainly, we would expect differences in the ways in which individuals growing up in different cultural contexts would construe themselves and their experiences (Oyserman & Markus, 1993), and there is accumulating data supporting the idea of cultural differences in presentation of self in autobiography (e.g., Han, Leichtman, & Wang, 1998; Mullen & Yi, 1995). Many of the chapters in this book discuss culture, self, and autobiography in detail, and as their contributions make clear, this is an important connection to consider. The way in which gender may be constructed within differing cultural identities is a critical aspect of autobiography.

Perhaps most important, what our research demonstrates is that gender, identity, and autobiography are intertwined, both developmentally and situationally. Rather than conceptualizing gender as a stable, essential aspect of identity that is reflected in autobiographical narratives, our research indicates that the ways in which individuals construe and display gendered identities are influenced specifically by the people and contexts of interaction in which we participate. In this regard, the particular meaning of our gendered selves changes with the goals and partners with whom we negotiate our everyday lives. Thus, although we may perceive our experiences as maintaining a continuous, persistent sense of self across different activities and developmental seasons, we often overlook the rich nuances and subtleties of identity that are linked inextricably to both the significant and seemingly mundane settings in which the moments of our life stories unfold.

REFERENCES

Adams, S., Kuebli, J., Boyle, P., & Fivush, R. (1995). Gender differences in parent–child conversations about past emotions: A longitudinal investigation. *Sex Roles, 33,* 309–323.
Aukett, R., Ritchie, J., & Mill, K. (1988). Gender differences in friendship patterns. *Sex Roles, 19,* 57–66.
Bretherton, I., Fritz, J., Zahn-Waxler, C., & Ridgeway, D. (1986). Learning to talk about emotions: A functionalist perspective. *Child Development, 57,* 529–548.

Buckner, J. P. (2000). *The remembering self.* Unpublished dissertation, Emory University, Atlanta, GA.

Buckner, J. P., & Fivush, R. (1997). Gender and self in children's autobiographical narratives. *Applied Cognitive Psychology, 12,* 407–429

Buckner, J. P., & Fivush, R. (in press). Gendered themes in family reminiscing. *Memory.*

Campos, J. J., & Barrett, K. C. (1984). Toward a new understanding of emotions and their development. In C. E. Izard, J. Kagen, & R. B. Zajonc (Eds.), *Emotions, cognition and behavior* (pp. 229–263). New York: Cambridge University Press.

Chodorow, N. J. (1978). *The reproduction of mothering: Psychoanalysis and the socialization of gender.* Berkeley: University of California Press.

Cross, S. E., & Madson, L. (1997). Models of the self: Self-construals and gender. *Psychological Bulletin, 122,* 5–37.

Davis, P. J. (1990). Gender differences in autobiographical memories for childhood emotional experiences. *Journal of Personality and Social Psychology, 76,* 498–510.

Deaux, K., & Major, B. (1987). Putting gender into context: An interactional model of gender-related behavior. *Psychological Review, 94,* 369–389.

Erikson, E. (1968). *Youth and identity crisis.* New York: Norton.

Fabes, R. A., & Martin, C. L. (1991). Gender and age stereotypes of emotionality. *Personality and Social Psychology Bulletin, 17,* 532–540.

Fiese, B. H., Hooker, K. A., Kotary, L., Schwagler, J., & Rimmer, M. (1995). Family stories in the early stages of parenthood. *Journal of Marriage and the Family, 57,* 763–770.

Fischer, A. H. (2000). *Gender and emotion: Social psychological perspectives.* New York: Cambridge University Press.

Fivush, R. (1994). Constructing narrative, emotion and self in parent–child conversations about the past. In U. Neisser & R. Fivush (Eds.), *The remembering self: Accuracy and construction in the life narrative* (pp. 136–157). New York: Cambridge University press.

Fivush, R., Brotman, M., Buckner, J. P., & Goodman, S. (2000). Gender differences in parent–child emotion narratives. *Sex Roles, 42,* 233–254.

Fivush, R., & Buckner, J. P. (2000). Gender, sadness and depression: The development of emotional focus through gendered discourse. In A. H. Fischer (Ed.), *Gender and emotion: Social psychological perspectives* (pp. 232–253). New York: Cambridge University Press.

Fivush, R., Haden, C., & Adam, S. (1995). Structure and coherence of preschoolers' personal narratives over time: Implications for childhood amnesia. *Journal of Experimental Child Psychology, 60,* 32–56.

Fivush, R., Haden, C., & Reese, E. (1996). Remembering, recounting and reminiscing: The development of autobiographical memory in social context. In D. Rubin (Ed.), *Reconstructing our past: An overview of autobiographical memory* (pp. 341–359). New York: Cambridge University Press.

Fogel, A. (1993). *Developing through relationships.* Chicago: University of Chicago Press.

Gergen, M. (1992). Life stories: Pieces of a dream. In G. C. Rosenwald & R. L. Ochberg (Eds.), *Storied lives: The cultural politics of self-understanding* (pp. 127–143). New Haven, CT: Yale University Press.

Gilligan, C. (1982). *In a different voice: Psychological theory and women's development.* Cambridge, MA: Harvard University Press.

Han, J. J., Leichtman, M. D., & Wang, Q. (1998). Autobiographical memory in Korean, Chinese, and American children. *Developmental Psychology, 34,* 701–713.

Kohlberg, L. (1966). A cognitive–developmental analysis of children's sex-role concepts and attitudes. In E. E. Maccoby (Ed.), *The development of sex differences* (pp. 82–173). Stanford, CA: Stanford University Press.

Maccoby, E. E. (1988). Gender as a social category. *Developmental Psychology, 24,* 755–765.

Maccoby, E. E., & Jacklin, C. N. (1989). Gender segregation in children. In H. W. Reese (Ed.), Advances in child development and behavior (Vol. 20, pp. 239–287). New York: Academic Press.

Markus, H., & Oyserman, D. (1989). Gender and thought: The role of the self-concept. In M. Crawford & M. Gentry (Eds.), *Gender and thought: psychological perspectives.* New York: Springer-Verlag.

Martin, C. L. (1993). New directins for assessing children's gender knowledge. *Developmental Review, 13,* 184–204.

Merriman, S. B., & Cross, L. H. (1982). Adulthood and reminiscence: A descriptive study. *Educational Gerontology, 8,* 275–290.

Middleton, D., & Edwards, D. (1990). Conversational remembering: A social psychological approach. In D. Middleton & D. Edwards (Eds.), *Collective remembering* (pp. 23–45). London: Sage Publications.

Miller, P. H., & Scholnick, E. K. (2000). *Toward a feminist developmental psychology.* New York: Routledge.

Miller, P. J. (1994). Narrative practices: Their role in socialization and self-construction. In U. Neisser & R. Fivush (Eds.), *The remembering self: Construction and accuracy in the life narrative* (pp. 158–179). New York: Cambridge University Press.

Mullen, M., & Yi, S. (1995). The cultural context of talk about the past: Implications for the development of autobiographical memory. *Cognitive Development, 10,* 407–419.

Oyserman, D., & Markus, H. (1993). The sociocultural self. In J. Suls (Ed.), *Psychological perspectives on the self: The self in social perspective* (Vol. 4, pp. 187–220). Hillsdale, NJ: Lawrence Erlbaum Associates.

Reese, E., Haden, C., & Fivush, R. (1996). Mothers, father, daughters, sons: Gender differences in reminiscing. *Research on Language and Social Interaction, 29,* 27–56.

Rosenwald, G. C., & Ochberg, R. L. (1992). Introduction: Life stories, cultural politics, and self-understanding. In G. C. Rosenwald & R. L. Ochberg (Eds.), *Storied lives: The cultural politics of self-understanding* (pp. 1–18). New Haven, CT: Yale University Press.

Sachs, J. (1983). Talking about the there and then: The emergence of displaced reference in parent–child discourse. In K. Nelson (Ed.), *Children's language* (Vol. 4, pp. 1- 28). Hillsdale, NJ: Lawrence Erlbaum Associates.

Schieffelin, B. B., & Ochs, E. (1986). *Language socialization across cultures.* New York: Cambridge University Press.

Schwartz, A. E. (1984). Earliest memories: Sex differences and the meaning of experience. *Imagination, Cognition and Personality, 4,* 43–52.

Sehulster, J. R. (1996, July). Prospective and retrospective factors in the organization of autobiographical memory. In J. R. Sehulster & D. Bruce (Chairs), *Organization of autobiographical memory.* Symposium conducted at the International Conference on Memory, Abano Terme, Italy.

Signorella, M. L., Bigler, R. S., & Liben, L. (1993). Developmental differences in children's gender schemata about others: A meta-analytic review. *Developmental Review, 13,* 106–126.

Snell, W. E., Jr., Miller, R. S., Belk, S. S., Garcia-Falconi, R., & Hernandez-Sanchez, J. E. (1989). Men's and women's emotional self-disclosure: The impact of disclosure recipient, culture, and the masculine role. *Sex Roles, 21,* 467–486.

Stapley, J. C., & Haviland, J. M. (1989). Beyond depression: Gender differences in normal adolescents' emotional experience. *Sex Roles, 20,* 295–308.

Tan, A. L., Kendis, R. J., Fine, J. T., & Porac, J. (1977). A short measure of Eriksonian ego identity. *Journal of Personality Assessment, 41,* 279–284.

Tenney, Y. J. (1989). Predicting conversational reports of a personal event. *Cognitive Science, 13,* 213–233.

Tellegen, A., & Waller, N. G. (1997). Exploring personality through test construction: Development of the Multidimensional Personality Questionnaire. In S. R. Briggs & J. M. Cheek (Eds.), *Personality measures: Development and evaluation (Vol. 1).* Greenwich, CT: JAI Press.

Thorne, A. (1995). Developmental truths in memories of childhood and adolescence. *Journal of Personality, 63,* 139–163.

Chapter 8

Telling Traumatic Events in Adolescence: A Study of Master Narrative Positioning

Avril Thorne
Kate C. McLean
University of California, Santa Cruz

In thinking about culture and the autobiographical self, we feel tugged in two directions. "Culture" presses us to consider how people are similar, whereas "self" presses us to consider the uniqueness of individual lives. How can such seemingly oppositional concepts be connected in ways that appreciate both personal experience and the press of larger communities? Furthermore, how can the link be made *dynamically,* so that personal history and cultural values can be viewed as mutually emergent, and *contextually,* in order to preserve the richness of actual moments when self and culture meet?

Our approach to this problem centers on salient episodes of telling self-defining memories to others. Self-defining memories, like all personal memories, concern specific and memorable past events (Nelson, 1993). Self-defining memories, however, are particularly vivid, emotional, and familiar, revealing "affective patterns and themes that stamp an individual's most important concerns" (Singer & Salovey, 1993, p. 4). Self-defining memories are a central feature of the autobiographical self because they are essential for the development of the internalized life story, as well as for conveying one's personal past to others. We begin by introducing the two vehicles with which we approached the problem, the concepts of positioning and of master narrative, and then proceed to tell the empirical story.

169

Positioning: Conveying the Point of a Self-Defining Memory

Researchers usually determine the meaning of an event narrative by examining content within the narrative. Although the meaning sometimes seems very clear, this is not always the case. To illustrate, consider the following event narrative from one of our informants, a 20-year-old we call Henry. Henry responded to a questionnaire that elicited *self-defining memories*, which were defined as personal memories that are at least 1 year old, are highly vivid, continue to evoke strong feelings even now, and "convey powerfully how you have come to be the person you currently are" (Singer & Moffitt, 1991–1992, p. 242). One of Henry's self-defining memories concerned an event that reportedly occurred when he was 11 years old:

> [Event narrative:] When my father informed me that my uncle had died, we were working on a school science project. He answered the phone, told me that his brother had died, and that we should finish up the science project. Even though I was not close to my uncle, my tears streamed. My father told me that the long suffering from cancer was over, and that I shouldn't feel sad. Then he asked me to hold a flashlight so we could finish the science project.

In this memory narrative, Henry's feelings about his father are not very clear. How did Henry feel about his father's urging him not to feel sad? Why does he regard this memory as self-defining? Why is he telling us this story? These are the kinds of questions that a listener might ask of Henry.

In the last few years, we found that the point of a story, or what Labov and Waletsky (1967) called the *evaluative component,* can become clarified when the story is told to another person. Interlocutors often demand meanings; sooner or later, they insist on knowing why the speaker is telling them the story. Although psychotherapists and ethnographers have long understood that dialogue can help to clarify the meaning of events (e.g., Agar & Hobbs, 1982; Loewald, 1975), we came to this discovery only recently. Our discovery was prompted by survey findings that highly memorable events tend to be told soon after the event occurs and on multiple occasions thereafter, presumably to clarify the emotional meaning of the event (Rimé, Mesquita, Philippot, & Boca, 1991). Intrigued by these findings, we added another query to our self-defining memory questionnaire. We asked informants not only to describe a self-defining event, but also, if possible, to describe a specific episode in which they had told the event to someone else. We henceforth refer to the latter narrative as the *telling narrative,* to differentiate it from the narrative of the original event, or the *event narrative.*

Henry's telling narrative convinced us that addressing a story to a specific person can reveal and perhaps even promote the development of the point of the story:

> [Telling narrative:] I told my friend [Joe] because we were comparing our distant relationships. I told him that I can't take news like that with such a stoic nature. Joe felt the same way I did, and we concluded that we were different than our fathers. I told him 9 years later.

The point of the science project story was not clear in Henry's event narrative, but seemed much more clear in his telling narrative, which was addressed to his friend Joe. In the telling narrative, Henry positioned himself as unequivocally rejecting his father's edict not to feel sad, a position shared by his friend.

Positioning refers to the social and emotional stances that individuals take vis-à-vis real or imagined others (Bamberg, 1997; Davies & Harré, 1990). It is a dynamic rendition of the more static concept of role. Positioning can occur between characters within a story, as well as between the storyteller and the audience (Bamberg, 1997). The positions that we pursue in this chapter concern emotional stances with regard to momentous events. For example, Henry's position in the science project memory, as clarified in this case by the telling narrative, was one of sadness with respect to the death of a loved one. The position was endorsed by his college friend, but resisted by their fathers, who favored a more stoic position with regard to death.

Master Narratives: Culturally Valued Positions

The fathers' position that one should be stoic in the face of tragedy is an example of a *master narrative* (Boje, 1991). The term *master* conveys an essential feature of such positions: they are propounded by people who are granted some modicum of authority. Master narratives are not simply regarded as appropriate ways to experience the world; they are enforced in large and small ways. Master narratives are used by cultural stakeholders as strategies for the "management of sense-making" (Boje, 1991, p. 124). Consensus about the existence of a master narrative does not necessarily imply acceptance of the narrative. Tellers may resist the master narrative, but in so doing, they thereby acknowledge the existence of the narrative in justifying their alternative position (Schiffrin, 1996). Master narratives thus function as cultural standards against which community members feel compelled to position their personal experience. The minimal criterion for identifying a master narrative is the perception that a particular emotional position is acceptable to, or resisted by, a valued audience.

Boje introduced the concept of master narrative in a study of how members of organizations constructed company stories to legitimate particular values and actions. Similar emphases on the pragmatic use of narratives for managing sense making have been made in other cultural contexts, including studies of socializing physicians' case presentations (Hunter, 1986), kindergarten children's stories at sharing time (Michaels, 1991), and children's reporting of emotional events (Fivush, 1989). Studies of parental scaffolding of children's narratives found ample evidence that parents teach young children what events are reportable and how to report them (Fivush & Reese, 1992; Hudson, 1990; Nelson, 1993; Pillemer & White, 1989). To the extent that particular positions are promoted by people who are deemed to have cultural authority, such as parents, teachers, or valued peers, the constructions count as master narratives.

The fathers of Henry and Joe did not invent the edict that their sons should be stoic. Rather, their fathers' stoicism exemplifies a cultural convention about how European-American males are supposed to deal with tragic events: Keep a stiff upper lip and press on with the task at hand. Plentiful research has found that European-American parents encourage girls to produce more emotionally laden narratives than boys. The expression of sadness, in particular, is more emphasized for girls (Chance & Fiese, 1999; Dunn, Bretherton, & Munn, 1987; Fivush, 1991), as are expressions of care and concern for others (Ely, Melzi, Hadge, & McCabe, 1998; Gilligan, 1982). For boys, emotion talk is minimized by focusing on details of the setting and action, and on pragmatic solutions (Cervantes & Callanan, 1998; Chance & Fiese, 1999). These findings crosscut a variety of parents and children in European-American culture, suggesting a shared value that emotional events should be managed pragmatically by males and elaborately by females.

STUDYING MASTER NARRATIVE POSITIONING IN SELF-DEFINING MEMORIES

As personality and developmental psychologists, we have been struggling to understand how enduring personal memories serve the emerging sense of self in concrete moments of social life. We were attracted to the dynamic and contextual affordances of the notion of positioning with respect to master narratives, but had to rely on our own devices to apply these concepts to self-defining event and telling narratives. We first explain why we chose to study late adolescents and a particular kind of self-defining event. We then describe some of our findings with regard to master narrative positioning. A fuller account of the study can be found in Thorne and McLean (in press).

Why Study Late Adolescents

For cognitive, social, and emotional reasons, we expected late adolescence to be a prime time for struggling with master narrative positioning. By late adolescence, the cognitive capacity for abstract thinking is well developed, so that alternative interpretations of events can begin to be grappled with (e.g., Harter & Monsour, 1992; Inhelder & Piaget, 1958). Also in late adolescence, social networks begin to expand (Carstensen, 1995), and struggles with identity and intimacy become prominent developmental tasks (Erikson, 1968; McAdams, 1993). Socioculturally, the achievement of identity and intimacy can be viewed as pursuits of satisfying positions within a vast array of cultural values and practices (Thorne, 2000).

As adolescents tell their past to a broadening social network, they may come to recognize that the personal past can take on new meanings when viewed from alternative perspectives. Adolescence is also a highly emotional era that is packed with personal memories, a number of which may be considered self-defining (Rubin, Rahhal, & Poon, 1998; Singer & Salovey, 1993). Because highly emotional events are likely to be told to others soon after the events occur and on multiple occasions thereafter (Rimé et al., 1991), the late adolescent era seemed ripe for capturing highly salient episodes of master narrative positioning.

Why Study Life-Threatening Events

We had been collecting self-defining event and telling narratives from college students for a few years, and knew the general lay of the land in terms of events that were regarded as self-defining. Of the three self-defining events volunteered by our samples of 18- to 20-year-old European-American college students, the majority concerned either relationship events (often conflicts with parents or peers), or life-threatening events. Because parent and peer relationships undergo important transitions in adolescence, we were not surprised that relationship events often emerged as self-defining memories. However, the relatively high incidence of life-threatening events was surprising because such experiences have not been given a prominent place in theories of adolescent development (e.g., Erikson, 1968; Harter, 1998).

Although developmental theories have not emphasized mortality as a salient adolescent concern, life-threatening events have been found to be very potent for those who experience them. Pillemer (1998, p. 31) characterized traumatic events as having a "big bang" quality, in which "the survivor's life is abruptly and violently altered." Traumatic events can have lasting emotional salience, so that their recollection years later can result in an emotional reliving of the event (Langer, 1991). Research with children has also documented the potency of frightening events. For example, Ely, MacGibbon, and Hadge (2000) found that children produced more extensive verbal narratives about their injuries and illnesses than about happier topics such as trips and pets, and Terr (1990) found that children's reactions to traumatic events showed an urgency to explain the cause of the event, evoking the questions "why" and "why me?"

If traumatic events are so potent for individuals, they should also be important for the culture at large, and prime candidates for emotional regulation by others, such as caregivers. Making sense of life-threatening events probably begins early in childhood, when caregivers try to comfort children who are afraid of drowning, dog bites, bee stings, hospitals, and death. Fear and sadness are potent emotions that need to be managed for the benefit of children and caregivers. Parents are thus likely to be concerned about how the child experiences the event, and may try to help the child interpret the event in a satisfactory way. Statements such as, "You felt sad, didn't you?" or "Don't be afraid!" teach particular values and practices about how one is supposed to feel in the face of fear or sadness.

Because traumatic events were prominent in late adolescents' self-defining memories, and because communities can be expected to deem such events important to manage, we chose trauma narratives as the lens for pondering the usefulness of the concept of master narrative positioning for understanding the development of the autobiographical self in adolescence.

Features of Traumatic Event and Telling Narratives

Of the sample of 60 life-threatening events that were reported as self-defining, only 7 had reportedly never been told in the past. None of these reportedly nontold events involved the kind of physical or sexual abuse that might be likely to be silenced (Hanson, 1997). Several of the events involved deaths of family members or friends, one event was a physical assault in late childhood, another was a car accident involving several friends, and the other was a fall from a sixth-floor window. The latter event could possibly have been a suicide attempt, but this was our inference. All of these nontold events reportedly occurred in the presence of family members or friends, with whom some discussion probably occurred at the time of the event. Of the remaining 53 events, a few seemed to be the kinds of events that might result in shame and self-silencing: being raped by a stranger at a party, and being pursued by a sexual pervert in a park. However, both events had reportedly been told to others on multiple occasions in an effort to find sympathy and understanding. For these women, silencing was vigorously resisted. We return to such events later in the chapter.

For now, we want to emphasize that the large majority of traumatic events had reportedly been told at least once, and on multiple occasions. Furthermore, reminiscence about the traumatic event typically spanned the entire period of adolescence. The original events occurred on the average at age 13, the memorable tellings at age 16, and the reports were collected at age 19. The primary types of life-threatening events were deaths of loved ones, accidents (e.g., serious car wrecks and near-drownings), and physical attacks, including assault and rape.

Emotional Positions in Traumatic Event Narratives

Informed by findings from gender socialization research and by examining the content of the traumatic event narratives, we identified three kinds of emotional positions with regard to traumatic events: I was tough; I was concerned for others; and I was vulnerable. The "tough" position is reflected in what has been termed "John Wayne discourse" (Talbot, Bibace, Bokhour, & Bamberg, 1996). This position focused on action rather than emotion, and conveyed courage and fearlessness in the face of events that might make others cower and shake. The Vulnerable position emphasized one's own fear, sadness, and/or helplessness in the face of traumatic events. Concern for others, which we called the Florence Nightingale position, emphasized care and concern for the feelings of others. The categories were defined as mutually exclusive, and interrater agreement was acceptable, ranging from kappas of .82 to .93.

Gender socialization research, discussed previously, led us to expect that the John Wayne position would more often be voiced by young men, and that positions of vulnerability and concern for others would more often be voiced by young women. For several reasons, however, we did not expect our findings to directly parallel empirical trends in gender socialization research. Most gender socialization research has studied samples of children rather than late adolescents. By late adolescence, gender roles may loosen as positions with regard to emotional expression are reevaluated and realigned (Eccles & Bryan, 1994). In addition, our informants were enrolled at a politically liberal university founded on humanistic principles, a zeitgeist that is still detectable today. Within this humanistic community, tough John Wayne discourse might not be a very popular position, or at least might not be as gendered as one might expect in some other communities. Similarly, Vulnerable positions might be expected to be less gendered.

TABLE 8.1
Average Frequency of Traumatic Event Positions

	Males	Females	
Traumatic Position	M (SD)	M (SD)	t (43)
John Wayne	.37 (.60)	.27 (.67)	.51
Florence Nightingale	.16 (.38)	.50 (.65)	−2.06*
Vulnerability	.37 (.50)	.62 (.64)	−1.41

Note: Each informant reported an average of 1 traumatic event narrative, and positions were coded as mutually
exclusive. A fourth traumatic position, Existential Awe, was
infrequent and is not reported here. Standard deviations are
in parentheses. $N = 19$ males, 26 females.
*$p < .05$, two-tailed.

Findings with regard to gender differences in the three traumatic event
positions are shown in Table 8.1. The only significant gender difference was
that women voiced disproportionately more Florence Nightingale (FN) positions than did men. FN positions were particularly prevalent with regard to
reporting deaths, and deaths were also significantly more often reported by
women than by men, $t(43) = 2.25$, $p < .05$. Here is an example of an FN death
narrative from an informant we call Sue:

[FN event narrative:] I was in the seventh grade when a good friend called me
up after school crying. Her 24-year-old brother had been in a car accident and
was dead. Immediately I started crying and felt sick to my stomach. This was
not only my first experience with death, but it was someone that was too young
to die. . . . This experience changed me in that I was much more honest with
my feelings toward my friends and family. I remember my friend saying that
she had told her brother she loved him just before he left that night and how
glad she was she had gotten the chance to say it one last time. Now, even when
I'm fighting with loved ones I always let them know I care about them because
you never know what's going to happen.

It may seem strange that Sue chose the death of her friend's brother as a self-
defining memory, but the personal significance of the event is apparent at the
end of the narrative, when Sue casts the event as teaching her to be more open
in voicing her care for others. Some other FN narratives about experiences
with death also included comments on the deeper meanings of the experience, including a newfound awareness of the preciousness of life, and the
importance of living each day as if it were the last.

We were also impressed that FN narratives tended to be punctuated with
abrupt shifts between expressing one's own sadness and expressing concern

for others. The following narrative exemplifies such shifts. The narrative involved the death of the father of a best friend, called Dr. Schwarz and Ruth, respectively:

> [FN event narrative:] I was at college when I got the call to learn that my best friend's father had passed away. . . . I remember the feeling I got when I heard the voice on the other end of the line: "Dr. Schwarz has passed away . . ." *I froze and all I could think about was how worried I was for Ruth.* I couldn't imagine what I would do if one of my parents died. He had changed my life only months before he passed. I interviewed him for a class assignment and he told me all about the Nazi war camps and losing his whole family. It changed my life. I realized how cruel the world can be—then when he died I realized that people die. I had never known anyone to die before and it was very upsetting to me. I was baking cookies with two of my close friends, just seconds before we were laughing and having a good time . . . then I got the call. *I couldn't even stand up; I was in the fetal position on the floor bawling. I was so worried about her.* I walked down to a nearby garden to pick a flower—it was El Dia de Los Muertos and I put a flower on the altar. I learned a lot from Dr. Schwarz' death. I learned to seize the moment and most importantly to tell people when you love them, because death is not just something that happens in the movies. I learned that life is too short to hold grudges and that there is really no time to be mean to folks. [emphasis added]

Shifts from concern about self to concern for others were more apparent in women's traumatic event narratives than those of men and, as noted previously, particularly in narratives about deaths. The few men who did report deaths typically employed Vulnerability narratives, which focused on their own feelings of sadness. Henry's science project memory is a case in point. Henry reported that he cried in response to the death of his uncle. He did not say "I was concerned for my father, who had just lost his brother." But let us put ourselves in 11-year-old Henry's position: When Henry cried, his father told him not to feel sad and to get back to work on the science project. In this context, it is unlikely that Henry would have expressed concern for his father's feelings, inasmuch as his father did not seem to want to talk about feelings. Even if Henry had wanted to express concern for his father's feelings, the position seems likely to have been rejected.

Master Narratives in Listeners' Responses to Tellings of Traumatic Events

In concert with most master narrative literature, we pursued master narratives locally, in terms of the opinions of significant others with respect to the acceptability of a particular kind of story or position. After informants

described each self-defining event, they were asked to provide a telling narrative in response to the following query: Can you describe a specific episode in
which you remember telling this event to someone else? If so, please describe
that episode, including to whom you told the event, what led you to tell it, and
how you and others reacted to the telling.

However, unlike some master narrative researchers, we did not use inter-
viewers to probe informants further about their experience. The advantage of
using an open-ended questionnaire is that it is more anonymous and perhaps
less constraining than an interview. The downside of using a questionnaire is
that informants can more easily decline to answer. Although 53 of the events
had reportedly been told in the past, only 35 of these event narratives were
accompanied by a telling narrative that was codable. To be regarded as codable, the telling narrative had to indicate a clear audience response in terms of
acceptance or rejection of the teller's emotional position.

Despite this attrition, the telling narratives suggested some interesting
trends with regard to the composition of the telling audience and their
responses to particular traumatic positions. In the majority of cases (about
80% for both males and females), the memorable audience to whom informants had told their traumatic event was a peer rather than a parent. Because
the memorable telling episode tended to occur around age 16, this finding
supports prior findings that peer values are increasingly important by midadolescence (Buhrmester & Furman, 1987; Youniss & Smollar, 1985). The
memorable audience to whom one directed the story tended to be a same-sex
audience, which also supports prior findings regarding the importance of
same-sex peers in early and midadolescence (Bukowski, Sippola, & Hoza,
1999).

Although memorable episodes of having told the traumatic event tended
to be addressed to same-sex peers, no gender differences were discernible in
the listener's response to a particular traumatic position: Males were as likely
as females to accept particular traumatic event positions. We therefore col-
lapsed across gender to examine listener responses. Overall, we found that
positions of care and concern (FN) and toughness (JW) were accepted by at
least 80% of the listeners, but positions of vulnerability were less often
accepted (42%).

The greater acceptability of FN and JW positions seemed to pivot on their
placing less burden on the audience because the tellers seemed to have at least
partially resolved the trauma. *Florence Nightingale* event narratives revealed
some fear or sadness but also contained enough references to caring for others' feelings to suggest that the listener could respond without too much difficulty. For example, in the following telling narrative that accompanied the

account of a friend's (Ruth's) father, Dr. Schwartz, the boyfriend provided comfort, and then the teller proceeded to the funeral:

> [FN telling narrative:] On the way to get a flower I saw my boyfriend—I told him because I hadn't told anyone yet and I needed a shoulder to cry on. He was very concerned and loving. *He hugged me and told me it would be all right and I should drive back for Ruth and go to the funeral.* He made me feel better. People's reactions surprise me quite a bit. I expected people to say more, but when you say the word "death" people don't know what to do. [Emphasis added]

As was true of FN narratives, audience responses to *John Wayne* narratives were usually positive. However, JW narratives were never reportedly told in an effort to be comforted. Rather, JW narratives were told to entertain. JW narratives were highly detailed and action packed and rarely referred to emotion, especially pain. For example, one event narrative provided an elaborate description of the setting and the difficulty of a mountain bike ride, culminating in a severely fractured arm. At no point did the informant use any words explicitly referring to his own feelings of pain or fear, as seen in this description of the accident:

> [JW event narrative:] After about half-way down the 12-mile trail I was coming around a right turn going about 30 and there was a huge water bar across the trail, my front tire landed in it and stopped, and I kept going. My arm slapped the ground before I landed and that's when it broke. I knew it was broken the second it happened, before I even landed. I remember looking up at my arm and having it look like I had two elbows. The first thing when John rode up on me was "Oh shit, your arm's fucked up!" I had to walk half a mile of trail holding my arm while John rode ahead to call the ambulance and Al carried our bikes. Because of that day I now have two steel rods and 13 screws in my arm.

The telling narrative was exceedingly brief:

> [JW telling narrative:] I told the other guys I worked with at the bike shop, and they were amazed. But it was more fun hearing John and Al's versions.

The reporter estimated that he had told the event on about 10 occasions; obviously, however, the event was told more often than that because his friends also told it to others, sometimes in the presence of the hero, who clearly appreciated hearing the recount. The detailed plot and the survival of the hero seemed to account for the positive audience response to the tough-it-out position.

JW narratives featured the self-aggrandizing motives that tantalized Labov and Waletsky (1967), whose classic study of responses to the question, "Were

you ever in a situation where you were in serious danger of being killed?"
launched the study of personal narratives in sociolinguistics. Their claim that
the stories elicited by this probe displayed large doses of self-aggrandizement
holds true for this study, because no tellers of JW narratives went to any
lengths to apologize for the heroic tone of their rendition. The boisterous
bravery of the narratives seemed almost like a protest in itself, a protest against
displaying vulnerability, pain, or fear.

Vulnerability was the most risky traumatic event position in terms of audience response. More than half of the vulnerable event narratives were rejected
by the audience, apparently because the vulnerability seemed inappropriate
for the age of the teller, and/or placed too much burden on the listener. One
case of peer rejection occurred in response to a story about being attacked by
a dog at age 4. The event narrative was rife with expressions of fear and panic:
"screaming at the top of my lungs . . . to this day I have a fear of large dogs."
The telling event was actually a generic event and had reportedly happened
about 10 times since:

> [V telling narrative:] I always bring up the story if I am walking with a friend
> and we walk past a barking, hyper big dog. They always notice that I tense up
> so I get sucked into telling them why. I usually don't like to tell people because
> they usually tell me to get over it. But it is one of those memories that rises up
> every time I am around a large dog.

Possibly the reporter keeps telling the episode in hopes that somebody will
offer him a solution, or at least sympathy. So far, he seems to have had no luck
with audience acceptance; his peers seem to feel that he is too old to be afraid
of large dogs.

Another rejected Vulnerability narrative concerned an account of almost
being killed in a car accident: "I told my friends what happened but they didn't
want to hear about the 'almost dead' part. It was too depressing. So I felt
worse." This telling narrative was so sparse that it was not clear whether the
audience's primary concern was for the friend or for the negative mood that
the story induced. However, the narrative was sufficiently detailed to code the
audience response as rejection.

Several informants described a series of serial rejections of Vulnerable narratives. For example, one case involved multiple rejected tellings of a story
about being pursued by a pervert in a Tokyo park at age 11:

> [V event narrative:] I'm finally pretty comfortable telling people about this
> event. It happened when I was in fourth grade—living in Tokyo, Japan. . . . I
> walked to the park by myself and when I got there—a Japanese man showed
> me a map and rattled off in Japanese asking for directions. He seemed to need

my help. He asked me where the library was—and I told him that I didn't know. He insisted that I find it with him. I felt strange about the situation—and considered trying to duck away behind a bush as we walked deeper into the park. When we got to a bridge he knelt down to rest the map on his knees and take a closer look—but with one hand—he touched my vagina. I stepped back from him thinking that he had done it by accident—and he scooted forward. I stepped back again and he stood up and reached for me again. He continued to ask me for directions. I wanted to scream "tatsukete" (help) but could not remember the Japanese word for it. Instead I just ran away yelling "wakarimasen" (I don't understand).

The reporter estimated that she had told the event five times, after 4 years of silence:

[V telling narrative:] The first time I told this to anyone was four years after it happened. I told my best friend. I lied to her and told her that he had gone as far as unzipping himself. I guess I didn't think it was scary enough as it really happened. Since then, I've told my mother, two boyfriends, and another close friend as it actually did occur. Nobody really knows how to react to it—I usually end up teary eyed. It only comes up if somebody asks me directly if I've been sexually abused.

Unlike the bike accident JW narrative, which is easy on the ears, the above Vulnerability narrative is painful to hear and is still painful to tell. "Nobody really knows how to react to it," and the reporter also does not know how to react to it except by crying. Perhaps she does not know how to react because no one has helped her to make sense of the traumatic event.

Although the majority of Vulnerable event narratives were resisted by the telling audience, 42% were accepted. Accepted Vulnerability narratives seemed to place less burden on the listener. In some cases, the burden seemed less because the reporter seemed to have resolved the trauma; in other cases, the burden seemed less because the audience had experienced a similar traumatic event and had responded similarly. Henry's science project memory, discussed earlier, expressed sadness at the death of an uncle, a position that was accepted by a friend who also felt that sadness was an appropriate response to death.

Overall, the findings suggested that audiences were more willing to accept traumatic positions of toughness or concern for the feelings of others than positions of raw vulnerability—unmitigated fear or sadness. Based on their greater likelihood of being accepted by audiences, we speculate that for this sample of European-American college students, John Wayne and Florence Nightingale positions constituted culturally dominant narratives and Vulnerable positions did not. Vulnerability was a more narrowly acceptable narrative—sometimes accepted by family members and friends, but not always. A number of informants commented that listeners do not know how to respond to feelings of fear and sadness, suggesting that there is no general script for managing vulnerability in this sample of late adolescents.

CONCLUSIONS

We were surprised to find that life-threatening events were so prominent in late adolescents' self-defining memories because developmental theories have not emphasized mortality as a salient adolescent concern. According to Erik-sonian theory, adolescents are primarily concerned with identity, with unify-ing perceived disparities among who they have been, who they are now, and who they could be (McAdams, 1993). Viewed in this light, life-threatening events may promote awareness of the ultimate disparity, between life and death. When philosophical meanings were offered for life-threatening events, our informants referred to a newfound awareness of mortality, the precious-ness of friends, family, and life itself, and the importance of living each day as if it were the last.

We were also impressed at the ease with which we could apply the socio-linguistic concept of positioning to identify emotional stances with regard to life-threatening events. Positioning seemed a felicitous concept to apply because we were studying how people made sense of highly emotional past events, and emotion drives both memorability and sense making (Brewer, 1988; Rimé et al., 1991). We found that traumatic event narratives primarily displayed three kinds of emotional positions: a concern for the feelings of others (the empathetic Florence Nightingale position, more often expressed by women, and with regard to death); a preoccupation with one's own fear or sadness (the Vulnerability position); or one's courage or bravery (the tough, action-packed John Wayne position).

Master narratives were more difficult to discern because culturally domi-nant positions were not readily apparent in narratives of having told the event to someone else. Episodes of having told the event to others typically re-counted the response of particular peers, or in some cases, parents, but not the responses of larger communities. Because culturally dominant positions were not usually apparent in the telling narratives, we identified master narra-tives by majority vote: Positions that were reportedly accepted by a large majority of listeners were considered to be master narratives. In focusing on the majority response to traumatic positions, we emphasized two essential features of master narratives: their regulatory force, and their prevalence in the community.

On the basis of the most prevalent listener response to each traumatic position, we concluded that the John Wayne and Florence Nightingale positions counted as master narratives, and that the Vulnerability position did not. Vulnerable narratives were more often rejected than accepted by listeners, who preferred Vulnerability to be interlaced with concern for others, or to be dismissed altogether in lieu of an action-packed plot. Tough and empathetic positions seemed to place less burden on listeners because the teller seemed to have resolved the crisis more successfully. Some communities seem to recognize the burden of vulnerability and have developed specialized agents, such as priests and psychotherapists, to handle it. In our study, the audiences who accepted Vulnerability positions seemed to do so on the basis of having experienced a similar kind of suffering.

The present findings are derived from a small slice of European-American culture and may not generalize to other age groups or to other communities. Older adults may not resonate to the concept of a self-defining memory because forging an identity is not such a compelling issue. The concept of self-defining memories may also seem less compelling in cultures that do not emphasize personal event telling, such as Mayan and Japanese communities (Minami & McCabe, 1991; Rogoff & Mistry, 1990). Self-defining memories may make the most sense to European-Americans who are transitioning to adulthood and beginning to develop a personal life story.

However, we were pleased with the yield of the present findings and the promise of the overall approach. As applied to self-defining memories, the concept of master narrative positioning allows for considerable agency with regard to acceptance or rejection of community values. The approach also places lived experience squarely at the center: Individuals can be seen as continually striving to position themselves within the larger community in an effort to make satisfactory sense of their experiences. Examining how particular kinds of emotional positions are embraced or resisted within a community is a useful way of identifying the contours of the elusive creature that goes by the name of "culture." Similarly, examining how individuals within the "same" culture gradually establish niches for making sense of deeply emotional experiences can reveal diverse possibilities for human development.

REFERENCES

Agar, M., & Hobbs, J. (1982). Interpreting discourse: Coherence and the analysis of ethnographic interviews. *Discourse Processes, 5*, 1–32.
Bamberg, M. G. W. (1997). Positioning between structure and performance. *Journal of Narrative and Life History, 7*, 335–342.

Boje, D. (1991). The storytelling organization: A study of story performance in an office supply firm. *Administrative Science Quarterly, 36,* 106–126.

Brewer, W. F. (1988). Memory for randomly sampled autobiographical events. In U. Neisser & E. Winograd (Eds.), *Remembering reconsidered: Ecological and traditional approaches to the study of memory* (pp. 21–90). New York: Cambridge University Press.

Buhrmester, D., & Furman, W. (1987). The development of companionship and intimacy. *Child Development, 58,* 1101–1113.

Bukowski, W. M., Sippola, L. K., & Hoza, B. (1999). Same and other: Interdependency between participation in same- and other-sex friendships. *Journal of Youth & Adolescence, 28,* 439–459.

Carstensen, L. L. (1995). Evidence of a life-span theory of socioemotional selectivity. *Current Directions in Psychological Science, 4,* 151–156.

Cervantes, C. A., & Callanan, M. A. (1998). Labels and explanations in mother–child emotion talk: Age and gender differentiation. *Developmental Psychology, 34,* 88–98.

Chance, C., & Fiese, B. H. (1999). Gender-stereotyped lessons about emotion in family narratives. *Narrative Inquiry, 9,* 215–241.

Davies, B., & Harré, R. (1990). Positioning: The discursive production of selves. *Journal for the Theory of Social Behaviour, 20,* 43–63.

Dunn, J., Bretherton, I., & Munn, P. (1987). Conversations about feeling states between mothers and their young children. *Developmental Psychology, 23,* 132–139.

Eccles, J. S., & Bryan, J. (1994). Adolescence: Critical crossroad in the path of gender role development. In M. R. Stevenson (Ed.), *Gender roles through the lifespan* (pp. 111–148). Muncie, IN: Ball State University.

Ely, R., MacGibbon, A., & Hadge, L. (2000). I get scared all the time: Passivity and disaffiliation in children's personal narratives. *Narrative Inquiry, 10,* 453–473.

Ely, R., Melzi, G., Hadge, L., & McCabe, A. (1998). Being brave, being nice: Themes of agency and communion in children's narratives. *Journal of Personality, 66,* 257–284.

Erikson, E. H. (1968). *Identity, youth, and crisis.* New York: Norton.

Fivush, R. (1989). Exploring sex differences in the emotional content of mother–child conversations about the past, *Sex Roles, 20,* 675–691.

Fivush, R. (1991). Gender and emotion in mother–child conversations about the past. *Journal of Narrative & Life History, 1,* 325–341.

Fivush, R., & Reese, E. (1992). The social construction of autobiographical memory. In M. A. Conway, D. C. Rubin, & W. Wagewnaar (Eds.), *Theoretical perspectives on autobiographical memory* (pp. 1–28). Dordrecht, Netherlands: Kluwer Academic Publishers.

Gilligan, C. (1982). *In a different voice: Psychological theory and women's development.* Cambridge, MA: Harvard University Press.

Hanson, K. (1997). Reasons for shame, shame against reason. In M. R. Lansky & A. P. Morrison (Eds.), *The widening scope of shame* (pp. 155–179). Hillsdale, NJ: The Analytic Press.

Harter, S. (1998). The development of self-representations. In W. Damon (Ed.), *Handbook of child psychology* (Vol. 3, pp. 553–617). New York: Wiley.

Harter, S., & Monsour, A. (1992). Developmental analysis of conflict caused by opposing attributes in the adolescent self-portrait. *Developmental Psychology, 28,* 251–260.

Hudson, J. A. (1990). The emergence of autobiographic memory in mother–child conversation. In R. Fivush & J. A. Hudson (Eds.), *Knowing and remembering in young children* (pp. 166–196). New York: Cambridge University Press.

Hunter, K. M. (1986). "There was this one guy . . .": The uses of anecdotes in medicine. *Perspectives in Biology and Medicine, 29,* 619–630.

Inhelder, B., & Piaget, J. (1958). The growth of logical thinking from childhood to adolescence: An essay on the construction of formal operational structures. New York: NY: Basic Books.

Labov, W., & Waletsky, J. (1967). Narrative analysis: Oral versions of personal experience. In J. Helm (Ed.), *Essays on verbal and visual arts: Proceedings of the 1966 annual spring meeting of the American Ethnological Society* (pp. 12–44). Seattle, WA.: University of Washington Press.

Langer, L. L. (1991). *Holocaust testimonies: The ruins of memory.* New Haven, CT: Yale University Press.

Loewald, H. W. (1975). Psychoanalysis as an art and the fantasy character of the psychoanalytic situation. *Journal of the American Psychoanalytic Association, 23,* 277–299.

McAdams, D. P. (1993). *The stories we live by: Personal myths and the making of the self.* New York: William Morrow.

Michaels, S. (1991). The dismantling of narrative. In A. McCabe & C. Peterson (Eds.), *Developing narrative structure* (pp. 303–351). Hillsdale, NJ: Lawrence Erlbaum Associates.

Minami, M., & McCabe, A. (1991). Haiku as a discourse regulation device: A stanza analysis of Japanese children's personal narratives. *Language in Society, 20,* 577–599.

Nelson, K. (1993). The psychological and social origins of autobiographical memory. *Psychological Science, 4,* 7–14.

Pillemer, D. B. (1998). *Momentous events, vivid memories.* Cambridge, MA: Harvard University Press.

Pillemer, D. B., & White, S. H. (1989). Childhood events recalled by children and adults. In H. W. Reese (Ed.), *Advances in child development and behavior* (Vol. 21, pp. 297–340). New York: Academic Press.

Rimé, B., Mesquita, B., Philippot, P., & Boca, S. (1991). Beyond the emotional event: Six studies on the social sharing of emotion. *Cognition and Emotion, 5,* 435–465.

Rogoff, B., & Mistry, J. (1990). The social and functional context of children's remembering. In R. Fivush & J. A. Hudson (Eds.), *Knowing and remembering in young children* (pp. 197–222). New York: Cambridge University Press.

Rubin, D. C., Rahhal, T. A., & Poon, L. W. (1998). Things learned in early adulthood are remembered best. *Memory & Cognition, 26,* 3–19.

Schiffrin, D. (1996). Narrative as self-portrait: Sociolinguistic constructions of identity. *Language in Society, 25,*167–203.

Singer, J. A., & Moffitt, K. H. (1991–1992). An experimental investigation of specificity and generality in memory narratives. *Imagination, Cognition, and Personality, 11,* 233–257.

Singer, J.A., & Salovey, P. (1993). *The remembered self: Emotion and memory in personality.* New York: The Free Press.

Talbot, J., Bibace, R., Bokhour, B., & Bamberg, M. (1996). Affirmation and resistance of dominant discourses: The rhetorical construction of pregnancy. *Journal of Narrative and Life History, 6,* 225–251.

Terr, L. C. (1990). *Too scared to cry: Psychic trauma in childhood.* New York: Harper & Row.

Thorne, A. (2000). Personal memory telling and personality development. *Personality and Social Psychology Review, 4,* 45–56.

Thorne, A., & McLean, K. C. (in press). Gendered reminiscence practices and self-definition in late adolescence. *Sex Roles.*

Youniss, J., & Smollar, J. (1985). *Adolescent relations with mothers, fathers, and friends.* Chicago, IL: University of Chicago Press.

Chapter 9

Identity and the Life Story

Dan P. McAdams
Northwestern University

The *self* is many things, but *identity* is a life story. In my life-story theory of identity (e.g., McAdams, 1985, 1993, 1996), I argued that identity takes the form of a story, complete with setting, scenes, characters, plot, and themes. In late adolescence and young adulthood, people living in modern societies begin to reconstruct the personal past, perceive the present, and anticipate the future in terms of an internalized and evolving self-story, an integrative narrative of self that provides modern life with some modicum of psychosocial unity and purpose. Life stories are based on autobiographical facts, but they go considerably beyond the facts as people selectively appropriate aspects of their experience and imaginatively construe both past and future to construct stories that make sense to them and to their audiences, that vivify and integrate life and make it more or less meaningful. A person's evolving and dynamic life story is a key component of what constitutes the individuality of that particular person (McAdams, 2001; Singer, 1995), situated in a particular family and among particular friends and acquaintances (Thorne, 2000), and living in a particular society at a particular historical moment (Gregg, 1991). Life stories develop over time, and although identity itself does not become a salient psychosocial issue until the adolescent years (Erikson, 1963; Habermas & Bluck, 2000), the origins of life-story making and telling can be traced back to early childhood (Fivush, 1994), and traced forward to the last years in the human life course (Kenyon, 1996).

The idea that identity is an internalized and evolving life story resonates with a number of important themes in psychology and the social sciences today. This chapter explores the meaning and the implications of this idea in the contexts of contemporary research and theory on the development of self-understanding over the life course, connections between autobiographical memory and self, the place of life stories in human personality, and the relations between life stories on the one hand and culture and society on the other.

WHAT IS IDENTITY?

Social scientists and laypersons alike commonly use the terms *self* and *identity* interchangeably. Following Erikson (1963), however, I employ a sharp distinction between the two. As James (1892/1963) argued, the self may be viewed as both the subjective sense of "I" and the objective sense of "me." Accordingly, the "me" includes within it any and all things, features, and characteristics that the "I" may attribute to it—all that is me, all that is mine. By contrast, Erikson's conception of identity refers to a peculiar quality or flavoring of the self-as-me—a way that the "I" begins to arrange or configure the "me" in adolescence and young adulthood, when the standards for what constitutes an appropriate "me" change rather dramatically. It is at this time in the life course, Erikson maintained, that people first confront the problem of *identity versus role confusion*. In this, the fifth of Erikson's eight stages of life, people first explore ideological and occupational options available in society and experiment with a wide range of social roles, with the aim of eventually consolidating their beliefs and values into a personal ideology and making provisional commitments to life plans and projects that promise to situate them meaningfully into new societal niches (Marcia, 1980). It is during this developmental period, recently given the apt name of *emerging adulthood* by Arnett (2000), that people first seek to integrate their disparate roles, talents, proclivities, and social involvements into a patterned *configuration* of thought and activity that provides life with some semblance of psychosocial *unity and purpose* (Breger, 1974). That configuration is what identity is.

Employing Erikson's understanding of the term, then, identity is an integrative configuration of self-in-the-adult-world. This configuration integrates in two ways. First, in a synchronic sense, identity integrates the wide range of different, and likely conflicting, roles and relationships that characterize a given life in the here-and-now. "When I am with my father, I feel sullen and depressed; but when I talk with my friends, I feel a great surge of optimism and love for humankind." Identity needs to integrate these two things so that although they appear very different, they can be viewed as integral parts of the same self-configuration. Second, identity must integrate diachronically, that is, in time. "I used to love to play baseball, but now I want to be a social psychologist." Or, "I was a born-again Christian, but these days I feel I am an agnostic." Identity needs to integrate these kinds of contrasts so that although self elements are separated in time (and in content quality), they can be brought meaningfully together in a temporally organized whole. Put starkly, identity becomes a problem when the adolescent or young adult first realizes that he or she is, has been, and/or could be many different (and conflicting) things, and experiences a strong desire, encouraged by society, to be but *one* (large, integrated, and dynamic) thing. Young children have selves; they know who they are, and they can tell you. But they do not have identities, in Erikson's sense, in that they are not confronted with the problem of arranging the me into a unified and purposeful whole that specifies a meaningful niche in the emerging adult world. Selves begin to take identity shape in late adolescence and young adulthood.

Why does identity wait so long? The reasons are both cultural and cognitive. In Western societies, we expect adolescents to begin the process of taking stock of the material, ideological, occupational, and interpersonal resources in their worlds, and taking stock of themselves, in order to find a reasonably good match between what a person can do and believe on the one hand and what adult society enables a person to do and believe on the other. Identity exploration is considered an on-time developmental task for late adolescence and young adulthood (Cohler, 1982). Parents, high school teachers, siblings, friends, college admissions counselors, the business world, the media, and many other aspects and agents of modern society explicitly and implicitly urge adolescents and young adults to "get a life" (Habermas & Bluck, 2000). It is time to begin to examine what society has to offer, to explore (in both imagination and behavior) a wide range of ideological and life-style options, and, eventually, to make commitments, even if only temporary, to personalized niches in the adult world. This is to say that society and the emerging adult are ready for the individual's identity explorations by the time he or she has in fact become an emerging adult. Accordingly, Erikson (1959) wrote:

> The period can be viewed as a psychosocial moratorium during which the individual through free role experimentation may find a niche in some section of his society, a niche which is firmly defined and yet seems to be uniquely made for him. In finding it the young adult gains an assured sense of inner continuity and social sameness which will bridge what he was as a child and what he is about to become, and will reconcile his conception of himself and his community's recognition of him. (p. 111)

Although Erikson did not emphasize it, advances in cognitive development in the adolescent years are likely to be as important as any other forces in launching the identity project. Breger (1974) and Elkind (1981) argued that with the emergence of formal operations in adolescence, identity becomes an especially engaging abstraction for the abstract thinker: "[T]he idea of a unitary or whole self in which past memories of who one was, present experiences of who one is, and future expectations of who one will be, is the sort of abstraction that the child simply does not think about." But "with the emergence of formal operations in adolescence, wholeness, unity, and integration become introspectively real problems" (Breger, 1974, p. 330). The idea that one's life, as complex and dynamic as it increasingly appears to be, might be integrated into a meaningful and purposeful whole may represent, therefore, an especially appealing possibility to the self-reflective emerging adult.

During this developmental period, I have argued, people begin to put their lives together into self-defining stories. The process of constructing a life story may be incremental and uneven, subject to fits and starts, as the emerging adult tries out different kinds of characters, plots, and stories until he or she begins to settle on the kinds of narrative forms and contents that seem to work or fit. What gradually emerges is an internalized and evolving story of self that integrates the self synchronically and diachronically, explaining why it is that I am sullen with my father and euphoric with my friends and how it happened—step by step, scene by scene—that I went from being a born-again Christian who loved baseball to an agnostic social psychologist. According to Habermas and Bluck (2000), the construction of these kinds of integrative life stories requires a set of cognitive tools that are not fully accessible until adolescence. They argued that the full articulation of an integrative life story requires the understanding and utilization of four types of coherences: temporal, biographical, causal, and thematic coherence. The four begin to emerge in childhood, but they emerge at different points and develop at different rates. People can tell stories about themselves long before adolescence, but it is not until adolescence that they can effectively put their lives together into a story.

THE DEVELOPMENT OF THE LIFE STORY

Stories are fundamentally about the vicissitudes of human intention organized in time (Bruner, 1990; Ricoeur, 1984). In virtually all intelligible stories, humans or human-like characters act to accomplish intentions, generating a sequence of actions and reactions extended as a plot in time (Mandler, 1984). Human intentionality is at the heart of narrative, and therefore the development of intentionality in humans is of prime importance in establishing the mental conditions necessary for story telling and story comprehension. Recent research with infants suggests that by the end of the first or early in the second year of life, humans come to understand other persons as intentional agents (Tomasello, 2000). For example, 16-month-old infants will imitate complex behavioral sequences exhibited by other human beings only when those activities appear intentional. As Tomasello (2000) wrote, "Young children do not just mimic the limb movements of other persons; rather, they attempt to reproduce other persons' intended, goal-directed actions in the world" (p. 38). What emerges at this time, wrote Dennett (1987), is an *intentional stance* vis-à-vis the world. In other words, children in the second year of life come to experience the world from the subjective standpoint of an intentional, causal "I," able now to assume the existential position of a motivated human subject who appropriates experience as his or her own (Kagan, 1994; McAdams, 1997). This existential I-ness is tacitly and immediately grasped in and through intentional action (Blasi, 1988).

In James's terms, with the consolidation of the existential, intentional I comes the eventual formulation of the me. In the second year of life, children begin to attribute various distinguishing characteristics to themselves, including their names, their favorite toys, their likes and dislikes, and so on. With the development of language, the self-as-object grows rapidly to encompass a wide range of things "about me" that can be verbally described. To be included in the mix eventually are memories of events in which the self was involved. According to Howe and Courage (1997), *autobiographical memory* emerges toward the end of the second year of life when children have consolidated a basic sense of I and reflexively have begun to build up a rudimentary understanding of the me. Although infants can remember events (basic episodic memory) before this time, it is not until the end of the second year, Howe and Courage contended, that episodic memory becomes personalized and children begin to organize events that they experience as "things that happened to me." From this point onward, the me expands to include autobiographical recollections, recalled as little stories about what has transpired in "my life."

Autobiographical memory emerges and develops in a social context (Nelson, 1988; Welch-Ross, 1995). Parents typically encourage children to talk about their personal experiences as soon as children are verbally able to do so (Fivush & Kuebli, 1997). Early on, parents may take the lead in stimulating the child's recollection and telling of the past by reminding the child of recent events, such as this morning's breakfast or yesterday's visit to the doctor. Taking advantage of this initial conversational scaffolding provided by adults, the young child soon begins to take more initiative in sharing personal events. By the age of 3, children are actively engaged in coconstructing their past experience in conversations with adults. By the end of the preschool years, they are able to give a relatively coherent narrative account of the past. In conversations with adults about personal memories, young children become acquainted with the narrative structures through which events are typically discussed by people in their world. The sharing of personal experiences functions as a major mechanism of socialization (Miller, 1994) and helps to build an organized personal history from a growing base of autobiographical memories (Fivush, 1994).

As children move through elementary school, they come to narrate their own personal experiences in ways that conform to their implicit understandings of how good stories should be structured and what they should include. In this way, they imbue their experience with what Habermas and Bluck (2000) termed *temporal coherence*. Before adolescence, however, temporal coherence applies mainly to single autobiographical events rather than to connections between different events. In elementary school, furthermore, children begin to internalize their culture's norms concerning what the story of an entire life should itself contain. As they learn, for example, that a telling of a single life typically begins with, say, an account of birth and typically includes, say, early experiences in the family, eventual emergence out of the family, geographical moves, and so on, they acquire an understanding of what Habermas and Bluck (2000) called *biographical coherence*. Cultural norms define conventional phases of the life course and suggest what kinds of narrative forms make sense in telling a life (Denzin, 1989). As children learn the culture's biographical conventions, they begin to see how single events in their own lives might be sequenced and linked to conform to the culture's concept of biography.

Still, it is not until adolescence, Habermas and Bluck (2000) contended, that individuals craft causal narratives to explain how different events are linked together in the context of a biography. *Causal coherence* is exhibited in the increasing effort across adolescence to provide narrative accounts of one's life that explain how one event caused, led to, transformed, or in some way is meaningfully related to other events in one's life. Traits, attitudes, beliefs, and preferences may now be explained in terms of the life events that may have caused them. An adolescent may, for example, explain why she rejects her parents' liberal political values, or why she feels shy around members of the opposite sex, or how it came to be that her junior year in high school represented a turning point in her understanding of herself in terms of personal experiences from the past that have been selected and, in many cases, reconstructed to make a coherent explanation. In what Habermas and Bluck (2000) termed *thematic coherence,* furthermore, she may identify an overarching theme, value, or principle that integrates many different episodes in her life and conveys the gist of who she is and what her autobiography is all about. Studies reported by Habermas and Bluck (2000) suggest that causal and thematic coherence are rare in autobiographical accounts in early adolescence but increase substantially through the teen-aged years and into young adulthood. By the time individuals have reached the emerging adulthood years, therefore, they are typically able and eager to construct stories about the past and about the self that exhibit temporal, biographical, causal, and thematic coherence. Autobiographical memory and narrative understanding now have developed to the level whereby they can be called into service in the making of identity.

But identity is not made from scratch. Long before adolescence, children collect and process experiences of all kinds that may eventually make their way into or have some important influence on the integrative life stories they later construct to make sense of their lives (McAdams, 1993). Even early attachment patterns with caregivers may ultimately be reflected in the overall narrative tone and quality that adult life stories show (Main, Kaplan, & Cassidy, 1985). The dominant images and themes of adult life stories may reflect influences from the earliest years of life.

Over the adult life course, people continue to work on their life stories, reflecting various on-time and off-time transitions and happenings. In early to middle adulthood, for example, many American men and women appear to focus their identity work on articulating, expanding, and refining the story's main characters, or personal *imagoes*. An imago is an idealized personification of the self that functions as a protagonist in the narrative (McAdams, 1984). Akin to what Markus and Nurius (1986) called "possible selves," imagoes personify important motivational trends in the life story, such as strong needs for power, achievement, or intimacy (McAdams, 1985). The construction of imagoes helps to integrate a life by bringing into the same narrative format different personifications of the me—the self-as-loving-wife, the self-as-ardent-feminist, the self-as-devoted-mother, the self-as-the-young-girl-who-longed-to-escape-the-suburbs, the self-as-future-retiree-who-will-escape-to-that-country-home, and so on. By constructing a single life story that integrates a wide range of self-characterizations as interacting protagonists, or imagoes, the adult can resolve what William James first identified as the "one-in-many-selves paradox" (Knowles & Sibicky, 1990, p. 676). One's life becomes a story with a large cast of self-characters who assume different positions in the narrative, take on different voices, represent different self-facets, personify significant trends during different developmental chapters—all in the same evolving story, the same identity (Hermans, 1996).

The midlife years can be occasioned by considerable identity work for many modern adults. Of special interest are the ways in which what Erikson

(1963) termed *generativity* finds its way into life stories at midlife and beyond. As men and women move into and through midlife, themes of caring for the next generation, of leaving a positive legacy for the future, of giving something back to society become increasingly salient in life stories (McAdams, de St. Aubin, & Logan, 1993; McAdams, Hart, & Maruna, 1998). Furthermore, as adults move into and through midlife, they may become more and more concerned with the "endings" of their life stories. It is in the nature of stories that beginnings and middles lead inevitably to endings, and that endings provide a sense of closure and resolution (Kermode, 1967). The imagery and rhetoric of generativity provide adults with an especially compelling way to conceive of "the end," even as people are deeply immersed in the middle of the life course. By suggesting that one's own efforts may generate products and outcomes that will outlive the self, by framing a life story in terms of those good things (and people) that become the self's enduring legacy, life narrations that emphasize generativity implicitly provide stories with what may be perceived, consciously or unconsciously, as good and satisfying endings (Kotre, 1984; McAdams, 1985). These endings, in turn, feed back to influence beginnings and middles. Consequently, it should not be surprising to observe considerable revising and reworking of one's life story, even the reimagining of the distant past, in light of changing psychosocial concerns in the adult years and changing understandings of what the near and distant future may bring.

AUTOBIOGRAPHICAL MEMORY
AND THE LIFE STORY

An emerging theme in the study of memory for real-life and personal events is that autobiographical memory helps to locate and define the self within an ongoing life story that, simultaneously, is strongly oriented toward future goals (e.g., Pillemer, 1998; Schachter, 1996; Stein, Wade, & Liwag, 1997). For example, Conway and Pleydell-Pearce (2000) argued that a person's goals function as control processes in a self-memory system (SMS), modulating the construction of memories. Autobiographical memories are encoded and retrieved in ways that serve the goals of the current working self. As such, current goals influence how autobiographical information is absorbed and organized in the first place, and goals generate retrieval models to guide the search process later on.

In the SMS, personal goals are linked to an autobiographical knowledge base, which itself consists of information encoded at three levels of specificity: lifetime periods, general events, and event-specific knowledge (Conway &

Pleydell-Pearce, 2000). Lifetime periods mark off relatively large chunks of autobiographical time, such as "my childhood years" or "my first marriage," and they correspond roughly to what I have designated as main chapters in a person's life story (McAdams, 1985). General events (e.g., "parties I attended in college," "weekend nights spent babysitting") and event-specific knowledge (e.g., "the particular evening I proposed to my wife," "my father's funeral") cover the same ground as Pillemer's (1998) *personal event memories* and what I have called *nuclear episodes* in the life story (McAdams, 1985). Indeed, the interview methodology that my colleagues and I employ in life-story research begins with accounts of life chapters, moves to accounts of particular episodes that stand out in bold print in the life story (nuclear episodes such as life-story high points, low points, and turning points), and moves eventually to accounts of future goals and plans. The life story is an integration of the reconstructed past, represented mainly as chapters and episodes, and the anticipated future, represented mainly as goals.

Some remembered episodes are more central to self-definition than are others. For example, Singer and Salovey (1993) focused on *self-defining memories,* remembered episodes that are "vivid, affectively charged, repetitive, linked to other similar memories, and related to an important unresolved theme or enduring concern in an individual's life" (p. 13). It is these kinds of memories that occupy the most prominent positions within identity as a life story. In this regard, Robinson and Taylor (1998) made an important distinction between autobiographical memories and self-narratives. They point out that people remember many episodes in life that are mundane and appear to have little relevance to their self-concepts. Autobiographical memory, therefore, comprises a vast range of personal information and experience. Self-narratives, in contrast, "consist of a set of temporally and thematically organized salient experiences and concerns that constitute one's identity" (p. 126). Self-narratives include only a subset of the remembered events stored in autobiographical memory, Robinson and Taylor suggested, and, moreover, self-narratives may also include information that is not technically part of the autobiographical memory base. An example of the latter is the individual's imagined future—how I see myself in 10 years, what events I believe I will experience one day, what I leave behind.

Nonetheless, there is significant overlap between the episodic knowledge that cognitive psychologists position within autobiographical memory and the lifetime periods, general events, and event-specific knowledge that go into the making of identity as a life story. Like many cognitive approaches to autobiographical memory, furthermore, the life-story theory of identity adopts a moderately reconstructive view of autobiographical recollections (e.g.,

Brewer, 1986; Ross, 1997). Personal goals and other concerns shape the encoding and recollection of self-defining memories and other important features of the life story. Reconstruction exerts a distorting effect, especially with regard to memories from long ago (Thompson, Skowronski, Larsen, & Betz, 1996). But for life stories, the greatest degree of reconstruction may involve selection and interpretation, rather than outright distortion of the historical truth (Bluck & Levine, 1998). People select and interpret certain memories as self-defining, providing them with privileged status in the life story. Other potential candidates for such status are downgraded, relegated to the category of "oh yes, I remember that, but I don't think it is very important," or forgotten altogether. To a certain degree, then, identity is a product of choice. We choose the events that we consider most important for defining who we are and providing our lives with some semblance of unity and purpose, and we endow them with symbolism, lessons learned, integrative themes, and other personal meanings that make sense to us in the present as we survey the past and anticipate the future. Yet, identity choices are not a matter of "free choice." Instead, choices must be seen in the social/historical/political contexts that render some of them to be better or more appropriate choices than others. Furthermore, different people have access to dramatically different choices, reflecting constraints and opportunties that vary by social class, gender, race/ethnicity, and many other social–structural and cultural factors.

The power of narrative choice and selection is apparent in the well-documented phenomenon of the memory bump (Fitzgerald, 1988; Rubin, Weltzer, & Nebes, 1986). People tend to recall a disproportionately large number of autobiographical events from the ages of approximately 15 to 25 years. There is some indication, furthermore, that episodic memories from this period are especially rich in emotional and motivational content (Thorne, 2000). Consistent with what the life-story theory of identity predicts, Fitzgerald (1988) and Conway and Pleydell-Pearce (2000) argued that adults are wont to select events from this particular period in the life course because it is during adolescence and young adulthood that people are most preoccupied with forming their identities. It is indeed roughly during the period of the reminiscence bump that young people are first confronting the identity problem in modern society and actively formulating integrative life stories to address the psychosocial challenges they face. Consequently, they may be more likely to encode personal events occurring during these years as relevant to their psychosocial "goal" of formulating an identity. It may indeed be true, moreover, that the kinds of events that do tend to happen during this especially consequential period of the human life course are the kinds of autobiographical episodes that make for especially good stories (McAdams, 1993).

In this regard, it should not be surprising that the "coming of age story" is such a staple in contemporary fiction and cinema and that the myth of the hero—the adventurous transition from young-adolescent innocence to full-fledged adulthood—is a timeless and universally beloved mythic form (Campbell, 1949).

INDIVIDUAL DIFFERENCES IN STORIES

People differ from each other in a great many psychological ways, but among the most important arenas wherein human variability manifests itself is identity as a life story (McAdams, 1995, 2001). In recent years, a growing number of researchers have explored individual difference in life stories and related these differences to important aspects of personality and social functioning, to psychological well-being, and to important demographic and cultural trends (e.g., McAdams, 1999; Murray, 1989; Rosenwald & Ochberg, 1992; Singer, 1995; Thorne, 1995). As examples, Gergen and Gergen (1986) distinguished between stability, progressive, and regressive life narratives; Maruna (1997) identified a common reform story told by ex-convicts in narrating how they moved from a life of crime to desistance; Gregg (1996) discovered a hybrid life narrative that mixes themes of modernity and traditional Islamic faith among contemporary young Moroccans.

Early research employing the life-story theory of identity focused on the relations between social motives on the one hand and content themes in life stories on the other (McAdams, 1982, 1985; McAdams, Hoffman, Mansfield, & Day, 1996). My students and I conducted a series of studies demonstrating that individual differences in power motivation and intimacy motivation (both assessed via the Thematic Apperception Test, or TAT) are significantly related to content themes of *agency* and *communion* (Bakan, 1966), respectively, as manifest in people's life stories. People high in power motivation emphasize the agentic themes of self-mastery, status and victory, achievement and responsibility, and empowerment in significant autobiographical scenes, and they tend to conceive of the story's main characters (imagoes) in highly agentic terms, compared to people low in power motivation. By contrast, people high in intimacy motivation emphasize the communal themes of friendship and love, dialogue, caring for others, and sense of community in the significant scenes in their life stories, and they formulate highly communal imagoes, such as personifications of the self as the caregiver, the loyal friend, and the lover, compared to people low in intimacy motivation. Woike (1995; Woike, Gersekovich, Piorkowski, & Polo, 1999) showed that social motives link not only to the content of life stories but also to the cognitive style that the storyteller displays when describing a most memorable autobiographical event. People with strong power motivation tend to employ an analytic and differentiated style when describing agentic events, perceiving more differences, separations, and oppositions in the significant scenes in their life stories. By contrast, people high in intimacy motivation tend to employ a synthetic and integrated style when describing communal events, detecting similarities, connections, and congruence among different elements in significant life story scenes.

Individual differences in the structural complexity of life stories have been linked to Loevinger's (1976) concept of *ego development*. In Loevinger's developmental scheme, people at relatively high stages of ego development adopt a more nuanced and individuated framework for making sense of subjective experience, whereas people low in ego development tend to view experience in more black-and-white and conformist terms. In one study, we found that adults high in ego development tend to construct more different kinds of plots in their life stories, suggesting greater narrative complexity, compared to adults low in ego development (McAdams, 1985). Helson and Roberts (1994) found that midlife women high in ego development were more likely than those scoring low to narrate negative life scenes in ways suggesting that they changed considerably through the adversity. More complex life stories may involve greater levels of change in the characters. Differences in perceived change were also found in a study of Catholic and Protestant college students asked to narrate their own religious development (McAdams, Booth, & Selvik, 1981). The researchers found that students high in ego development were more likely to articulate a story of transformation and growth, suggesting that they had gone through significant religious doubts and uncertainties and were developing toward a new and more personalized ideological perspective. By contrast, students low in ego development tended to deny that they had ever gone through a crisis in faith or described a period of questioning in their lives that was then abandoned as they returned to their original beliefs. They tended to construct simpler faith narratives of stability and consistency.

In recent studies, my colleagues and I focused on the life stories constructed by adults who have distinguished themselves for their generative involvements, as parents, teachers, community volunteers, and so on. In one study, we contrasted the life stories constructed by adults scoring high on objective (behavioral and self-report) indices of generativity to those constructed by a matched sample of adults scoring in the intermediate to low range on generativity (McAdams, Diamond, de St. Aubin, & Mansfield, 1997). We found that as a group, the highly generative adults tended to formulate life narratives that more closely approximated a *commitment story* compared to their less generative counterparts. In the prototypical commitment story, the protagonist (a) enjoys an early family blessing or advantage, (b) is sensitized to the suffering of others at an early age, (c) is guided by a clear and compelling personal ideology that remains relatively stable over time, (d) transforms or redeems bad scenes into good outcomes (redemption sequences), and (e) sets goals for the future to benefit society. As an internalized narrative of the self, the commitment story may help to sustain and reinforce the generative adult's efforts to contribute in positive ways to the next generation. Although many different kinds of life stories might be constructed by highly generative people, the adult who works hard to guide and foster the next generation may make sense of his or her strong commitment in terms of an internalized narrative that suggests that he or she was "called" or destined to do good things for others, that such a personal destiny is deeply rooted in childhood, reinforced by a precocious sensitivity to the suffering of others, and bolstered by a clear and convincing belief system that remains steadfast over time. Perceiving one's life in terms of redemption sequences (bad scenes are transformed into good outcomes), furthermore, provides the hope that hard work today will yield positive dividends for the future, a hope that may sustain generative efforts as private as raising one's child and as public as committing oneself to the advancement of one's own society (Colby & Damon, 1992). Stories in literature, myth, and folklore that celebrate generativity often display the kinds of themes identified as part of the commitment story (McAdams, 1993).

A prominent theme in the commitment story is the transformation of bad events into good outcomes, what we have called a *redemption sequence.* The theme of redemption is a powerful motif, as well, in life stories of reformed alcoholics (Singer, 1997) and ex-convicts who have renounced a life of crime (Maruna, 1997). McAdams, Reynolds, Lewis, Patten, and Bowman (2001) coded narrative accounts of key life-story scenes among students and adults for redemption sequences and for the contrasting narrative form of *contamination sequences.* In a contamination sequence, an emotionally positive event goes suddenly bad. The results show that redemption sequences in life stories are positively associated with self-report measures of life satisfaction, self-esteem, and sense of life coherence, and negatively associated with depression. By contrast, contamination sequences are positively associated with depression and negatively associated with the three indices of well-being. The results are consistent with the literature in health psychology showing that people who construe benefits as having followed from their injuries, illnesses, or misfortunes tend to show faster recovery from their setbacks and more positive well-being overall (Affleck & Tennen, 1996). Although life-story telling functions to provide the self with identity, therefore, it can is also be instrumental in the overall maintenance of mental health.

IDENTITY AND CULTURE

People tell stories in all human cultures. They tell them to other people. The very concept of a story is inherently social in that stories exist to be told in a social context. "The narrative structure of autobiographical memory appears indistinguishable from the narrative structure of other social communications," wrote Rubin (1998), "and the recall of autobiographical memories is usually a social act that can define a social group" (p. 54). As noted earlier, developmental psychologists such as Fivush (1994) and Nelson (1988) emphasized the ways in which children and adults share personal memories in conversation, how autobiographical memory is socially constructed. Thorne (2000) argued that the term "personal memory" is a misnomer, for the majority of important memories are shared with other people. A better term might be "intimate memories," she suggested. For Thorne (2000), the construction of self-defining memories and life stories is always a social enterprise, and "families and friends collude in self-making" (p. 45). Even when families and friends are absent, however, life stories may retain their social character. Hermans (1996) viewed the self as akin to a *polyphonic novel,* containing within it a multitude of internalized voices that "speak" to each other in dialogue.

Life stories mirror the culture wherein the story is made and told. Stories live in culture. They are born, they grow, they proliferate, and they eventually die according to the norms, rules, and traditions that prevail in a given society, according to a society's implicit understandings of what counts as a tellable story, a tellable life. As Rosenwald (1992) put it, "When people tell life stories, they do so in accordance with the models of intelligibility specific to the culture" (p. 265). As previously noted, Habermas and Bluck (2000) contended that before a person can formulate a convincing life story, he or she must become acquainted with the culture's concept of biography. In modern Western cultures, Denzin (1989) suggested, biographies are expected to begin in the family, to involve growth and expansion in the early years, to trace later problems back to earlier conflicts, to incorporate epiphanies and turning points that mark changes in the protagonist's quest, and to be couched in the discourse of progress versus decline. But other societies tell lives in different ways, and have different views of what constitutes a good story to tell (Gregg, 1991; Markus & Kitayama, 1991).

Even in a given society, furthermore, different stories compete for dominance and acceptance. Feminists such as Heilbrun (1988) argued that in Western societies, many women "have been deprived of the narratives, or the texts, plots, or examples, by which they might assume power over—take control over—their lives" (p. 17). It is painfully clear that life stories echo gender and class constructions in society and reflect, in one way or another, prevailing patterns of hegemony in the economic, political, and cultural contexts wherein human lives are situated. Power elites in society privilege certain life stories over others, and therefore a number of narrative researchers and clinicians seek to give voice and expression to forms of life narrative that have traditionally been suppressed or marginalized (Franz & Stewart, 1994; Gergen & Gergen, 1993; White & Epston, 1990).

A wide-ranging and loosely coordinated movement in the social sciences, the *narrative study of lives*, has emerged in recent years as an interdisciplinary effort to write, interpret, and disseminate people's life stories, with special attention paid to the accounts of women, people of color, and representatives of other groups whose lives and whose stories have historically been ignored or even suppressed (Josselson & Lieblich, 1993). Many of the studies undertaken by scholars in this arena utilize inductive and hermeneutical methods to examine in depth small samples of life stories collected from clearly defined sociodemographic and cultural groups. For instance, Modell (1992) identified common themes and narrative strategies in the stories that birth parents tell about why they gave up their children for adoption. Walkover (1992) found that married couples on the edge of parenthood crafted stories about their imagined future in which they romanticized and idealized the children they were about to have, suggesting an implicit (but irrational) belief in the perfectibility of childhood. Linn (1997) identified common life-narrative types among Israeli soldiers who refused to engage in what they believed to be immoral acts of aggression. Cohler, Hostetler, and Boxer (1998) analyzed conflicts, frustrations, and potentialities in generativity in the life stories of gay couples. Crossley (2001) explored how HIV patients thematized the sense of place and the meaning of home in their life stories.

Anthropologists and cross-cultural psychologists have long been interested in what stories can reveal about the similarities and differences among cultures. Folk tales, legends, sacred myths, and biographical stories have been viewed as windows into patterns of culture and into the complex (and sometimes contested) relations between culture and self (Geertz, 1973; Shweder & Sullivan, 1993). What has sometimes gone unrecognized, however, is how psychosocially crucial life-story telling is in contemporary modern cultures. Following Giddens (1991) and Taylor (1989), I argued that the unique problems that cultural modernity poses for human selfhood require modern men and women to become especially adept at assimilating their lives to culturally intelligible stories (McAdams, 1996, 1997). In the modern world, the self is a reflexive project that a person is expected to "work on," to develop, improve, expand, and strive to perfect. The emphasis on individualism that so pervades contemporary Western life urges modern adults to find or create their "true" and "authentic" selves, to be all they can be, to fully actualize their vast inner potentials. Accordingly, modern people see the self as complex and multi-faceted, as containing many layers and depth, and as changing relentlessly over time (Giddens, 1991). At the same time, they feel a strong urge to find some coherence in the self, to fashion a self that is more or less unified and pur-poseful within the discordant cultural parameters that situate their lives. From the media to everyday discourse, modern life is filled with models and exam-ples of how to live a meaningful life, and how not to. Yet virtually every posi-tive model has its drawbacks, nothing close to a consensus exists, and even if some modest level of cultural consensus could be reached, modern people are socialized anyway to find their own way, to craft a self that is true to who one "really" is (Gergen, 1992). As a consequence, people pick and choose and plagiarize selectively from the many stories and images they find in culture in order to formulate a narrative identity.

Identity is not a problem unique to contemporary cultural life in the West, but it is especially characteristic of it. In modern life, constructing a meaning-ful life story is a veritable cultural imperative. Identity continues to be one of the most challenging psychosocial problems for contemporary cultural life, as people struggle and strive to make narrative sense of their lives during a time of rapid, and sometimes unpredictable, cultural change (Gergen, 1992). It behooves psychologists and social scientists, therefore, to redouble their efforts to understand the nature of life stories, how stories develop over time, the relations between autobiographical memory and the narration of selves, individual differences in the stories people construct, and the complex rela-tions between individual stories and the larger and ever-changing narrative texts that characterize society and culture.

ACKNOWLEDGMENTS

Preparation of this chapter was greatly aided by a grant from the Foley Family Foundation to establish the Foley Center for the Study of Lives at Northwest-ern University.

REFERENCES

Affleck, G., & Tennen, H. (1996). Construing benefits from adversity: Adaptational signifi-cance and dispositional underpinnings. *Journal of Personality, 64,* 899–922.

Arnett, J. J. (2000). Emerging adulthood: A theory of development from the late teens through the twenties. *American Psychologist, 55,* 469–480.

Bakan, D. (1966). *The duality of human existence: Isolation and communion in Western man.* Boston: Beacon Press.

Blasi, A. (1988). Identity and the development of the self. In D. K. Lapsley and F. C. Power (Eds.), *Self, ego, identity: Integrative approaches* (pp. 226–242). New York: Springer-Verlag.

Bluck, S., & Levine, L. J. (1998). Reminscence as autobiographical memory: A catalyst for reminscence theory development. *Ageing and Society, 18,* 185–208.

Breger, L. (1974). *From instinct to identity: The development of personality.* Englewood Cliffs, NJ: Prentice-Hall.

Brewer, W. F. (1986). What is autobiographical memory? In D. Rubin (Ed.), *Autobiographical memory* (pp. 25–49). New York: Cambridge University Press.

Bruner, J. S. (1990). *Acts of meaning.* Cambridge, MA: Harvard University Press.

Campbell, J. (1949). *The hero with a thousand faces.* New York: Bollingen Foundation.

Cohler, B. J. (1982). Personal narrative and the life course. In P. Baltes & O. G. Brim, Jr. (Eds.), *Life span development and behavior* (Vol. 4, pp. 205–241). New York: Academic Press.

Cohler, B. J., Hostetler, A. J., & Boxer, A. (1998). Generativity, social context, and lived experi-ence: Narratives of gay men in middle adulthood. In D. P. McAdams and E. de St. Aubin (Eds.), *Generativity and adult development* (pp. 265–309). Washington, DC: American Psy-chological Association.

Colby, A., & Damon, W. (1992). *Some do care: Contemporary lives of moral commitment.* New York: The Free Press.

Conway, M. A., & Pleydell-Pearce, C. W. (2000). The construction of autobiographical memo-ries in the self-memory system. *Psychological Review, 107,* 261–288.

Crossley, M. (2001). Sense of place and its import for life transitions: The case of HIV positive individuals. In D. P. McAdams, R. Josselson, & A. Lieblich (Eds.), *Turns in the road: Narra-tive studies of lives in transition* (pp. 279–296). Washington, DC: American Psychological Association.

Dennett, D. (1987). *The intentional stance.* Cambridge, MA.: MIT Press.

Denzin, N. (1989). *Interpretive biography.* Newbury Park, CA: Sage.

Elkind, D. (1981). *Children and adolescents* (3rd Ed.). New York: Oxford University Press.

Erikson, E. H. (1959). Identity and the life cycle: Selected papers. *Psychological Issues, 1*(1), 5–165.

Erikson, E. H. (1963). *Childhood and society* (2nd Ed.). New York: Norton.

Fivush, R. (1994). Constructing narrative, emotion, and self in parent–child conversations about the past. In U. Neisser & R. Fivush (Eds.), *The remembering self* (pp. 136–157). New York: Cambridge University Press.

Fivush, R., & Kuebli, J. (1997). Making everyday events emotional: The construal of emotion in parent–child conversations about the past. In N. L. Stein, P. A. Ornstein, B. Tversky, & C. Brainerd (Eds.), *Memory for everyday and emotional events* (pp. 239–266). Mahwah, NJ: Lawrence Erlbaum Associates.

Fitzgerald, J. M. (1988). Vivid memories and the reminscence phenomenon: The role of a self-narrative. *Human Development, 31,* 261–273.

Franz, C., & Stewart, A. J. (Eds.). (1994). *Women creating lives: Identities, resilience, and resistance.* Boulder, CO: Westview.

Geertz, C. (1973). *The interpretation of cultures.* New York: Basic Books.

Gergen, K. J. (1992). *The saturated self: Dilemmas of identity in contemporary life.* New York: Basic Books.

Gergen, K. J., & Gergen, M. M. (1986). Narrative form and the construction of psychological science. In T. Sarbin (Ed.), *Narrative psychology: The storied nature of human conduct* (pp. 22–44). New York: Praeger.

Gergen, M. M., & Gergen, K. J. (1993). Narratives of the gendered body in popular autobiography. In R. Josselson & A. Lieblich (Eds.), *The narrative study of lives* (Vol. 1, pp. 191–218). Thousand Oaks, CA: Sage.

Giddens, A. (1991). *Modernity and self-identity: Self and society in the late modern age.* Stanford, CA: Stanford University Press.

Gregg, G. (1991). *Self-representation: Life narrative studies in identity and ideology.* New York: Greenwood Press.

Gregg, G. (1996). Themes of authority in life-histories of young Moroccans. In S. Miller & R. Bourgia (Eds.), *Representations of power in Morocco.* Cambridge, MA: Harvard University Press.

Habermas, T., & Bluck, S. (2000). Getting a life: The emergence of the life story in adolescence. *Psychological Bulletin, 126,* 748–769.

Heilbrun, C. G. (1988). *Writing a woman's life.* New York: Norton.

Helson, R., & Roberts, B. W. (1994). Ego development and personality change in adulthood. *Journal of Personality and Social Psychology, 66,* 911–920.

Hermans, H. J. M. (1996). Voicing the self: From information processing to dialogical interchange. *Psychological Bulletin, 119,* 31–50.

Howe, M. L., & Courage, M. L. (1997). The emergence and early development of autobiographical memory. *Psychological Review, 104,* 499–523.

James, W. (1963). *Psychology.* Greenwich, CT: Fawcett. (Original work published 1892)

Josselson, R., & Lieblich, A. (Eds.). (1993). *The narrative study of lives* (Vol. 1). Thousand Oaks, CA: Sage.

Kagan, J. (1994). *Galen's prophecy.* New York: Basic Books.

Kenyon, G. M. (1996). The meaning/value of personal storytelling. In J. E. Birren, G. M. Kenyon, J-E. Ruth, J. J. F. Schroots, and T. Svennson (Eds.), *Aging and biography: Explorations in adult development* (pp. 21–38). New York: Springer.

Kermode, F. (1967). *The sense of an ending.* New York: Oxford University Press.

Knowles, E. S., & Sibicky, M. E. (1990). Continuity and diversity in the stream of selves: Metaphorical resolutions of William James's one-in-many-selves paradox. *Personality and Social Psychology Bulletin, 16,* 676–687.

Kotre, J. (1984). *Outliving the self: Generativity and the interpretation of lives.* Baltimore, MD: Johns Hopkins University Press.

Linn, R. (1997). Soldiers' narrative of selective moral resistance: A separate position of the connected self? In A. Lieblich & R. Josselson (Eds.), *The narrative study of lives* (Vol. 5, pp. 94–112). Thousand Oaks, CA: Sage.

Loevinger, J. (1976). *Ego development.* San Francisco, CA: Jossey-Bass.

Main, M., Kaplan, N., & Cassidy, J. (1985). Security in infancy, childhood, and adulthood: A move to the level of representation. *Monographs for the Society for Research in Child Development, 50*(1 & 2), 66–104.

Mandler, J. M. (1984). *Stories, scripts, and scenes: Aspects of schema theory.* Hillsdale, NJ: Lawrence Erlbaum Associates.

Marcia, J. E. (1980). *Identity in adolescence.* In J. Adelson (Ed.), *Handbook of adolescent psychology* (pp. 159–187). New York: Wiley.

Markus, H., & Kitayama, S. (1991). Culture and the self: Implications for cognition, emotion, and motivation. *Psychological Review, 98,* 224–253.

Markus, H., & Nurius, P. (1986). Possible selves. *American Psychologist, 41,* 954–969.

Maruna, S. (1997). Going straight: Desistance from crime and life narratives of reform. In A. Lieblich & R. Josselson (Eds.), *The narrative study of lives* (Vol. 5, pp. 59–93). Thousand Oaks, CA: Sage.

McAdams, D. P. (1982). Experiences of intimacy and power: Relationships between social motives and autobiographical memory. *Journal of Personality and Social Psychology, 42,* 292–302.

McAdams, D. P. (1984). Love, power, and images of the self. In C. Z. Malatesta & C. E. Izard (Eds.), *Emotion in adult development* (pp. 159–174). Beverly Hills, CA: Sage.

McAdams, D. P. (1985). *Power, intimacy, and the life story: Personological inquiries into identity.* New York: Guilford Press.

McAdams, D. P. (1993). *The stories we live by: Personal myths and the making of the self.* New York: William Morrow.

McAdams, D. P. (1995). What do we know when we know a person? *Journal of Personality, 63,* 365–396.

McAdams, D. P. (1996). Personality, modernity, and the storied self: A contemporary framework for studying persons. *Psychological Inquiry, 7,* 295–321.

McAdams, D. P. (1997). The case for unity in the (post)modern self: A modest proposal. In R. Ashmore and L. Jussim (Eds.), *Self and identity: Fundamental issues* (pp. 46–78). New York: Oxford University Press.

McAdams, D. P. (1999). Personal narratives and the life story. In L. Pervin & O. John (Eds.), *Handbook of personality: Theory and research* (2nd ed., pp. 478–500). New York: Guilford.

McAdams, D. P. (2001). *The person: An integrated introduction to personality psychology* (3rd ed.). Fort Worth, TX: Harcourt.

McAdams, D. P., Booth, L., & Selvik, R. (1981). Religious identity among students at a private college: Social motives, ego stage, and development. *Merrill-Palmer Quarterly, 27,* 219–239.

McAdams, D. P., de St. Aubin, E., & Logan, R. (1993). Generativity among young, midlife, and older adults. *Psychology and Aging, 8,* 221–230.

McAdams, D. P., Diamond, A., de St. Aubin, E., & Mansfield, E. (1997). Stories of commitment: The psychosocial construction of generative lives. *Journal of Personality and Social Psychology, 72,* 678–694.

McAdams, D. P., Hart, H., & Maruna, S. (1998). The anatomy of generativity. In D. P. McAdams & E. de St. Aubin (Eds.), *Generativity and adult development* (pp. 7–43). Washington, DC: American Psychological Association.

McAdams, D. P., Hoffman, B. J., Mansfield, E. D., & Day, R. (1996). Themes of agency and communion in significant autobiographical scenes. *Journal of Personality, 64,* 339–378.

McAdams, D. P., Reynolds, J., Lewis, M. L., Patten, A., & Bowman, P. T. (2001). When bad things turn good and good things turn bad: Sequences of redemption and contamination in life narrative, and their relation to psychosocial adaptation in midlife adults and in students. *Personality and Social Psychology Bulletin, 27,* 472–483.

Miller, P. J. (1994). Narrative practices: Their role in socialization and self-construction. In U. Neisser & R. Fivush (Eds.), *The remembering self* (pp. 158–179). New York: Oxford University Press.

Modell, J. (1992). "How do you introduce yourself as a childless mother?" Birthparent interpretations of parenthood. In G. C. Rosenwald & R. L. Ochberg (Eds.), *Storied lives: The cultural politics of self-understanding* (pp. 76–94). New Haven, CT: Yale University Press.

Murray, K. (1989). The construction of identity in the narratives of romance and comedy. In J. Shotter & K. J. Gergen (Eds.), *Texts of identity* (pp. 176–205). London: Sage.

Nelson, K. (1988). The ontogeny of memory for real events. In U. Neisser & E. Winograd (Eds.), *Remembering reconsidered* (pp. 244–276). New York: Cambridge University Press.

Pillemer, D. B. (1998). *Momentous events, vivid memories.* Cambridge, MA: Harvard University Press.

Ricoeur, P. (1984). *Time and narrative.* Chicago: University of Chicago Press.

Robinson, J. A., & Taylor, L. R. (1998). Autobiographical memory and self-narratives: A tale of two stories. In C. P. Thompson, D. J. Hermann, D. Bruce, J. D. Read, D. G. Payne, & M. P. Toglia (Eds.), *Autobiographical memory: Theoretical and applied perspectives* (pp. 125–143). Mahwah, NJ: Lawrence Erlbaum Associates.

Rosenwald, G. C. (1992). Conclusion: Reflections on narrative self-understanding. In G. C. Rosenwald & R. L. Ochberg (Eds.), *Storied lives: The cultural politics of self-understanding* (pp. 265–289). New Haven, CT: Yale University Press.

Rosenwald, G. C., & Ochberg, R. L. (1992). (Eds.). *Storied lives.* New Haven, CT: Yale University Press.

Ross, M. (1997). Validating memories. In N. L. Stein, P. A. Ornstein, B. Tversky, & C. Brainerd (Eds.), *Memory for everyday and emotional events* (pp. 49–81). Mahwah, NJ: Lawrence Erlbaum Associates.

Rubin, D. C. (1998). Beginnings of a theory of autobiographical remembering. In C. P. Thompson, D. J. Hermann, D. Bruce, J. D. Read, D. G. Payne, & M. P. Toglia (Eds.), *Autobiographical memory: Theoretical and applied perspectives* (pp. 47–67). Mahwah, NJ: Lawrence Erlbaum Associates.

Rubin, D. C., Wetzler, S. E., & Nebes, R. D. (1986). Autobiographical memory across the lifespan. In D. C. Rubin (Ed.), *Autobiographical memory.* New York: Cambridge University Press.

Schachter, D. L. (1996). *Searching for memory: The brain, the mind, and the past.* New York: Basic Books.

Shweder, R. A., & Sullivan, M. A. (1993). Cultural psychology: Who needs it? *Annual Review of Psychology, 44,* 497–523.

Singer, J. A. (1995). Seeing one's self: Locating narrative memory in a framework of personality. *Journal of Personality, 63,* 429–457.

Singer, J. A. (1997). *Message in a bottle: Stories of men and addiction.* New York: The Free Press.

Singer, J. A., & Salovey, P. (1993). *The remembered self.* New York: The Free Press.

Stein, N. L., Wade, E., & Liwag, M. C. (1997). A theoretical approach to understanding and remembering emotional events. In N. L. Stein, P. A. Ornstein, B. Tversky, & C. Brainerd (Eds.), *Memory for everyday and emotional events* (pp. 15–47). Mahwah, NJ: Lawrence Erlbaum Associates.

Taylor, C. (1989). *Sources of the self: The making of the modern identity.* Cambridge, MA: Harvard University Press.

Thompson, C. P., Skowronski, J. J., Larsen, S. F., & Betz, A. L. (1996). (Eds.). *Autobiographical memory: Remembering what and remembering when.* Mahwah, NJ: Lawrence Erlbaum Associates.

Thorne, A. (1995). Developmental truths in memories of childhood and adolescence. *Journal of Personality, 63,* 139–163.

Thorne, A. (2000). Personal memory telling and personality development. *Personality and Social Psychology Review, 4,* 45–56.

Tomasello, M. (2000). Culture and cognitive development. *Current Directions in Psychological Science, 9,* 37–40.

Walkover, B. C. (1992). The family as an overwrought object of desire. In G. C. Rosenwald & R. L. Ochberg (Eds.), *Storied lives: The cultural politics of self-understanding* (pp. 178–191). New Haven, CT: Yale University Press.

Welch-Ross, M. K. (1995). An integrative model of the development of autobiographical memory. *Developmental Review, 15,* 338–365.

White, M., & Epston, D. (1990). *Narrative means to therapeutic ends.* New York: Norton.

Woike, B. A. (1995). Most-memorable experiences: Evidence for a link between implicit and explicit motives and social cognitive processes in everyday life. *Journal of Personality and Social Psychology, 68,* 1081–1091.

Woike, B. A., Gersekovich, I., Piorkowski, R., & Polo, M. (1999). The role of motives in the content and structure of autobiographical memory. *Journal of Personality and Social Psychology, 76,* 600–612.

Chapter 10

Self-Making Narratives*

Jerome Bruner
New York University

"Self" is a surprisingly quirky idea—intuitively obvious to commonsense, yet notoriously evasive to definition by the fastidious philosopher. The best we seem able to do when asked what it is is to point a finger at our forehead or our chest. Yet, self is common coin: No conversation goes long without its being unapologetically invoked. And the legal code simply takes it for granted when it invokes such legal concepts as "responsibility" and "privacy." So we would do well, then, to have a brief look at what the "self" is that self narratives are supposed to be about.

Is it that there is some essential self inside us that we need to put into words? If that were so, why would we ever need to tell ourselves about ourselves—or why would there be such injunctions as "Know thyself" or "To thine own self be true." Surely, if our selves were transparent to us, we would have no need to *tell* ourselves about them. Yet we spend a good deal of time doing just that, either alone, or vicariously at the psychiatrist's, or at confession if we are believers. So what function does such self-telling serve?

The standard 20th-century answer to this question was, of course, that much of ourselves was unconscious and adroitly defended from our conscious probings by various mechanisms for concealing or distorting it. We needed, as it were, to find ways around these defenses—with the help of a psychoanalyst in interaction with whom we would reenact the past and overcome our resistance to discovering ourselves. Where there was id, now there

---

*This chapter is reprinted with permission from "The Narrative Creation of Self" from MAKING STORIES: LAW, LITERATURE, LIFE by Jerome Bruner. Copyright © 2002 by Jerome Bruner. Reprinted by permission of Farrar, Straus and Giroux, LLC.

shall be ego, to paraphrase Freud. Little question that Freud's solution to our puzzle was a brilliant metaphor and that it had profound effects on our image of man (Bruner, 1958).

Yet, we do well to continue our inquiry. Freud's struggle drama of ego, superego, and id, for all its metaphoric brilliance, should not blind us to the unfinished business that remains. And it is to the pursuit of this unfinished business that this chapter is dedicated. More precisely, why do we need to tell stories in order to elucidate what we mean by "self"? Indeed, it is a question that has even come to preoccupy mainstream psychoanalysis itself (Spence, 1982, 1987).

I begin by proposing boldly that, in effect, there is no such thing as an intuitively obvious and essential self to know, one that just sits there to be portrayed in words. Rather, we constantly construct and reconstruct a self to meet the needs of the situations we encounter, and do so with the guidance of our memories of the past and our hopes and fears for the future.[1] Telling oneself about oneself is rather like making up a story about who and what we are, what has happened, and why we are doing what we are doing.

It is not that we have to make up these stories from scratch each time. We develop habits. Our self-making stories cumulate over time, even begin to fall into genres. They get out of date, and not just because we grow older or wiser, but because our self-making stories need to fit new circumstances, new friends, new enterprises. Our very memories become victims of our self-making stories. It is not that I can no longer tell you (or myself) the "original, true story" about my desolation in the bleak summer after my father died. Rather, I would be telling you (or myself) a new one about a 12-year-old "once upon a time." And I could tell it several ways, all of them shaped as much by my life since then as by the circumstances of that long-ago summer.

Self-making is a narrative art, and although it is more constrained by memory than fiction, it is uneasily constrained, a matter we come to presently. Self-making, anomalously, is from both the inside and the outside. The inside of it, we like to say in our Cartesian way, is memory, feelings, ideas, beliefs, subjectivity. A part of its insidedness is almost certainly innate and species-specific in origin, like our irresistible sense of continuity over time and place, our postural sense of ourselves, and the like. But much of self-making is based on outside sources as well—on the apparent esteem of others, and on the myriad expectations that we early, even mindlessly, pick up from the culture in which we are immersed. For with respect to those expectations, "the fish will be the last to discover water."

Besides, narrative acts of self-making are typically guided by unspoken, implicit cultural models of what selfhood should be and what it might be—

and, of course, what it should not be. Not that we are slaves of culture, as even the most dedicated cultural anthropologists now appreciate (Clifford, 1988; Kuper, 1999). Rather, there are too many possible, ambiguous models of selfhood on offer even in simple or ritualized cultures. Yet, all cultures provide presuppositions and perspectives about selfhood, rather like plot summaries or homilies for telling oneself or others about oneself, ranging from the locative ("A man's home is his castle") to the affectional ("Love thy neighbor as thyself").

But they are not all of a piece, these self-making precepts—like those last two homilies, for example. They leave ample room for maneuver. Self making is, after all, our principal means for establishing our own uniqueness. And a moment's thought makes plain that our uniqueness comes from distinguishing ourselves from others, which we do by comparing our self-told accounts of ourselves with the accounts that others give us of themselves—which add further ambiguity. For we are forever mindful of the difference between what we tell ourselves about ourselves and what we reveal to others.

Telling others about oneself is, then, no simple matter; it depends on what *we* think *they* think we ought to be like. Nor do such calculations end when we come to telling ourselves about ourselves. Our own self-making narratives soon come to reflect what we think others expect us to be like. Without much awareness of it, we develop a decorum for telling ourself about ourself: how to be frank with ourselves, how not to offend others. A thoughtful student of autobiography proposed that self narratives (at least those in the genre of written autobiography) conform to a tacit *pacte autobiographique* governing what constitutes appropriate public self-telling (Lejeune, 1989). We follow some variant of it even when we are only telling ourselves about ourselves. In the process, selfhood becomes *res publica*, even when talking to ourselves.

It hardly requires a postmodern leap to conclude, then, that self is also other (Ricoeur, 1962). Classicists, interestingly, see this phenomenon even in the ancient world. Did the Roman art of rhetoric, originally designed to aid in arguing convincingly to others, not eventually get turned inward to self-telling? And may that have produced the resoluteness so characteristic of Roman masculinity? (Gunderson, 1999) Who would doubt John Donne any longer that "No man is an islande entyre to himself"?

Yet, a haunting question remains. Is there some sort of spiraling effect in all this? Does so private a process as self making become the sport of the tools and institutions that a culture creates? Take rhetoric as a case in point. It is part of a culture's tool kit for bettering how we convince the other fellow in argument. Eventually, we are told, it was turned inward as an adjunct to self making, yielding the sharp-minded Roman, clear about who and what he was and what was expected of him. Did that self-certainty shape the Emperor Justinian, pushing him at the peak of his career to cleanse all local ambiguity from the administration of Roman law? Is Empire affected by the long reach of self narratives?

Take another example from antiquity, this one offered by the distinguished Cambridge classicist, Sir Geoffrey Lloyd. He noted, with impressive evidence, that the ancient Greeks were much more confrontational and autonomy-driven in their conduct of life than the then-contemporary Chinese (Lloyd, 1979, 1998, 1999). The Greeks, not the Chinese, invented the "winner-take-all" syllogism for resolving their arguments, whereas the Chinese, surely as gifted mathematically, avoided such show-down procedures like the plague. Showdowns fit Chinese decorum properly. Did their methods of proof make the Greeks even more confrontational, until, as with the rhetoric of the later Romans, it even sharpened their sense of their own selfhood? Do we invent tools to further our cultural bent, and then become servants of those tools, even developing selves to fit?

Americans, it has been said, no longer show as much overt affection toward each other as they used to: men worry that it might be taken as sexual harassment if directed toward women, adults that it might appear like child abuse if toward kids, all of it the side-effect of well-intended prohibitive statutes. A posted notice in one California school district expressly forbids "showing your affections" (on a list of prohibitions that includes "Don't spit" as well!). Will our new guardedness end up obscuring the tender side of selfhood? At least one commentator thinks so (Oxenhandler, 2001). Or does global mobility affect our attachments, our empathy for others? The shape of selfhood is not as private an issue as it once seemed.

Selfhood seems to have become an astonishingly public issue in our times. Endless books tell us how to improve it: how to keep from becoming "divided," narcissistic, isolated, or unsituated. Research psychologists, ordinarily proud of their neutrality, warn us of our "errors" in judging self, that we usually "see" others as guided by enduring beliefs and dispositions while seeing ourselves as more subtly steered by our circumstances—what they call the primary attribution error.

But has not self always been a matter of public, moral concern, even a topic of debate? Self and soul have forever been yin and yang in the Judeo–Christian tradition. Confession of sins and appropriate penance purged the soul—and raised the spirits of one's secular self. Doctrinally, the soul was cursed with original sin, and we know from magisterial works on the history of childhood how important it was to purge that sin from selfhood. Calvin's version of original sin was so compelling that it took Rousseau's (1979) irony and courage to bid it bitter farewell in *Emile*.

But the good self has also been an issue in that perpetual cockpit of secular moral debate called pedagogy. Does education make the spirit more generous by broadening the mind? Does selfhood become the richer by exposure, in Arnold's (1993) classic phrase, to "all that was best" is a society's tradition? Education was *Bildung,* character building, not just subject matter. Hegel (1995) thought he had diagnosed the difficulty: the young (or anybody) had to be inspired to rise above immediate demands by being instructed in the culture's a noble history. He went so far as to suggest that pedagogy should "alienate one from the present." Even the allegedly pragmatic Dewey in his time debated the issue of how to create a self fit for a good society (Ryan, 2001).

No generation, it seems, has even been able to heed the advice of the title of Thurber's (1986) little classic of a generation ago, *Leave Your Self Alone!* Am I any freer of value judgments writing about selfhood than anybody before me? I hold the Western liberal view that inviolate selfhood is the base of human freedom, or the rather odd esthetic view that our selves are among the most impressive works of literary art we human beings create. Surely, I am not above the fray. The only hope I can harbor, perhaps, is that I may help myself become more aware of what the contending values are—and even make the reader so.

Yes, self-making and self-telling are about as public an activity as any private acts can be. And so are the critiques of them.

Why do we naturally portray ourselves through story, so naturally indeed that selfhood itself seems like a product of our own story making? Does the research literature of psychology provide any answers? One gifted psychologist, Neisser, has done us the favor of gathering much of that literature together in several learned volumes containing articles by leading scholars in the field (Neisser, 1993; Neisser & Fivush, 1994; Neisser & Jopling, 1997; Neisser & Winograd, 1988). I have gone back over those volumes with our question in mind, "Why narrative?" Let me condense what I found into a dozen psychological one-liners about selfhood of "The Self."

1. It is teleological, replete with desires, intentions, aspirations, endlessly in pursuit of goals.
2. In consequence, it is sensitive to obstacles: responsive to success or failure, unsteady in handling uncertain outcomes.
3. It responds to its judged successes and failures by altering its aspirations and ambitions and changing its reference group (Bruner, 1991).
4. It relies on selective remembering to adjust the past to the demands of the present and the anticipated future.

5. It is oriented toward "reference groups" and "significant others" who provide the cultural standards by which it judges itself.[2]
6. It is possessive and extensible, adopting beliefs, values, loyalties, even objects as aspects of its own identity.
7. Yet, it seems able to shed these values and possessions as required by circumstances without losing its continuity.
8. It is experientially continuous over time and circumstances, despite striking transformations in its contents and activities.
9. It is sensitive to where and with whom it finds itself in the world.
10. It is accountable and sometimes responsible for formulating itself in words, becoming troubled when words cannot be found.[3]
11. It is moody, affective, labile, and situation sensitive.
12. It is coherence seeking and coherence guarding, eschewing dissonance and contradiction through highly developed psychic procedures.

It is not a very surprising list, hardly counterintuitive in the smallest detail. It becomes somewhat more interesting, though, if you translate it into a set of reminders about how to tell a good story. Something like:

13. A story needs a plot.
14. Plots need obstacles to goal.
15. Obstacles make people reconsider.
16. Tell only about the story-relevant past.
17. Give your characters allies and connections.
18. Let your characters grow.
19. But keep their identity intact.
20. And also keep their continuity evident.
21. Locate your characters in the world of people.
22. Let your characters explain themselves as needed.
23. Let your characters suffer moods.
24. Characters should worry when not making sense.

Should we say, then, that all the psychological research on selfhood has rediscovered the wheel, that all we have learned from it is that most people have learned how to tell passable stories, with themselves as the chief protagonist? That would surely be unjust and, besides, just plain untrue. But we could certainly fault the psychologists responsible for those findings with a failure to tell the dancer from the dance, the medium from the message, or however one puts it. For the self of the psychologists comes out to be little more than a standard protagonist in a standard story of a standard genre. She sets out on some quest, runs into obstacles and has second thoughts about her aims in life, remembers what's needed as needed, has allies and people she cares about, yet grows without losing herself in the process. She lives in a recognizable world, speaks her own mind when she needs to, but is thrown when words fail her, and wonders whether her life makes sense. It can be tragic, comic, a *Bildungsroman*, whatever. Does selfhood require more than a reasonably well-wrought story, a story whose continuing episodes tie together (like continued stories generally, or like lines of precedent in the law)?

Maybe we're faced with another chicken-and-egg puzzle. Is our sense of selfhood the *fons et origio* of story telling, or is it the human gift of narrative that endows selfhood with the shape it has taken? But perhaps that oversimplifies. There is an old adage in linguistics that "thinking is for speaking"—that we come to think in a certain way in order to say it in the language we have learned to use, which hardly means that *all* thinking is shaped just for the sake of talking. Slobin (2000), a gifted scholar and a seasoned student of how language and thought influence each other, put it well:

> . . . one cannot verbalize experience without taking a *perspective,* and . . . the language being used often favors particular perspectives. The world does not present "events" to be encoded in language. Rather, in the process of speaking or writing, experiences are filtered through language into *verbalized events.*

Selfhood can surely be thought of as one of those verbalized events, a kind of metaevent that provides coherence and continuity to the scramble of experience. But it is not just language per se but narrative that shapes its use—particularly its use in self making. Is it so surprising? Physicists come to think in those scrawls they put on the blackboard for each other. Musicians are so adept at thinking musically that (to cite a sometimes cellist in his orchestra), the conductor Dmitri Miropoulos would, in rehearsal, hum his way backward through a passage to get to where he felt the orchestra's playing had gone off! Are we any less adept in those acts of retrospect by which we try to decide whether, after all, "this is the kind of person I really mean to be"?

Most people never get around to composing a full-scale autobiography. Self-telling, rather, is mostly provoked by episodes related to some longer term concern. Although linked to or provoked by particular happenings, it ordinarily presupposes those longer term, larger scale concerns—much as history writing where the *annales* record of particular events is already somehow determined or shaped by a more encompassing *chronique,* which itself bears the stamp of an over-arching *historie*. An account of a battle takes for granted the existence of a war which takes for granted the even larger notion of competitive nation-states and a world order.

No autobiography is completed, only ended. No autobiographer is free of questions about which self his autobiography is about, composed from what perspective, for whom. The one we actually write is only one version, one way of achieving coherence. Autobiography turns even a seasoned writer into a *Doppelganger*—and turns its readers into sleuths. How can any version of an autobiography strike a balance between what one actually was and what one might have been? And we play games with ourselves about this would-be balance. A writer friend and neighbor of mine, a gifted journalist engaged in writing an autobiography as was I, responded to my doubts with: "No problem for me; I am faithful to memory." Yet she was renowned locally as a delicious fabulist who, in the words of a witty fellow townsman, "could make a shopping trip to Skibbereen sound like a visit to ancient Rome itself." Like her, we are forever balancing what was with what might have been—and, in the main, mercifully unaware of how we do it.

Literally, autobiography, for all it pitfalls, has much to teach us about what we leave implicit in our more spontaneous, episode-linked, briefer self-accounts. It can even provide hints about a writer's cryptophilosophical notion of what a self is! And that is no idle question.

A recent book highlights this point vividly—Olney's thoughtful *Memory and Narrative: The Weave of Life-Writing* (1998). Olney is particularly concerned with the rise and fall of the narrative form in self-accounting, and with why, in recent times, it has begun losing its allure for literary autobiographers, even if they cannot escape it in their more spontaneous and episodic self-telling.

Four famous life-writers come under his scrutiny, their work extending over more than a millennium, starting with St. Augustine, whose *Confessions* virtually pioneered the autobiographical genre in the 4th century, and ending with Samuel Beckett. Augustine saw his as a search for his true life, his true self, and conceived of autobiography as a quest for true memory, for reality. For Augustine, one's true life is that which has been given us by God and Providence, and narrative's inherent and unique orderliness reflects the natural form of memory, the form truest to Providence—given being. True memory mirrors the real world, and Augustine accepted narrative as its medium. His was a "narrative realism" and the Self that emerges is the gift of Revelation, leavened by Reason.

Contrast Giambattista Vico in the 17th century, next on Olney's historical trajectory. Vico's reflections on the powers of mind itself led him to cock his eye at Augustine's narrative realism. For him, a life is crafted by the mental acts of those who live it, not by an act of God. Its story-likeness is of our doing, not God's. Vico was perhaps the first radical constructivist, though he was protected by a rationalism that guarded him from the skepticism usually associated with that radical stance.

Enter Jean-Jacques Rosseau a century later, who, alerted by Vico's reflections and emboldened by the new skepticism of his own revolutionary times, set out to raise new doubts about Augustine's stable and innocent narrative realism. Rosseau's *Confessions* are laced with high-spirited skepticism. Yes, acts-of-mind, not Providence, shape an autobiography, but Rousseau also poked fun at our acts-of-mind—their passionate follies and vanity-serving uses. Life stories for Rousseau became rather more like social games than quests for some higher truth, and that may be one reason he had little patience with notions like original sin. He turned Vico's respect for reason into a somewhat rueful and impious skepticism.

Jump two centuries now to Samuel Beckett and our own times. Beckett was at one with Vico's reasoned rejection of Augustine's narrative realism and even more in sympathy with Rosseau's wry skepticism. But he explicitly rejected narrative as reflecting that inherent order or life. Indeed, he denied the very notion that there is any inherent order. His was a thoroughgoing factionalism, his mission to free life-writing (as well at literature) of its narrative straitjacket. Life is problematic, not to be shackled in conventional genres. So even his somewhat autobiographical dramas, like *Waiting for Godot*, pose problems rather than answer them. For him, the road was better than the inn: let one be not lulled by the illusion of narrative.

Each—Augustine, Vico, Rousseau, and Beckett—is a child of his historical time, each cultivating a fresh image of childhood and rejecting what for him was a stale one. For Augustine, at the start, self was the product of revelation-guided narrative, revealing what God had wrought; by the time we reach Beckett, a millennium later, the self-told narrative was a mere *façon d'écrire*, a man-made noose strangling the imagination. But for each of them, the issue of selfhood, its nature and origin, were matters of deep and debatable concern, a concern that seems not to have diminished over a millennium, although issues changed drastically. Why did Thomas à Kempis call his account of true monastic selfhood the *Imitation Christi*? Was he pushing Augustinian narrative realism, proposing Christ's depiction of the serving self as the true model? And were the monks and nuns of his times convinced that their selves were truly imitations of Christ's? Reading Thomas with modern eyes, one even senses that he is rather like a recruiter glorifying the kind of selfhood that might lure novices into the monastic life—or justify staying in it. The contrast implied throughout his stirring little book is of the selfish, secular self. And so it seems to be the case for all disquisitions about selfhood. In some indirect way, they are also advertisements about the *right* selfhood, each age with its own version of the competition.

So it is, also, with Virginia Woolf's metaphoric "room of one's own," her new feminist appeal for a change in women's conceptions of their selfhood. Was Jack Kerouac's *On The Road* turned to reducing the teleological intensity in his generation's style of self-telling and self-making?

Olney's account of the great innovations in conceptions of selfhood is brilliant. One regrets only that he did not explore more fully the struggles his heroic authors suffered in their times—Augustine's against Christian blind faith, Rousseau's against an oppressive *ancien regime,* Vico's against the spirit of the Enlightenment, and Beckett's against literary realism. The four of them obviously shaped new images of selfhood. But their images, indeed, no image of selfhood ever gains a monopoly.

We would do well to inquire why this is so.

A self-making narrative is something of a balancing act. It must, on the one hand, create a conviction of autonomy, that one has a will of one's own, a certain freedom of choice, a degree of possibility. However, it must also relate one to a world of others—to friends and family, to institutions, to the past, to reference groups. But there is an implicit commitment to others in relating oneself to others that, of course, limits our autonomy. We seem virtually unable to live without both, autonomy and commitment, and our lives strive to balance the two. So do the self-narratives we tell ourselves.

Not everyone succeeds. Take one Christopher McCandless, a 23-year-old whose dead body was found several years ago in a deserted bus in the Alaska wilderness. Some autobiographical fragments showed up among his meager possessions, and they tell the story of a "radically autonomous identity gone wrong" (Eakin, 1999). "Dealing with things on his own" was his ideal, and he translated Thoreau's injunction, "simplify, simplify," to mean he should depend on nobody, strive for unfettered autonomy. And his self-narrative fit this formula: At the end of his days, he was living in remote Alaska entirely on edible plants, and after 3 months he died of starvation. Shortly before his death, he went to the trouble of taking a self-portrait, the film of which was found in his camera. In it the young man is seated, with one hand raised and holding in the other a block-letter note on which he has written, "I have had a happy life and Thank the Lord. Goodbye and may God Bless All." On a plywood-covered window of the deserted bus that became his last refuge, he scratched this message: "Two Years He walks the Earth . . . Ultimate Freedom. An Extremist. An Aesthetic Voyager Whose Home is *The Road* . . . No Longer

To Be Poisoned By Civilization He Flees, And Walks Alone Upon the Land To Become *Lost* in the *Wild*."

In the end, even poor Christopher McCandless felt some commitment to others, his commitment offered, mind you, as an act of free will. As he lay alone, starving to death, he still felt impelled to offer God's blessings to those he had spurned—an act of grace, a balancing act. Then, perhaps nostalgically, perhaps bitterly, he died. Was he victim or victor in his own story? A generation ago, the great Vladimir Propp (Bruner, 1958) demonstrated how characters and events in folk-stories serve as functions in narrative plots: They do not exist on their own. What function did poor Christopher McCandless's final act play in his story, and how did he tell it to himself?

I once knew a young doctor, disillusioned with the humdrum of private practice, who, on hearing about the organization Médecins sans Frontières, began reading their literature and raising money for them at his county medical association meetings. Finally, he himself spent 2 years doctoring in Africa. On his return, I asked him if he had changed. "Yes," he said, "my life's more all of a piece now." All of a piece? Scattered over two continents? Yes, for now my physician friend is not only practicing medicine back where he'd started, but researching the roiling history of the town he'd left to go off to Africa, better to find the sources of his discontent, to reconcile his autonomy with his commitment to a town that he is making part of the wider world he had longed for. In doing so, has he created a viable Self? He has even enlisted the local town fathers as his allies in the effort!

So how indeed does one balance autonomy and commitment in one's sense of self—let alone making it all of a piece? I had studied that question as a psychologist in the usual indirect way we psychologists do, and dutifully contributed my chapter to one of those Neisser volumes mentioned earlier. But somehow the balance comes out more plainly in just ordinary conversation. So I have been asking people about it casually when the topic seemed right— friends, people with whom I work, acquaintances with whom I have become familiar. I simply ask them outright about themselves whenever the topic of balancing seems natural. One was a third-year law student, a young woman who was deeply committed to child advocacy in support of parents during child-related litigation. I had met her at a conference and asked her how she had gotten into that work, which seemed to suit her to a T. She said she would send me an e-mail, and here in effect is what it said:

> It was in some ways inadvert. I had graduated from college on the West Coast with a B.A. in English and Creative Writing, and didn't want to go into education or publishing, etc. but did want to do something . . . to better the lives of poor children. By a peculiar turn of circumstances (too long and

boring to go into) I fell into a internship with the Community Legal Aid Society in a middle-sized city back East, where I worked closely with an attorney who was representing parents (often with mental disabilities) in abuse and neglect cases. I was immediately drawn to the work. Most of all, I was astounded by the strength of these parents in the face of tremendous environmental adversity, but also by the way their voices were heard by no one. When they encountered someone (the attorney I worked with, myself) who was truly interested in listening to them, they often weren't able to trust the relationship and this in turn interfered with effective [legal] representation. Having done a lot of my own work "finding my voice" and learning firsthand the healing, even transformative power of being in relationship with someone who really listened, I felt very connected to these parents, despite our differences in background, etc. So, in the end, it is a continuation of my very deep, very personal interest . . .

Both the doctor and the child advocate had reached impasses: bored and discontented, going on and on with foreseeable duties to fulfill previously established commitments. Medical school, then internship, then small-town private practice. The well-brought-up daughter of literary bent, on to college, on into teaching high school English. Both were on trajectories shaped by conventional commitment, early commitment. Neither was in material need; they did not have to continue. Both foresaw the next step too clearly, as if possibility had been closed off by the sheer predictability of what lay ahead.

Commitment under these conditions is a narrative reminiscent of law stories. It is dominated by precedent-obligations in one's own life. Medical graduates go on to internships and then into practice—with hometown practice perhaps providing an off-the-track fillip. Circumstances change. The balancing act between commitment and autonomy no longer satisfies as the range of possibilities narrow. One's self narrative seems lacking in those imagined possible worlds that imagination generates—and that novelists and dramatists cultivate.

We can think of these times in life in several ways that are familiar. For example, we can think of them as akin to times at which things are ripe for a landmark decision by a court of law. And, like landmark decisions, where a prior doctrinal principle is expanded to take account of new conditions, turning points in a life honor an old aspiration in a new way. Medical care is not just for the safe and hometown familiars, but for the deprived and beleaguered beyond a horizon one had not realized existed earlier. Or one gives one's more developed voice to those who need it in their defense, not just to those who would routinely find it on their own. Or poor Christopher McCandless: if self-sufficiency is good, then total self-sufficiency is its epitome. Or one can conceive of turning points in one's self-telling as rather like a self-generated *peripéteia,* one's previously coping with trouble having now generated trouble of its own.

The bald fact of the matter is that one rarely encounters autobiographies, whether written or spontaneously told in interview, that are without turning points. And they are almost always accompanied by some such remark as "I became a new woman," or "I found a new voice," or "It was a new me after I walked out." Are they an integral part of growing up—like the sturm und drang of adolescence? Perhaps, although they certainly are not a product of youth, for turning points occur often later in life, particularly as retirement approaches. It may well be that Erikson's (1966) renowned "life stages," marked by a shift in concern from autonomy to competence to intimacy and then to continuity, provide stage settings for our autobiographical turning points.

Some cultures seem to provide for them ritually, as *rites de passage,* and they are often sufficiently painful or taxing to get the idea across. A !Kung Bushman boy is put through a painful ceremonial (including fresh ashes rubbed into fresh gashes in his cheeks, tomorrows proud scars of manhood) designed to mark his passage out of childhood. Now he is fit to be a hunter, ready to reject the ways of childhood. He is even taken on a hunt soon after, and much hoopla is made about his role in killing the giraffe, or whatever gets snagged on the hunt. The rite of passage not only encourages but legitimates change.[4]

But it is only in *rites de passage* (or in Erikson's life stages) that turning points are conventionalized. Self-narrating (if I may be permitted to say it again) is from the outside in as well as from the inside out. When circumstances ready us for change, we turn to others who have lived through one, become open to new trends and new ways of looking at oneself in the world. We read novels with new interest, go to demos, listen with a more open ear. Lawyers bored with the routines of mergers and copyright infringement suits pay new attention to what the Civil Liberties Union is up to. A rising and discontented Jane Fonda, on her own testimony, begins reading the "new" feminist literature to help her understand a divorce through which she has just suffered. And, indeed feminism itself offers changing versions of a woman's selfhood: from feminine consciousness in a Willa Cather or Katherine Mansfield to the protest feminism of a Simone de Beauvoir or Germaine Greer to today's activist "equality" feminists.

Self-making through self-narrating is restless and endless. It is probably more so now than ever before. It is a dialectical process, a balancing act. And despite our self-assuring homilies about people never changing, they do. They rebalance their autonomy and their commitments, most usually in a form that honors what they were before. The decorum of self-making keeps most of us from the sorts of wild adventure in self-making that brought Christopher McCandless down.

What is there to say in conclusion about the narrative art of self-making?

Sigmund Freud (1956) in an interesting book too seldom read, remarked that we are rather like a "cast of characters" in a novel or play. Novelists and playwrights, he remarked, construct their works of art by decomposing their own interior cast of characters, putting them on stage or on the page to work out their relations with each other. Those characters can also be heard in the pages of any autobiography. Perhaps it is a literary exaggeration to call our multiple inner voices "characters." But they are there to be heard, trying to come to terms with each other, sometimes at loggerheads. An extensive self-making narrative will try to speak for them all, but we know already that there is no single all-purpose story that can do that. To whom are you telling it, and to what end? Besides, we are too Hamlet-like to make it all-of-a-piece—too torn between the familiar and the possible.

None of which seems to discourage us. We go on, constructing ourselves through narrative. Why is narrative so essential, why do we need it for self-definition? Although I turn to that question at the end, let me make one simple point now. The narrative gift is as distinctively human as our upright posture and our opposable thumb and forefinger. It seems to be our "natural" way of using language for characterizing those ever-present deviations from the expected state of things that characterizes living in a human culture. None of us knows the just-so evolutionary story of its rise and survival. But what we do know is that it is irresistible as our way of making sense of human interaction.

I have argued that it is through narrative that we create and recreate selfhood, that self is a product of our telling and not some essence to be delved for in the recesses of subjectivity. There is now evidence that without the capacity to make stories about ourselves, there would be no such thing as selfhood. So let me offer the evidence that exists on this point.

There is a neurological disorder called *dysnarrativia* (Eakin, 1999), a severe impairment in the ability to tell or understand stories. It is associated with neuropathies like Korsakov's or Alzheimer's syndrome. But it is more than an impairment of memory about the past, which is itself highly disruptive of one's sense of self, as Sacks's (1973) work made plain. In Korsakov's syndrome particularly, where affect as well as memory is severely impaired, selfhood virtually vanishes. Sacks describes one of his severe Korsakov patients as "scooped out, de-souled" (Sacks, 1987).

One of the most characteristic symptoms in such cases is an almost complete loss of ability to read other minds, to tell what others might have been thinking, feeling, even seeing. They seem to have lost a sense of self, but also a sense of other. An astute critic of autobiography, Paul John Eakin, commenting on this literature, took this evidence as further proof that selfhood is profoundly relational, that self, as noted earlier, is also other. These are the patients who suffer what I referred to earlier as dysnarrativia.

The emerging view seems to be that dysnarrativia is deadly for selfhood. Eakin (1999) cited the conclusion of an unpublished paper by Young and Saver (1995): "Individuals who have lost the ability to construct narratives have lost their selves." The construction of selfhood, it seems, cannot proceed without a capacity to narrate.

Once we are equipped with that capacity, then we can produce a selfhood that joins us with others, that permits us to hark back selectively to our past while shaping ourselves for the possibilities of an imagined future. But the self-told narratives that make and remake our selves are ones we gain from the culture in which we live. However much we may rely on a functioning brain to achieve our selfhood, we are virtually from the start expressions of the culture that nurtures us. But culture itself is a dialectic, replete with alternative narratives about what self is or might be. And the stories we tell to create ourselves reflect that dialectic.

REFERENCES

Arnold, M. (1993). *Culture and anarchy and other writings.* New York: Cambridge University Press.
Bruner, J. (1958). The Freudian conception of man. *Daedalus, 8,* 77–84.
Clifford, J. (1988). *The predicament of culture.* Cambridge: Harvard University Press.
Eakin, P. J. (1999). *How our lives become stories: Making selves.* Ithaca, NY: Cornell University Press.
Erikson, E. (1966). Eight ages of man. *International Journal of Psychiatry, 2,* 281–300.
Freud, S. (1956). *Delusion and dream: An interpretation in the light of psychoanalysis of Gradiva, a novel by Wilhelm Jensen* (P. Reiff, Ed.). Boston: Beacon Press.
Gunderson, E. (1999). *Staging masculinity: The rhetoric of performance in the Roman world.* Ann Arbor: University of Michigan Press.
Hegel, G. W. F. (1995). *Lectures on natural rights and political science.* Berkeley: University of California Press.
Kuper, A. (1999). *Culture: The anthropologist's account.* Cambridge: Harvard University Press.
Lejeune, P. (1989). *On autobiography.* Minneapolis: University of Minnesota Press.
Lloyd, G. E. R. (1979). *Magic, reason, and experience.* Cambridge: Cambridge University Press.
Lloyd, G. E. R. (1998). Lecture at the University of Toronto.
Lloyd, G. E. R. (1999). *Science, folklore, and ideology.* Indianapolis: Hackett.
Neisser, U., & Fivush, R. (1994). *The remembered self: Accuracy and construction in the life narrative.* New York: Cambridge University Press.

Neisser, U., & Jopling, D. (1997). *The conceptual self in context: Culture, experience, self-understanding.* New York: Cambridge University Press.

Neisser, U. (Ed.). (1993). *The perceived self.* New York: Cambridge University Press.

Neisser, U., & Winograd, E. (1988). (Eds.) *Remembering reconsidered.* Cambridge: Cambridge University Press.

Olney, J. (1998). *Memory and narrative: The weave of life writing.* Chicago: University of Chicago Press.

Oxenhandler, N. (2001). *The eros of parenthood.* New York: St. Martin's Press.

Ricoeur, P. (1962). *Oneself as another.* Chicago: University of Chicago Press.

Rousseau, J. J. (1979). *Emile: or, On education.* New York: Basic Books.

Ryan, A. (2001). Schools: the price of "progress" (a review of Diane Ravitch's *Left Back: A century of failed school reforms*) in the *New York Review of Books, 48*(3), 22, 18ff.

Sacks, O. (1973). *Awakenings.* London: Duckworth.

Sacks, O. (1987). *The man who mistook his wife for a hat and other clinical tales.* New York: Harpers.

Schweder, R. (2000). The psychology of practice and the practice of three psychologies. *Asian Journal of Social Psychology, 3,* 207–222.

Slobin, D. E. (2000). Verbalized events: A dynamic approach to linguistic relativity and determinism. *Current Issues in Linguistic Theory, 198,* p. 107.

Spence, D. (1982). *Narrative truth and historical truth: meaning and interpretation in psychoanalysis.* New York: Norton.

Spence, D. (1987). *The Freudian metaphor: Toward paradigm change in psychoanalysis.* New York: Norton.

Thurber, J. (1986). *The works of James Thurber: Complete and unabridged.* New York: Longmeadow Press.

Wang, Q. (in press). Culture effects of adults' earliest childhood recollection and self-description. *Journal of Personality and Social Psychology.*

Young, K., & Saver, J. L. (1995, December). *The neurology of narrative.* Paper presented at Modern Languages Association Convention, New York.

ENDNOTES

[1] Plainly, there are certain "features" of selfhood that are innate: for example, we locate ourselves posturally at the "zero point" of personal space and time, something we share with most mammals. But we rise above that primitive identity almost from the start. Even as young children, we master "Peekaboo" and then go on, once language begins, to the mastery of such daunting tasks as *deictic reference:* when I say *here* it means something near me; when you use it, it means something near to you. My *here* is your *there,* a self-switcher found nowhere else in the animal kingdom. How the primitive, postural, and preconceptual self is transformed into a conceptual self is interestingly discussed in Neisser, 1993.

[2] The anthropologist Richard Shweder argued (on comparative evidence) that there seem to be three normative or "ethical" criteria by which human beings, whatever their culture, judge themselves and others. He spoke of them as relating to "the ethics of autonomy, the ethics of community, and the ethics of divinity." Each has its particularized expression in different cultures, with each given different weightings. So, for example, more communitarian

Asian cultures differ strikingly from more autonomy-oriented western cultures, with even the earliest autobiographical memories of Chinese adults containing more community-related self-judging episodes than do the early memories of Americans, the latter tending to remember more episodes related to autonomy (Shweder, 2000). The data on early autobiographical memories is to be found in Wang (in press).

[3] While self-telling ordinarily proceeds in ordinary language, ordinary language also sports the genres and fashions of its time. Has the so-called "inward turn" of the novel pulled self-telling inward? Or what of the lexical "self explosion" in 17th-century England, replete with new reflexive compounds like *self-conscious, self-reliant, self-possessed,* and the like? Did those words appear in response to a turbulent century of Hobbes and Locke, Cromwell's Puritan uprising, two Stuart kings dethroned, the Glorious Revolution? Did the spate of reflexive compounds appear in response to change in the world, and did it alter the way people looked at and told about themselves?

[4] Inadvertent trauma often produces disruptive and profound turning points in self-narrative, but they are in sharp contrast to the communally supported orderly change of the *rite de passage.* Trauma typically alienates and isolates those who have suffered it. Victims of rape, for example, are often so consumed by self-blame and guilt that they can scarcely face their community. They are gently aided by group therapy with other victims, in the course of which they discover that their fellow victims suffer the same sense of isolation as they do.

Author Index

A

Adam, S., 55, 67, 152, 165
Adams, S., 156, 164
Affleck, G., 200, 203
Agar, M., 170, 183
Ainsworth, M. D. S., 38, 45
Arend, R. A., 39, 47
Arnett, J. J., 188, 203
Arnold, M., 213, 223
Attinasi, J., 122, 134, 142
Aukett, R., 156, 164

B

Backman, L., 93, 95
Bakan, D., 197, 203
Bamberg, M., 175, 185
Bamberg, M. G. W., 171, 183
Barnes, H. E., viii, xiii
Baron, R. M., 35, 45
Barrett, K. C., 156, 165
Bartlett, F. C., 20, 24
Bartsch, K., 18, 25
Bates, E., 46
Bauer, P. J., 8, 16, 25
Becker, A., 142
Bekerian, D. A., 89, 94
Belk, S. S., 156, 166
Belsky, J., 39, 44, 46
Betz, A. L., 196, 207
Bhogle, S., 79, 95
Bibace, R., 175, 185
Biggs, B., 100, 116
Bigler, R. S., 154, 166

Blasi, A., 191, 203
Blehar, M., 38, 45
Bluck, S., xiii, 187, 189, 190, 192, 193, 196, 200, 203, 204
Boca, S., 170, 185
Bochner, S., 87, 94
Boje, D., 171, 184
Bokhour, B., 175, 185
Booth, L., 198, 205
Borke, H., 90, 94
Bowlby, J., 38, 46
Bowman, P. T., 199, 205
Boxer, A., 201, 203
Boyle, P., 156, 164
Breger, L., 188, 190, 203
Bretherton, I., 39, 46, 157, 164, 172, 184
Brewer, W. F., 136, 142, 182, 184, 196, 203
Brotman, M., 157, 165
Brown, J., 54, 66
Brown, N., 31, 32, 47
Bruner, J., vii, xiii, 20, 25, 78, 94, 210, 213, 219, 223
Bruner, J. S., 190, 203
Bryan, J., 175, 184
Buckner, J. P., 150, 152, 153, 154, 157, 159, 160, 161, 165
Buhrmester, D., 178, 184
Bukowski, W. M., 178, 184
Butler, S., 102, 116
Butterworth, G., 25

C

Callanan, M. A., 172, 184
Campbell, J., 197, 203

Subject Index